TREATING ADHD/ADD IN CHILDREN AND ADOLESCENTS

ABOUT THE AUTHOR

Gene Carroccia, Psy.D. earned his Bachelor of Arts in psychology from the University of Delaware in Newark, Delaware where he was inducted into Phi Beta Kappa. He obtained his doctorate in clinical psychology from the Illinois School of Professional Psychology in Chicago, Illinois in 1998. Dr. Carroccia is a licensed clinical psychologist in Illinois who has extensive experience working with individuals with ADHD, as well as other conditions, including psychological trauma and maltreatment. For over twenty years, he has evaluated and treated hundreds of children, adolescents, and adults with ADHD. He works at a large not-for-profit health care system as a vice president of behavioral health care services. For many years prior to this he supervised doctoral interns and was the training director of an accredited doctoral clinical psychology internship training program. He was the editor of the clinical workbook *Treating Sexual Abuse and Trauma with Children, Adolescents, and Young Adults with Developmental Disabilities*, published by Charles C. Thomas in 2017. He resides in the suburbs of Chicago with his wife and two sons. For more information about his books, please visit adhdology.com.

TREATING ADHD/ADD IN CHILDREN AND ADOLESCENTS

Solutions for Parents and Clinicians

An ADHD*ology* Book

By

GENE CARROCCIA, PSY.D.

With a Foreword by
Patricia O. Quinn, M.D.

CHARLES C THOMAS • PUBLISHER • LTD.
Springfield • Illinois • U.S.A.

Published and Distributed Throughout the World by

CHARLES C THOMAS • PUBLISHER, LTD.
2600 South First Street
Springfield, Illinois 62704

This book is protected by copyright. No part of
it may be reproduced in any manner without written
permission from the publisher. All rights reserved.

© 2019 by CHARLES C THOMAS • PUBLISHER, LTD.

ISBN 978-0-398-09265-8 (paper)
ISBN 978-0-398-09266-5 (ebook)

Library of Congress Catalog Card Number: 2018057385 (paper)
2019000656 (ebook)

With THOMAS BOOKS *careful attention is given to all details of manufacturing and design. It is the Publisher's desire to present books that are satisfactory as to their physical qualities and artistic possibilities and appropriate for their particular use.* THOMAS BOOKS *will be true to those laws of quality that assure a good name and good will.*

Printed in the United States of America
MM-C-1

Library of Congress Cataloging-in-Publication Data

Names: Carroccia, Gene, author.
Title: Treating ADHD/ADD in children and adolescents : solutions for
   parents and clinicians : an ADHDology book / by Gene Carroccia,
   Psy.D.
Description: Springfield, Illinois : Charles C Thomas, Publisher, Ltd.,
   [2019] | Includes bibliographical references and index.
Identifiers: LCCN 2018057385 (print) | LCCN 2019000656 (ebook) |
   ISBN 9780398092665 (ebook) | ISBN 9780398092658 (paper)
Subjects: LCSH: Attention-deficit hyperactivity disorder—Treatment.
Classification: LCC RJ506.H9 (ebook) | LCC RJ506.H9 C374 2019
   (print) | DDC 618.92/8589—dc23
LC record available at https://lccnloc.gov/2018057385

This book is dedicated to Kirsten, my amazing wife, who has supported and encouraged me on this journey, and to all the families who are touched by ADHD.

FOREWORD

Parents raising a child with ADHD can often feel quite lost and alone, and may struggle with the many difficulties they face. ADHD is a chronic, neurobiological condition and the great variability in symptom presentations can often cause confusion in both parents, educators, and professionals. The diagnosis of ADHD is made by a professional using a set of criteria that look at specific symptoms and their pervasiveness across a variety of settings over time. However, once a diagnosis is made, the prognosis for a positive outcome is extremely hopeful as ADHD can in most cases be effectively managed with a comprehensive treatment program.

Dr. Carroccia provides such a program with his ADHD*ology* approach to ADHD. In *Treating ADHD/ADD in Children and Adolescents: Solutions for Parents and Clinicians*, this approach is covered in detail and is one of the few books on the topic that presents a long-term, organized, and comprehensive view on the treatment of ADHD.

Treating ADHD/ADD in Children and Adolescents will not only help parents navigate the evaluation process, but also assists them in finding the most effective ways of dealing with ADHD at home and at school. This includes strategies to manage behaviors, handle sleep issues, and choose a medication to treat ADHD symptoms. Clinicians may also find this book to be useful in their diagnostic and treatment approaches with children, adolescents and families who are struggling with the challenges of ADHD. *Treating ADHD/ADD in Children and Adolescents: Solutions for Parents and Clinicians* is highly recommended to help families find a path to success!

Patricia O. Quinn, M.D.

Behavioral Pediatrician; Co-Founder and Director of the Center for Girls and Women with ADHD; Author and co-author of multiple books on ADHD, including *Putting on the Brakes: Understanding and Taking Control of Your ADD or ADHD* and *Understanding Girls with ADHD*.

PREFACE

We are all surrounded by one or more children, adolescents, and adults who struggle with ADHD. As a licensed clinical psychologist and doctor of clinical psychology, I have evaluated and treated hundreds of children, adolescents, families and adults with ADHD, as well as ADHD-like presentations and other co-existing conditions and disorders. I discovered that parents and clinicians needed an effective treatment framework to navigate the ways to address and manage ADHD. I have seen many children and teens with long treatment histories who were not diagnosed with ADHD when they had true ADHD. Some were also misdiagnosed with ADHD when they really had other medical, sleep, neurodevelopmental, and/or psychological conditions, or had undiagnosed co-existing conditions along with true ADHD. Over time, I have realized that many clinicians and parents did not understand or address ADHD sufficiently because they were not aware of these many other conditions.

Whether new or seasoned to ADHD challenges, this book is for parents and close relatives of children and teens with ADHD. Behavioral and medical practitioners, teachers and education professionals should also find this book useful in addressing the different facets of ADHD. For the most effective results, this book is best used along with clinicians as part of the diagnostic and treatment process. It provides the information and teaches skills to be more effective in addressing the many hurdles that ADHD presents. To accomplish this, the comprehensive ADHD*ology* treatment model is presented. This powerful six phase approach can help families successfully address, manage and transform ADHD. This treatment model approach should help maximize results in the following ways:

1. Know how to obtain an accurate ADHD evaluation or assessment, including exploring the numerous medical, sleep, psychological, and neurodevelopmental conditions that may be causing ADHD-like symptoms or co-exist along with true ADHD.
2. Assist parents to better understand and accept a child or teen with ADHD.

3. Become more focused and effective in the management of difficult behaviors at home, including sleep challenges.
4. Better address homework and school challenges, as well as obtaining appropriate official school plans and services.
5. Partner with physicians to get the most from ADHD medication.
6. Learn about potent additional and alternative ADHD treatment approaches.

There's another ADHD*ology* book that compliments this work. It is entitled *Evaluating ADHD in Children and Adolescents: A Comprehensive Diagnostic Screening Tool*. It addresses how to comprehensively evaluate ADHD in children and teens. While *Evaluating ADHD* is mostly for clinicians, it has diagnostic checklists for the many other medical, sleep, psychological, and neurodevelopmental conditions that can cause ADHD-like symptoms or coexist with ADHD. It teaches readers how to efficiently evaluate ADHD, and parents may use these checklists to assist clinicians working with their children and teens. If children or teens have ADHD, but are still struggling and not improving with treatment, parents and clinicians are urged to consider obtaining further evaluations or psychological testing to explore and treat other possible conditions.

G.C.

INTRODUCTION

I knew the Unger family (not their real name) was going to be a handful only moments into my first phone conversation with the mother. I just started discussing my evaluation and therapy services for children and teens with behavioral difficulties when I started to hear the chaos in the background. The mother said she needed help with Jimmy, her nine-year-old son. She said Jimmy was getting D and F grades at school and had frequent visits to the principal's office. His behavioral problems at home were escalating as well, while she and his father were arguing more and more about his difficulties. This took her some time to relate due to the screaming and yelling in the background. "See," his mother said in a sarcastic tone, "this is what I deal with every day." She asked when was my soonest appointment.

I have worked with many families like Jimmy's, so I wasn't surprised by what I heard. As a clinical psychologist working with children and teens who have behavioral problems and ADHD, my job is to figure out what is going on diagnostically, provide psychotherapy treatment, and possibly make additional referrals for other needed services. I also help families better understand the child's behavioral health conditions, motivate the parents to become more effective in their parenting, and assist the family to obtain appropriate school services and accommodations. To accomplish all of this for children and teens with ADHD, I use the comprehensive ADHD*ology* treatment model, which is the core of this book. Each chapter of the book discusses aspects of the six phases of this approach.

The first is the evaluation phase. The mother, father, Jimmy and his older sister came to my office for the initial session. They were a Caucasian family and the parents were in their early forties. The mother was a mid-level manager at a successful technology company, the father was "between jobs," and the sister was sixteen. As I walked into the waiting room to greet them, the mother and Jimmy were bickering viciously because Jimmy was begging for snacks from the vending machine in the hall. "No, I said no! Why do I have to keep repeating myself!! No means no! I told you this a thousand times!" The father was busy doing something on his cell phone.

As I introduced myself and ushered them to my office, the family seemed irritated and frustrated. I noticed the boy had a large carrying case that had a zippered mesh top. I asked about the case. Jimmy said proudly that this was his pet iguana "Ziggy" who just came from an appointment with a veterinarian. Jimmy held the case up so I could see him better. "Can Ziggy learn to calm down too?" Jimmy asked me. "I hope so" I replied.

After they all sat down in my office, his mother immediately informed me that Jimmy had a long history of behavioral problems and complaints from teachers that started in preschool. She said his reading has been terrible, and he didn't seem to understand much of what he read. Also, he had difficulties with his homework. She said he often wouldn't bring it home and took hours to complete it when he did. Jimmy's handwriting was awful as well, and he struggled to stay in the lines when writing or coloring pictures. Additionally, he had trouble sitting still. In prior years he had run out of the classroom, would hit peers, and even hit the teacher when upset. The mother complained that the school hadn't done anything to help him, despite promising this for years. His current teacher seemed overwhelmed by his behaviors.

At this point in the session the father looked up from his phone and said their home was "a disaster." Jimmy refused to go to bed when asked and had been "staying up way too late." Also, he often would sneak his cell phone into bed to play games and listen to music. His mother said he was often irritable and he could argue "forever" when he was confronted about his misbehavior. Additionally, he had terrible tantrums when things didn't go his way or when he heard "No!" Further he had been lying about his homework and when things were missing at home. His older sister said that she often found her stolen things hidden in his room. He refused to do chores and had a habit of running out the door when confronted. Both parents agreed he was very clumsy at home, and did poorly at sports, avoiding them whenever he could.

"Sports aren't for me," Jimmy said dryly. He was kicking his chair and looked bored. "And everyone hates me anyway, you know."

I asked how the family addressed and handled his unwanted behavior. The sister said, "Oh, that's easy. My parents yell and threaten to take away his phone, but never do. Then they go in the basement and start screaming at each other."

The mother shared that the father "doesn't do a damn thing about it," and complained that she is the bad guy at home. She added, "His father is just another child I have at home. He doesn't help with anything. Look at him now! He's selfish and keeps losing jobs!"

The father looked up from his phone and gave her a dirty look. He turned to me and said, "Look, I was just like him when I was a kid. This kid doesn't need all this nagging and strict rules that make him worse. He just needs some encouragement." Eventually both parents agreed they can be "hot heads," and needed to calm down more. But because they can't agree on how to handle his behaviors, they would just lecture, yell, and give up.

I asked Jimmy for his perspectives on the situation. He said that when his parents argued with each other, his mom would bring up divorce. He said he knew he was going to make the divorce happen. Jimmy said he didn't know why he hated school and homework so much, but that it was just too boring. Reading was "way too much work" and he only liked fun things. He said he wanted more friends and knew he had to stop hitting others. He also felt badly about stealing things at home, and tried to apologize, but no one believed him. Jimmy told me he knew he was a bad kid. "Only music makes me feel good at night in bed. That, and holding Ziggy." The lizard made some noise in the case.

I asked everyone if they knew what was going on with Jimmy. His mother said he had an anger management problem. His father said Jimmy was a slow reader and had a bad teacher. His sister said he was brat and got away with everything. In the past, his teachers were vague with his mother when she asked them why he had school problems. Several years ago, his pediatrician said he was immature for his age, and the family should "wait and see" for his difficulties to improve. At the last visit however, the pediatrician suggested he receive some counseling to address his low self-esteem and anger issues. This is why the mother called me.

I have seen many similar variations of this family's situation. It is always sad to see an entire family suffering. However, I know that there is often a way for a better life for all if they can hang in there and work with me.

Using the ADHD*ology* treatment model, we completed the first phase after five sessions. During this evaluation period, I used a diagnostic approach to explore if Jimmy truly had ADHD, which I suspected, as well as check to see if he had any other conditions. During the ADHD evaluation process, I reviewed the child and family's history, gathered more information about the problems at home and school, and obtained ADHD and other psychological measures completed by his parents and teachers. I also used the ADHD*ology* Comprehensive Diagnostic ADHD Screening Tool (CDAST) to explore if he had any potential medical, sleep, psychological, or neurodevelopmental conditions that may be co-existing or causing his ADHD-like symptoms.

I determined that Jimmy did truly have Combined ADHD, which means he had a brain-functioning condition that caused his inattention, hyperactivity, and impulsivity difficulties. However, like many other children and teens with true ADHD, Jimmy had additional undetected conditions as well. He also had oppositional defiant disorder (ODD), a secondary behavioral condition that seems to grow out of ADHD and causes children to be much more difficult to manage. Also, he appeared to have signs of a visual processing disorder, which is a sensory processing condition that affects the eye-to-brain connection. It can cause serious reading difficulties, sloppy handwriting, and clumsiness with sports. Additionally, Jimmy had partial sleep deprivation, getting only about seven hours of sleep a night when a boy his age required between 9 to 12 hours per night. I believed this chronic lack of sleep was worsening to his inattention, irritability, and low frustration tolerance at school and home. He also suffered from negative peer and familial relations, low self-esteem, and exposure to parental discord.

I suspected that his father had an undiagnosed ADHD-Combined condition as well, due to his apparent childhood and adult ADHD-like difficulties. Since ADHD is highly genetically transmitted and more common in males than females, it is not uncommon for fathers to have ADHD when their children have this.

I shared my diagnostic findings with the family. The parents were amazed to learn that Jimmy had specific conditions causing many of his problems. I informed them that I only screened him for a visual processing disorder, but a specially-trained optometrist would need to evaluate him further. I said the good news is that this condition may be improved with vision therapy. I also discussed his other difficulties, and what could be done to address and improve these.

We moved to the second phase of ADHD treatment, which was education for the family. When they received the handouts about ADHD and ODD, they said the descriptions sounded exactly like Jimmy and they better understood how his conditions impacted him and the family. We discussed the grieving process of accepting his conditions. After learning that ADHD is a neurobiological brain functioning condition that is a disability, and that his behavior was often not his choosing to be difficult, his parents seemed to have more compassion for him. The mother shared that she believed his father had ADHD as well. The father reluctantly agreed.

Next, we began addressing and managing ADHD at home, which was the third treatment phase. His parents acknowledged they were ineffective in dealing with Jimmy's unwanted behaviors, and they learned more productive parental behavioral management approaches. They were taught how to stop yelling and lecturing, use of time outs for misbehavior, and how to use a written plan of behavioral expectations and consequences for his unwanted and positive behaviors. They also learned about using sleep hygiene practices, and immediately changed their bedtime approach with him. He started going to bed earlier with a set time and without his cell phone or electronic screen devices in his room.

As part of the fourth treatment phase of addressing school problems, I instructed the family how to request a case study evaluation from his school to obtain special school services. I wrote a letter to the school with my clinical findings to aid them in this process. The school responded and he received an Individual Education Plan (IEP) that provided individual tutoring for reading and social work services to improve his social skills. His teachers seemed to respond to him more positively as well. His mother also utilized an effective homework notebook system that improved his daily homework challenges.

During this time, Jimmy obtained a visual processing evaluation from a developmental optometrist who diagnosed him with a visual processing disorder. The optometrist explained that his eyes and brain were not working together properly, and he began twice a week vision therapy with the optometrist.

Eventually, his father agreed to obtain his own treatment for ADHD. He told me he was tired of struggling with many things in his own life, and wanted to "see what can be done." He went to a psychiatrist, was also diagnosed with Combined ADHD, and received a prescription for ADHD medication. The father shared that after a few days of staring at the bottle, he tried it and it helped enormously. "I feel normal now, for the first time in forever. I can think clearly and get things done much more easily." After this success, Jimmy saw a pediatric psychiatrist to receive his own medication. With some tweaking, he received an effective ADHD stimulant and dose that helped him. This medication focus was the fifth phase of the treatment model.

After about a month, Jimmy started obtaining better grades and had far fewer behavioral complaints at school. Over time, the vision therapy seemed to improve his reading skills, and his medication appeared to reduce his hyperactivity, impulsivity, and oppositional defiant problems at home and school. The lying and stealing behaviors ended. The family greatly enjoyed these improvements. The mother and father learned how to work together more with the behavioral techniques to better respond to his difficulties. The mother stopped threatening divorce, and the father got a new job, and kept it.

As our sessions tapered down, Jimmy still had some remaining inattention and behavioral difficulties. We entered into the sixth phase of the ADHD*ology* treatment approach, which is utilizing additional and alternative ADHD approaches and treatment options. I shared how improving his diet and obtaining neurofeedback, a special form of biofeedback, could help him. Neurofeedback is an alternative treatment that can improve ADHD for children and adolescents. The mother read about this and agreed to try it. We discussed other options to potentially address his ADHD, including increasing protein in his diet, taking Omega-3 fish oil supplements, eating more organic foods, and reducing and eliminating foods with additives and preservatives. I encouraged the family to first discuss the food and supplement changes with his pediatrician or a dietitian. We had already addressed his sleep issues, and he was now consistently getting a solid ten hours of sleep per night. After four months of these new efforts, Jimmy improved even more. He started keeping friends in his neighborhood, and his grades continued to increase. He also joined a soccer team and was earning allowance each week for doing his chores. Due to this progress, we decided to end our ADHD therapy treatment. At our last session, Jimmy gave me a picture that he drew. I smiled as I saw that the green coloring was completely within the lines of a happy lizard sitting on a rock. "Ziggy thanks you!" was written under the image of the iguana.

Throughout this book I will use the term "ADHD." Some readers may say "my child has ADD and not ADHD. They aren't hyperactive or impulsive." The term "ADD" indicates Attention Deficit Disorder for a child or teen who has inattention problems without significant hyperactivity and impulsivity difficulties. However, for decades the correct term for this disorder has been "ADHD - Predominantly Inattentive Presentation." Therefore, in this book the term ADHD will refer to all the ADHD types, including ADHD with impulsivity and hyperactivity (Combined ADHD) and without these two difficulties (Inattentive ADHD). These conditions can present differently, have distinct brain signatures, and may require somewhat differing treatments. Children, teens, and adults with Inattentive ADHD often have fewer behavioral problems. However, since Combined and Inattentive ADHD conditions share many similarities, unless stated otherwise, the information presented on ADHD should be applicable to all forms of ADHD.

ACKNOWLEDGMENTS

I would like to warmly thank a number of people that supported me on this long journey. I cannot express enough gratitude to my wife, Kirsten, for her intelligent perspectives, love, and endless patience during my weary hours of writing. My father, Eugene C. Carroccia, M.D., was encouraging and tirelessly contributed many essential editorial hours. Thanks so very much, Dad. My mother, Sharon Carroccia, LCSW, was warmly supportive of my efforts. Michael Thomas, publisher at Charles C Thomas Ltd., was supportive and helpful with my detailed questions. My good friends Albert Spicer, Psy.D. and Laura Spicer, Psy.D. contributed keen insights, morale support, and assistance with many parts of this process. Mark Berman, Psy.D. shared valuable information about neurofeedback. I would like to give a hearty thanks to my colleagues Vanessa Houdek, Psy.D., Sara Skinner, Psy.D., Schaelyn McFadden, Psy.D., Jenna Berberich, Psy.D., Michael Ingersoll, Psy.D. and Huda Abuasi, Psy.D. for their support. A special thanks to John F. Smith, Ph.D. for his wisdom and friendship. Gregg Rzepczynski, J.D. and Susan Meade were generous with their perspectives. I wish to thank Kevin Leehey, M.D. for giving me permission to reproduce his wonderful ADHD medication tables, and William Walsh, Ph.D. for his permission to share his important contributions to the field. Finally, thanks to Patricia Quinn, M.D. for her kind words in the Foreword.

CONTENTS

Page

Foreword by Patricia Quinn, M.D. vii
Preface ix
Introduction xi

Chapter
1. Toward a Better Understanding of Attention-Deficit/
   Hyperactivity Disorder (ADHD) 3
2. Overview of The ADHD*ology* Treatment Approach 22
3. Evaluating ADHD and Other Co-Existing Conditions 27
4. Education about ADHD 43
5. ADHD Behavior Management Essentials 49
6. Maximizing Parental Effectiveness at Home 76
7. Additional Ways to Address ADHD at Home 93
8. Addressing Sleep Problems 115
9. The Homework and School Behavioral Notebook Systems 122
10. Official School Plans: 504s and Individualized Education
    Programs (IEPs) 138
11. Additional Ways to Address ADHD School Issues 156
12. Medication Treatment for ADHD 168
    Table 1: Methylphenidate-based Medications for ADHD 182
    Table 2: Amphetamine-based Medications for ADHD 186
    Table 3: Non-Stimulant Medications for ADHD 189
13. ADHD Approaches That Require Minimal Assistance from
    Providers 192
14. Alternative ADHD Treatments from Providers 222

Index 241

TREATING ADHD/ADD IN CHILDREN AND ADOLESCENTS

Chapter 1

TOWARD A BETTER UNDERSTANDING OF ATTENTION-DEFICIT/HYPERACTIVITY DISORDER (ADHD)

We all know one or more children, adolescents, and adults who have ADHD. With ADHD occurring in about one in every ten children and teens, and approximately one in every twenty adults, ADHD touches us all. This book is designed to help readers better understand and overcome the challenges associated with children and teens with ADHD.

While some parts of this chapter may seem pessimistic or overwhelming, the hope is that the reader will learn and appreciate the realities of untreated ADHD. The more severe the ADHD, the more problems that can occur. Although this chapter presents some difficult facts about untreated ADHD, the rest of the book provides the answers, tools, and solutions to improve this condition. Just like Jimmy and the Unger family in the introduction, children and families with ADHD can make tremendous improvements and even thrive with the proper help and support.

ADHD IS A COMPLEX BRAIN-FUNCTIONING CONDITION

Understanding ADHD is one of the most essential aspects of addressing this condition. While almost all children and adolescents can present occasional signs or phases of ADHD-like symptoms, most individuals with true ADHD conditions have difficulties that persist over time and eventually impair their functioning. Those with ADHD have a complex neurobiological disorder that can affect their ability to control themselves, their behaviors, and their ability to focus their attention on things they are not interested in or don't like. Since ADHD can affect any age, from very young to the elderly, it is critical to understand that ADHD is not an emotional disorder, but a brain-functioning condition where parts of the brain are underfunctioning and not working properly. People with ADHD have specific parts of their brains that are smaller, underactive, or underdeveloped in certain ways. They can also have networks of brain parts that are imbalanced and certain important brain chemicals called neurotransmitters that are not working correctly. For more details about ADHD braining functioning, please refer to the last section in this chapter.

Yet, ADHD is not just a condition that affects a person's attention, focus, or ability to sit still; rather, it is a chronic brain problem of executive functioning that impairs important areas of daily behavior. The impairments impact their organizational skills, concentration, motivation, self-discipline, time management, relationships with others, and performance at school and work. As a result of these challenges, ADHD can cause significant individual, family, and societal problems. Children and teens with ADHD can also suffer from additional co-existing disorders, academic and learning problems that require greater school needs, twice the health care costs than those without ADHD, and more injuries and accidents. Teens and adults with ADHD often have greater employment, substance abuse, and relationship difficulties. In addition to the psychological costs, the financial costs of ADHD are staggering. Collectively, the cross-sector costs associated with ADHD in the United States were conservatively estimated to be more than $78 billion each year (Visser et al., 2014).

THE PREVELANCE OF ADHD

ADHD exists all over the world, and not just in the United States. Studies have shown that it has been found in similar rates of children and adolescents worldwide (Polanczyk et al., 2007). Research presented by the Centers for Disease Control and Prevention (CDC) in 2016 found that about 9.4 percent of children and teens ages 2 to 17 in the United States had ever been diagnosed with ADHD. This is about one child in ten, about two children in every school classroom, and 6.1 million children nationwide. This rate has also increased since 2003 (Center for Disease Control and Prevention, 2018) and earlier. The rise may be a result of better awareness of ADHD by providers, but also possibly from increasing neurotoxins in the environment (Dendy, 2006). A Center for Disease Control and Prevention study from 2011 found that ADHD was two to three times more common in males than females. Additionally, the average ages for ADHD diagnoses appear to decrease with severity, with mild ADHD diagnosed at age 7, moderate ADHD at about age 6, and severe cases diagnosed at age 4-1/2 (Visser et al., 2014).

It seems that ADHD is both over diagnosed and under-diagnosed by some professionals. Some reasons include improper or less thorough evaluations due to lack of time or inadequate training; ignoring or inappropriately delaying the diagnosis; lack of understanding ADHD (Hallowell & Ratey, 2005); and/or inaccurate diagnosing when other conditions are causing the ADHD-like difficulties.

CAUSES OF ADHD

ADHD has been correlated with a number of influences, including genetic factors, environmental components, as well as deficiencies involving neural brain pathways, brain structures, and brain chemicals called neurotransmitters (Herbert & Esparham, 2017). But despite being one of the most researched psychological disorders, the exact cause of ADHD is still not known. How ADHD develops is complicated, and multiple risk factors and causes seem responsible. ADHD is most commonly caused by heredity and a positive family history. It is considered one of the most heritable of all psychological disorders, with heritability estimates of about 70 percent. This means that for all the children and adults with ADHD, this condition is a result of genetic factors seven out of 10 times. For the remaining 30 percent, the ADHD is likely due to other factors, such as environmental influences. Research has suggested that ADHD seems to develop from a complicated interaction between a number of genetic risk variants (Tarver, Daley, & Sayal, 2014). It is considered a complex trait disorder affected by many susceptibility genes, with each gene contributing to the risk (Herbert & Esparham, 2017). If one parent has ADHD, the odds of a child inheriting this can range from about 30 to 50 percent (Dendy, 2006; Hallowell & Ratey, 2005). If both parents have ADHD, the risk is 50 percent or greater. If a sibling has ADHD, there is 30 percent probability that other siblings will have the condition (Hallowell & Ratey, 2005).

In addition to genetics, environmental factors can play a significant role in the development of ADHD, including exposure to alcohol, cigarettes or illicit drugs during pregnancy. Other causes or factors associated with increased rates of ADHD include head injuries (causing mild or traumatic brain injuries), premature births (about 36 weeks or earlier) and/or low birth weight (about 5 to 5.5 pounds or less), certain birth or pregnancy conditions (such as oxygen deprivation in infants with neonatal respiratory distress syndrome, preeclampsia, or inadequate oxygen before or after birth), certain vitamin and mineral imbalances (such as iron, zinc, magnesium, B and D vitamins, and copper), exposure to neurotoxic substances (such as lead, mercury, or cadmium), and exposure to certain artificial food and beverage additives and preservatives.

Since ADHD is not one single entity, it seems to be caused in complex ways. The interaction of multiple genetic and environmental factors appears to act together to create a spectrum of potential for its development. There is a growing amount of evidence that supports the idea that a number of these genetic and environmental factors interact during a child's early development to create a neurobiological vulnerability to the condition. This means that the more genetic and environmental risk factors a child experiences, the greater the potential for ADHD to occur (Curatolo, D'agassi, & Mover, 2010).

TYPES OF ADHD

The two most common types of ADHD are ADHD-Combined and ADHD-Inattentive presentations. ADHD-Combined is most prevalent, and causes the classic problems with inattention, hyperactivity, and impulsivity. Individuals with this condition are more disruptive, excessively active, messy, noisy, immature, and more irresponsible than others their age. However, the hyperactivity and impulsivity symptoms may decrease to some degree by adolescence or young adulthood. While there is another type called ADHD-Predominantly Hyperactive/Impulsive, this form of ADHD mostly appears in younger, preschool, or kindergarten-aged children who have not yet had to demonstrate the longer attention spans required in first grade and beyond.

ADHD-Inattentive presentation is sometimes called "ADD." However, ADD is not the technical term, so it should not be used. Inattentive ADHD mostly causes problems with attention, daydreaming, motivation, and remaining focused, and typically has lesser to no hyperactivity or impulsivity problems. Inattentive ADHD tends to emerge around ages 8-12, and is often identified later or never. They tend to have less behavioral, defiance, and social problems. They are more passive and apathetic, and experience more depression and anxiety than those with Combined ADHD. Some with Inattentive ADHD may have had hyperactivity and impulsivity that decreased over time (Barkley, 2013). Inattentive ADHD may be underdiagnosed in females due to their desires to please others and lesser behavioral problems (Dendy, 2006).

Finally, there is another more recently researched but less recognized condition that appears similar to Inattentive ADHD known as Sluggish Cognitive Tempo (SCT) or Concentration Deficit Disorder (CDD). While additional research on this topic is needed, it is believed that many individuals who appear to have Inattentive ADHD really have SCT (Barkley, 2010). SCT will be addressed further in Chapter 3.

PROBLEMS ASSOCIATED WITH ADHD

ADHD can be dramatically complex. The most difficult dimensions can be hidden unless it is really understood (Dendy, 2006). It is not a common sense or straight forward condition. Those with ADHD often are confusing and frustrating to parents, teachers, and others who have not been educated about ADHD. Many people mistakenly think they know about ADHD. However, when people do not understand that ADHD is caused by brain problems, they may use inaccurate perspectives and labels such as "lazy," "a bad kid," or "they just aren't trying hard enough." Shifting perspectives to appreciate how the brain condition of ADHD is a disability that causes performance and behavioral issues is critical in obtaining a better understanding. It is important to remember that just because we cannot see these brain difficulties, it does not mean that they do not exist or are not real.

ADHD is a disability that can impact many areas of life. The difficulties listed in the following sections pertain more to those with untreated and unmanaged ADHD. They are generalizations, and the degree and types of problems will result from the type of ADHD and its severity. Those with Inattentive ADHD often have lesser levels of these difficulties than those with Combined ADHD. Obviously, each person is different and will have their own unique strengths and weaknesses.

ADHD is a Motivation Disorder

People with untreated ADHD have serious motivation problems and are usually not motivated to do things except what interests them in the moment. However, if they do like something, then they can often do it for longer periods. This is confusing because adults can witness children and teens with ADHD easily doing the things they enjoy, but then struggle with routine chores, tasks at home, school activities, following rules, and completing homework. Children and adolescents with ADHD are usually computer, screen media, and video game fanatics, and love to do these for hours each day. The way they approach life is "What's in it for me?" and "I want to do what I want to do right now!" They are often pleasure-seeking missiles who can become easily frustrated and confused when adults do not allow them to do what they want. Those with ADHD can be over-focused on the things they are interested in, and ignore or lack adequate focus on daily routine demands, causing them to be ineffective and unproductive.

ADHD is a Performance Disorder

Individuals with untreated ADHD have difficulty persisting with activities for as long as others, unless they like the activity. Therefore, they will pay more attention to things that are new, highly stimulating, or interesting. In contrast, they struggle with maintaining their attention and focus on activities that are routine, ordinary, boring, repetitive, or tedious, such as schoolwork, chores, or lectures from adults. They are easily distracted and have difficulty staying on task to get things done in a timely way. People with ADHD have more memory problems, forget to complete tasks, and leave tasks unfinished.

Much to the aggravation of parents and teachers, children and adolescents with ADHD are often highly inconsistent in their performance of daily activities. One day they will be able to do a chore or task, while on another day they can struggle with the same task, avoid it or procrastinate. They have a hard time "keeping their word" about doing or finishing what they said they will do. As a result, they often appear as lazy, selfish, insensitive to others, and self-centered. They may often appear to have many excuses as well. Those with ADHD work more effectively under close supervision and when instructions are repeated more frequently. They require others to help supervise, guide, and structure their work and behavior for them. However, they often resent this structure because they want to do what they want, and many do not like rules. Curiously, if they are interested in something, they will temporarily be able to override their ADHD with naturally-occurring higher levels of adrenaline that will increase their ability to stay focused and persist.

ADHD is a Boredom Disorder

They can become more easily bored with routine activities than other people and will struggle with remaining interested and staying focused on things they don't enjoy. People with untreated ADHD have more difficulty persisting in their efforts and find themselves drawn away by more interesting things. They can become easily distracted and struggle to complete tasks they consider less stimulating. Unfortunately, this causes them to be less productive and experience more conflict with parents and teachers. Their difficulties with boredom also impact their performance and motivation across a range of life activities.

ADHD is an Organization Disorder

Individuals with untreated ADHD often are quite disorganized and messy. Most with normal functioning brains will take for granted their automatic ability to be organized and complete multistep everyday tasks, like doing homework, studying for tests, getting ready in the morning, or completing a project. These are activities that require performing multiple steps to produce an end result. However, for a person with an ADHD brain, it is harder to remain focused on less-interesting things. As a result, they have trouble starting a project or activity, remaining focused on each step, remembering to do the multiple behaviors needed for each step, and persisting to complete the entire task. They have more difficulties planning and thinking ahead as well. Because of these organizational difficulties, people with ADHD are notorious procrastinators with activities and projects. They will also struggle to maintain things in neat or orderly ways, and so they often have messy rooms, desks, closets, and book bags.

ADHD is a Frustration Disorder

Many individuals with untreated ADHD, and particularly those with ADHD-Combined, have poor frustration tolerance. They do not handle stress or frustration as well as others their age. While they can appear angry, frequently it is really frustration. Tolerating frustration is a brain-functioning ability, and ADHD can greatly lower this. Often parents who initiate therapy for the first time will say their child or teen has "anger problems." However, when explored, many times they actually have poor frustration tolerance resulting from their ADHD, and not simply anger difficulties. When things don't go their way or when they hear "no" to what they want, they can become easily overwhelmed, and exhibit temper tantrums or outbursts. Some can even become aggressive or destructive.

ADHD is a Self-Control Disorder

Due to their brain-functioning problems, those with untreated ADHD can have a harder time controlling themselves and their emotions. They have more behavioral problems, are more hyperreponsive, and are excessively reactive to others and events around them. They are impulsive, highly active and reactive, struggle with remaining seated, and talk too much. These difficulties cause them to be irresponsible and inconsistent. They do and say things without thinking about the consequences and make poor choices. This can cause them to be rude, annoying, and get into trouble more than others. These factors can greatly contribute to their social problems as well. They tend to have difficulties controlling their urges to do what they feel like doing, and avoid completing their responsibilities. Those with Combined ADHD often have much greater self-control challenges. While those with Inattentive ADHD tend to have fewer difficulties, they can struggle to control themselves with staying on task, avoiding procrastination, remaining motivated, and completing tasks on time.

ADHD is a Time-Disorder

Individuals with untreated ADHD often have time management problems due to their poor perception of time, forgetfulness, having difficulties with planning ahead, being easily distracted, having excessive daydreaming tendencies, excessive rushing, and poorly anticipating how long tasks take. They frequently lose track of time and are often late. By procrastinating, they can run out of time to complete tasks. This can cause them to submit school work and homework late, and be tardy to school, jobs and meetings. Ultimately, their struggles with time can cause further stresses, unreliability and conflict with others, and overall ineffectiveness in their lives.

ADHD is a Disorder of Poor Self-Awareness

Those with untreated ADHD tend to have lower levels of self-awareness. They tend to view themselves as having fewer difficulties than others around them (Barkley, 2015). They often do not see how they annoy or upset others. While individuals with ADHD may regret their behaviors after confronted, they often continue to demonstrate these tendencies and lack the insight on how to change their unproductive patterns. Children with ADHD in particular can have little to no awareness of their difficult behaviors. A number of these children can deny having struggles, and some may really believe that they have no problems at all.

ADHD AND ACADEMIC PROBLEMS

ADHD causes a number of academic difficulties and problems. Most untreated children and teens with ADHD become academic underachievers, and eventually obtain lower grades as they become older. Teachers commonly say they are "not living up to their potential," "bright but could be doing better," and "not applying themselves." Two large contributors to their lower grades are difficulties with homework and reading. Their problems with boredom and not persisting with less interesting academic tasks can lead them to struggle with reading and homework. They often have problems initiating, organizing, completing, and submitting their homework. Additionally, many can have reading problems due to their trouble staying focused, higher levels of distraction, struggles to remain seated, slower information processing speeds, forgetfulness, and working memory limitations. All of these can reduce their understanding and reading comprehension. Thus, it is no surprise that many children and adults with ADHD do not like to read unless the subject is stimulating to them.

More intelligent children with ADHD can do adequately or even well in the lower school grades by half-paying attention in class and when the homework is less frequent or demanding. However, often by 7th or 8th grade and usually by high school, even the most intelligent students with ADHD begin to suffer from lower grades due to the greater homework and organizational demands. Many times, the brighter the child, the later they are diagnosed with ADHD. Because homework is required as an essential part of their high school grades, they often have lower grades, despite at times doing well on tests. As they age, they will be required to study more, and many with ADHD lack effective study skills. These factors can contribute to lower test scores as grades advance. Children and teens with ADHD have much higher rates of failing one or more grades. Additionally, a number of teens with ADHD do not finish high school, particularly if it is untreated and more severe (Lawlis, 2004). But despite these challenges, adolescents and adults with ADHD can succeed in high school, college, and even graduate programs. Most of these individuals are highly motivated and typically work much harder at their studies than their peers to overcompensate for their condition. Individuals with ADHD who succeed in high school or beyond often report it takes them multiple times the effort as their peers.

ADHD AND SOCIAL PROBLEMS

Some children and adolescents with ADHD can connect well with others and may have some positive social skills. Those with hyperactivity and impulsivity can be outgoing, fun, socially engaging, and chatty. However, ADHD may create a number of concerning social challenges. ADHD can often cause significant interpersonal difficulties with peers, family relationships, and teachers. Children and teens with Combined ADHD tend to experience greater conflict with others. Those with Inattentive ADHD tend to exhibit more social reserve and withdrawal, and less overt discord in relationships.

Children and teens with ADHD-Combined can be disliked and rejected at higher levels due to their greater aggression, provocative and controlling behaviors, lower frustration tolerance, and lesser ability to cooperate and be flexible in play and interactions. They can blurt out hurtful or inappropriate statements, become rigid in their demands, and have problems with sharing and taking turns. They may act immaturely, excessively silly, and self-centered. They may also dominate conversations and be less responsive to nonverbal cues from others, which can further contribute to negative social outcomes. Due to their lesser social skills and abilities to resolve conflict, they may resort to more verbal or physical aggression.

As a result of their social challenges, children with ADHD can become increasingly delayed in their social and interpersonal skills, which in turn may generate additional rejection, relational problems, deficit skills, and eventually lower self-esteem. Families may struggle with the child's ongoing difficulties with peers and friends, as well as the fluctuations in their own relationships. Some children may gravitate towards playing with younger children because they can more easily dominate and relate to them. Those with Combined ADHD may bully more, while they and those with Inattentive ADHD can be bullied by peers at higher rates as well.

Due to the poor social skills and other difficulties caused by ADHD, this condition often creates significant interpersonal problems in families. Unfortunately, increased levels of chronic arguing, discord, and resentment often exist in homes with ADHD. Parents and their children with ADHD can experience ongoing negative relational dynamics. Sibling relationships can be impacted as well. As a result of these greater behavioral and family challenges, parents of children with ADHD divorce three times more frequently than families without ADHD (Lawlis, 2004).

OPPOSITIONAL DEFIANT DISORDER (ODD)

Combined ADHD often causes ODD, which is a behavioral disorder that can make those with ADHD more difficult to live with and manage. ODD is a pattern of anger, irritability, argumentativeness, and defiance lasting for a minimum of six months. These behaviors are beyond what is considered normal for the child's peers, occur with at least one person that is not their sibling, and cause significant difficulties at home or school. Symptoms include temper problems, being easily annoyed or touchy, angry mood, resents others, arguing with adults, defiance or doesn't respect adults' rules or requests, intentionally annoys, blames other people for their misbehaviors or errors, and revengeful or cruel behaviors (Mayo Clinic Staff, 2015).

About 54 to 67 percent of people with ADHD have ODD (Barkley, 2015), and it is much more common in those with Combined than Inattentive ADHD. Also, 50 percent of children diagnosed with ODD continue to have this condition into adulthood. ODD can result from the pattern of rebelliousness and arguing that some children with ADHD demonstrate with adults (Barkley, 2010). ODD can be seen as a secondary behavioral condition to ADHD. It seems to grow out of ADHD because individuals with untreated ADHD have more difficulties complying with adults to complete tasks, chores, and activities they do not like. ODD behaviors in people with ADHD occur partially due to their poor frustration tolerance. It is easier for them to say "No!," argue or complain about adults' requests, such as doing homework or chores. When parents and teachers ask them to do things, their ADHD brain-functioning problems can cause them to become easily stressed, overwhelmed, and frustrated. This can then cause them to be more non-compliant, oppositional, and defiant.

Children and teens with ODD often lie, blame others for their misbehavior, swear and deny doing things that they actually did. They can appear chronically angry and frequently display bad attitudes. A negative cycle can form because the more difficult they become, the more adults give up and stop asking them to do things. Their non-compliance then becomes reinforced and more ingrained. Children and teens with ODD are typically more defiant and difficult with parents they interact with the most, particularly mothers, and those they do not like. Also, the ODD behaviors may not be seen with all adults or at school. Fortunately, children and teens with ADHD often experience improvements in their ODD when they are on effective ADHD medications. Additional treatment for ODD involves implementing specific behavioral management approaches and family therapy.

ADHD AND OTHER DISORDERS

In addition to ODD, those with ADHD are at increased risk for having other co-existing psychological, sleep, and neurodevelopmental conditions. This unfortunately adds to the challenges and problems they confront daily. Research has found that as many as 67 to 80 percent of clinic-referred children with ADHD have at least one other psychological disorder, as many as half have two or more other disorders (Pliszka, 2015), and 20 percent have three or more co-existing disorders (Spruyt & Gozal, 2011). ADHD is a foundational disorder that greatly increases the risk of having other conditions over a lifetime. More than any other psychological condition, ADHD appears in combinations with other disorders (Brown, 2009).

Due to their lower frustration tolerance and other brain functioning difficulties, those with ADHD can be more overwhelmed by their daily challenges and stressors. They tend to struggle more with depression, worry, and anxiety. About 20 to 25 percent of people with ADHD have anxiety disorders (Spruyt & Gozal, 2011). Barkley (2015) reported that about 20 to 30 percent of people with ADHD have depressive disorders. Those with inattention tend to have more depression and general unhappiness, while adolescent girls with ADHD can have higher rates of depression and anxiety. Further, children and teens with ADHD and anxiety or depression can have even higher levels of ADHD symptoms when these other conditions worsen. Finally, children and teens with ADHD have much higher rates of sleep problems, and these can further negatively impact their ADHD and daily functioning.

Conservative estimates indicate that 25 to 40 percent of those with ADHD also have learning disorders (Tannock & Brown, 2009). These include reading and math disorders, as well as poor motor coordination or developmental coordination disorder. Those with ADHD also can have dysgraphia, or significantly messy handwriting, and these tend to be somewhat higher in those with Combined versus Inattentive ADHD (Barkley, 2015).

HOW ADHD PROGRESSES

There are a number of factors that can affect the impact and progression of ADHD. It exists on a continuum, with mild, moderate, or severe symptoms and impairments which may decrease over time. The degree of ADHD, amount of support, and effectiveness of treatments will usually determine the problems that will be experienced at home, school, and in other life areas. Also, those with Inattentive ADHD tend to have fewer difficulties than those with Combined ADHD. If co-existing conditions exist, the ADHD can be more complicated.

It can be normal for pre-school age children to demonstrate developmentally appropriate ADHD-like behaviors. Over half of parents tend to rate children as inattentive and overactive by age 4, and up to 40 percent may demonstrate inattention that is concerning to parents and teachers. However, many 6-year-olds and younger with ADHD-like traits can improve within 3 to 6 months. For younger children with an ADHD diagnosis, about 50 percent will have ADHD by later childhood or early adolescence. Preschool aged children with inattentiveness and hyperactivity that persists for at least a year are much more likely to have ADHD through adolescence (Barkley, 2013). Parents of children with Combined ADHD typically notice traits between ages 2 to 4 (Kelly, Pressman, & Greenhill, 2009). As a general rule, if ADHD symptoms persist for at least one year and beyond ages 6 to 7 (or by the end of first grade), then the condition can be more likely to continue over time. Also, the earlier and more severe the symptoms, the greater the likelihood of more chronic ADHD.

Younger children with impulsivity and hyperactivity can demonstrate self-management problems when they begin school due to classroom restrictions. For some without true ADHD, these difficulties can reflect a developmental lag, and they may need one or two years to mature. However, for those with true ADHD, the self-regulation difficulties remain and intensify with age. Others may not demonstrate significant ADHD difficulties until middle or high school when they switch classrooms, and experience greater homework and organizational demands. Some teens may not clearly demonstrate ADHD difficulties until high school because their parents heavily managed their academics (Brown, 2009).

It is estimated that 70 to 80 percent of children diagnosed with Combined and Inattentive ADHD in childhood will continue to have symptoms by adolescence (Dendy, 2006). As teens with ADHD age, between 60 to 70 percent will have symptoms that continue into adulthood and the rest may still experience some traits (Hallowell & Ratey, 2005). As children and teens with ADHD-Combined mature into adulthood, the inattention often remains, but hyperactive and disinhibition symptoms can decline. Others can improve to various degrees, but may still be affected by ADHD (Barkley, 2015). It is possible for some children to outgrow the disorder completely by later childhood, adolescence, or adulthood. However, it is more common that some symptoms remain through adulthood. Since each person is different, the best practice is to evaluate and monitor ADHD over time.

ADOLESCENTS WITH ADHD

As children with ADHD grow older, the condition and types of problems can change. Typically, the hyperactivity decreases in Combined ADHD, but the inattention and impulsivity problems persist. Adolescents with ADHD tend to experience higher rates of risky and unsafe behaviors, including starting sexual activity earlier, lesser use of birth control, and higher rates of sexually transmitted diseases and teen pregnancies. They have more speeding tickets and automotive accidents than adolescents without ADHD. Studies of teens with ADHD show that they were twice as likely to have abused alcohol within the last six months, and three times as likely to abuse drugs other than marijuana ("ADHD in Teens," 2014). Untreated teens with ADHD also have higher rates of nicotine and cigarette use and criminal arrests.

Adolescents with untreated ADHD can commit these risky behaviors due to their impulsivity, thrill seeking tendencies, poorer judgement, and lesser anticipation of consequences. They may also experience lower grades, greater relational discord with parents, and peer difficulties and rejection. By adolescence, many will have experienced years of these challenges, and depression, anxiety, and self-esteem problems can result. Fortunately, however, teens who take ADHD medication can have lower rates of these difficulties. Dendy (2006) reported ADHD can also be affected by hormonal influences, and may become worse during puberty. For females, ADHD symptoms can worsen during the week before their menstrual period. For more information on adolescents with ADHD, see Chapter 7.

ADULTS WITH ADHD

Any book about children and adolescents with ADHD should address the likelihood of future adult ADHD. It is believed that over 4 percent of adults in the United States have ADHD, and many have not been diagnosed or treated. Adults with ADHD must have had symptoms beginning in their childhood. Like children and teens, adults with ADHD may have ADHD-Combined or ADHD-Inattentive conditions. Common complaints from adults with ADHD are feeling chronically ineffective, relationship problems, work-related difficulties, and excessive struggles with the daily challenges of life.

Depending on the severity, adults with untreated ADHD can experience persistent challenges, including constantly living in the moment without planning ahead or being responsible; organizational problems; messy rooms, closets, desks, and cars; procrastination; poor follow through with tasks; making poor choices; being late for appointments and meetings; misplacing and losing things; poor self-discipline to complete chores and home activities; being easily distracted; and forgetting to do or finish tasks. Additionally, adults with untreated ADHD often have serious money management problems, including excessive debt, overspending, making impulsive purchases they do not need or cannot afford, abusing credit cards, and not paying bills on time.

These adults can have higher rates of addictive behaviors, substance abuse problems, speeding tickets, arrests, sexually transmitted diseases, aggressive incidents, car accidents, and injuries. Because of their chronic and numerous difficulties and disappointments, many adults with ADHD tend to suffer from lower self-esteem and higher rates of depression, anxiety, and substance abuse. Lawlis (2004) reported that 50 to 75 percent of adults in prison have some form of ADHD.

Adults with ADHD tend to be underachievers who frequently have more employment and work-related problems. These can include difficulties keeping jobs, becoming bored or easily overwhelmed by work positions, being late, social problems at work, and being inefficient on the job. Adults with ADHD are three times as likely to be unemployed. Just like children and teens, they will complete tasks and succeed more at jobs that they like, but will avoid, procrastinate, and struggle with work duties and responsibilities that are boring and tasks they do not enjoy. At home or work they may also become less productive or distracted by overfocusing on the things they enjoy.

Adults with untreated ADHD often suffer from numerous and serious relationship, social and family problems. They tend to have impaired marriages and relationships related to their impulsivity, inattention, excessive talking, disorganization, unreliability, lack of completion of home chores, financial problems, employment limitations, problematic substance use, negative communication, and mood and frustration difficulties. Adults with ADHD struggle with time management, and this makes them inconsistent and unable to keep their commitments. They often seem selfish and insensitive to others and are often unaware of others' needs or difficulties. Sadly, these relationship and other related ADHD problems cause higher rates of divorce.

In marriages or relationships with untreated ADHD, the spouse or partner without the disorder (typically a female) often experiences chronic resentment. Over time, the spouse without ADHD tends to "burn out" from overcompensating for the person with ADHD. The partner without ADHD commonly believes they do more at home and for the family, and often feel like a "parent" to the partner. Communication in ADHD marriages is challenging because the partner without ADHD often believes the other is selfish, stubborn, or doesn't listen during conversations, is excessively insensitive and defensive, and interrupts too frequently. The adult with ADHD may have unpredictable moodiness and irritability, and can be highly overreactive. They may have intense or abusive outbursts with their partners, but then calm down in a short time and expect all to be forgotten, while the spouse feels disrespected and remains upset about the interaction.

Parents with ADHD often struggle with their parenting abilities due to strained connections with their children, inconsistencies in their disciplining efforts, as well as the other aforementioned traits. To make things more complicated, ADHD often genetically "runs" in families, so adults with ADHD frequently have children with ADHD. Their children can have more challenges and special needs, and thus may be more difficult to parent. Collectively, this may generate even more stress and difficulties for everyone in the home.

BRAIN-FUNCTIONING DETAILS ABOUT ADHD

The neurochemical, structural, and systemic brain deficits in children and adults who have ADHD have been studied intensely. The reality of these brain-functioning deficits has been observed with a variety of measures, including genetics, quantitative electroencephalograph (QEEG), single photo emission computed tomography (SPECT), and positron emission tomography (PET), and higher resolution magnetic resonance imaging (MRI).

ADHD is not just a single neurobiological problem. Individuals with ADHD tend to have a variety of foundational brain-functioning issues. One difficulty that has been extensively studied involves imbalances and deficiencies in neurotransmitters in the brain's frontal cortex, and particularly the neurotransmitters dopamine and norepinephrine (Brown, 2009). Brain imaging, pharmacological, genetic, and animal models all indicate how dopamine plays an important role in ADHD (Curatolo, D'agassi, & Mover, 2010). Neurotransmitters send signals between nerve cells by crossing gaps or synapses. These neurochemicals are necessary for learning, motivation, self-control, staying alert, and processing information. Individuals with ADHD create dopamine and norepinephrine like everyone else. The difficulties occur with the dynamics of the excessive reloading or inadequate releasing of these neurotransmitters in the synapses of certain brain regions responsible for attention, self-management, and motivation. Stimulants do not just create more neurotransmitters. They temporarily stimulate and correct neurotransmitter dysfunction by enhancing the release and continued action of these chemicals in specific brain circuits (Brown, 2009).

White matter and grey matter are the two types of brain tissue in the central nervous system. Grey matter contains many brain cell bodies and processes information. White matter is composed millions of nerve fibers or axons that connect the various brain and grey matter parts with each other. Research using brain imaging has identified specific regional brain abnormalities in children with ADHD, including reduced grey matter in portions of the frontostriatal circuits, cortical thinning, and atypical white matter volumes in many neural tracts. These may also suggest deficit communication between certain brain areas (Tarver, Daley, & Sayal, 2014). Evidence is also emerging that reduced connectivity in the white matter in essential brain areas occurs in people with ADHD (Curatolo, D'agassi, & Mover, 2010).

Additionally, children with ADHD seem to be about three years behind in their brain's cortical development when compared to neurotypical children. The cerebral cortex is the brain's outer layer which is composed of grey matter. It is essential for a number of cognitive functions, such as attention, memory, language, and perception. Advanced cortical thinning is seen in some brain disorders, including Alzheimer's disease. Similarly, ADHD seems likely to result from intricate structural abnormalities of a number of brain regions and their connecting circuitry (Tarver, Daley, & Sayal, 2014).

Structural brain imaging studies have confirmed that the brains of children with ADHD are significantly smaller than children without ADHD. Additionally, the brain areas of the prefrontal cortex, cerebellum, and the basal ganglia in children with ADHD are negatively impacted in different ways (Curatolo, D'agassi, & Mover, 2010). Earlier research found that individuals with ADHD had underactive brain functioning, particularly in the frontal brain regions of the prefrontal and anterior cingulate cortex (Yang et al., 2015) as well as the frontostriatal and parietal brain regions (Cortese et al., 2012).

In the past, ADHD was believed to just be a result of dysfunction in the frontostriatal circuits, or the neural pathways connecting the brain's frontal lobe with the basal ganglia that controls behavioral, motor, and cognitive activities. The basal ganglia is the brain region responsible for producing dopamine which drives the prefrontal cortex. However, more recent neuroimaging studies have indicated that ADHD is a complex result of a number of brain areas dysfunctions, including the anterior cingulum, dorsolateral and ventrolateral prefrontal cortex, orbitofrontal cortex, the caudate nucleus, thalamus, amygdala and cerebellum. There also seems to be a shift towards viewing ADHD as a systemic problem within neuronal networks of the brain (Kasparek, Theiner, & Filova, 2015). Indeed, ADHD is being increasingly understood as problems with altered connectivity within and among multiple large-scale brain networks, rather than just difficulties in distinct and isolated brain regions (Cortese et al., 2012).

Further emerging research has indicated ADHD is associated with systemic difficulties across regions of the brain. One study found that children with ADHD had inefficient neural circuits that exerted less influence and lead to increased inattention and daydreaming when compared to neurotypical children. Interactions between three brain networks that govern attention abilities were found to be weaker in children with ADHD. These deficiencies were found in the salience network, which is a set of brain regions that work together through well-synchronized neural activity that determines where attention is directed and how focus is maintained. The study found that in a healthy functioning brain, focusing attention occurs through the salience network by decreasing the activity of the default mode while increasing the activity of the central executive network. However, children with ADHD were found to have weaker interactions between these brain networks which caused greater attention problems (Stanford Medicine, 2015).

THE ADHD*OLOGY* TREATMENT MODEL

So, what can be done to address these challenges? How can children and teens with ADHD be helped and succeed? Fortunately, there are effective approaches and treatments for ADHD. The rest of this book focuses upon solutions so that children and teens with ADHD can enjoy the lives they deserve. The next chapter presents the ADHD*ology* treatment model approach to offer a guiding framework of the six specific phases to address and positively transform ADHD.

SUMMARY POINTS

- ADHD is a complex brain-functioning condition which causes attention, hyperactivity, impulsivity, behavioral, motivational, organizational, academic, and social difficulties.
- ADHD is one of the most common child and adolescent neurodevelopmental conditions occurring in about 10 percent of children and adolescents in the United States.
- While genetics is the largest cause of ADHD, certain environmental factors can also contribute to its development.
- The most common type of ADHD is Combined ADHD, which causes significant inattentiveness, hyperactivity, and impulsivity. Inattentive ADHD creates mostly attention difficulties.
- Many with Combined ADHD also have oppositional defiant disorder which increases behavioral and relational challenges.
- Some may "grow out" of ADHD, but most will have at least some symptoms persisting into adulthood.
- Adolescents and adults with untreated ADHD can experience difficulties that can seriously impact scholastic and work performance, relationships, and life satisfaction.

REFERENCES

ADHD in Teens. (reviewed 2014, August 08). Retrieved from www.webmd.com/add-adhd/childhood-adhd/adhd-teens

Barkley, R. (2010). *Taking charge of adult ADHD.* New York, NY: The Guilford Press.

Barkley, R. (2013). *Taking charge of ADHD* (3rd ed.). New York, NY: The Guilford Press.

Barkley, R. (2015, March 19). *ADHD: Nature, course, outcomes, and comorbidity.* Retrieved from www.continuingedcourses.net/active/courses/course003.php

Brown, T. E. (2009). Developmental complexities of attentional disorders. In T. E. Brown (Ed.), *ADHD comorbidities: Handbook for ADHD complications in children and adults* (pp. 3–22). Arlington, VA: American Psychiatric Publishing, Inc.

Centers for Disease Control and Prevention. (2018, March 20). *Data and statistics (for ADHD).* Retrieved from www.cdc.gov/ncbddd/adhd/data.html

Cortese, S., Kelly, C., Chabernaud, C., Proal, E., Di Martino, A., Milham, M. P., & Castellanos, F. X. (2012, October). Toward systems neuroscience of ADHD: A meta-analysis of 55 fmri studies. *American Journal of Psychiatry, 169*(10), 1038–1055.

Curatolo, P., D'Agati, E., & Moavero, R. (2010). The neurobiological basis of ADHD. *Italian Journal of Pediatrics, 36*(1), 79. doi: 10.1186/1824-7288-36-79

Dendy, C. Z. (2006). *Teenagers with ADD and ADHD: A guide for parents and professsionals* (2nd ed.). Bethesda, MD: Woodbine House.

Hallowell, E. D., & Ratey, J. J. (2005). *Delivered from distraction.* New York: Ballantine Books.

Herbert, A., & Esparham, A. (2017, April 25). Mind-body therapy for children with attention-deficit/hyperactivity disorder. *Children, 4*(5), 31. Retrieved from https://www.ncbi.nlm.nih.gov/pubmed/28441363

Kasparek, T., Theiner, P., & Filova, A. (2015). Neurobiology of ADD from childhood to adulthood: Findings of imaging methods. *Journal of Attention Disorders, 19*(11), 931–943.

Kelly, P., Pressman, A. W., & Greenhill, L. L. (2009). ADHD in preschool children. In T. E. Brown (Ed.), *ADHD comorbidities: Handbook for ADHD complications in children and adults* (pp. 37–53). Arlington, VA: American Psychiatric Publishing, Inc.

Lawlis, F. (2004). *The ADD answer.* New York, NY: Viking/The Penguin Group.

Mayo Clinic Staff. (2015, February, 06). *Oppositional defiant disorder (ODD)–symptoms.* Retrieved from https://www.mayoclinic.org/diseases-conditions/oppositional-defiant-disorder/basics/symptoms/con-20024559

Pliszka, S. (2015). Comorbid psychiatric disorders in children with ADHD. In R. Barkley (Ed.), *Attention deficit hyperactivity disorder: A handbook for diagnosis and treatment* (4th ed., pp 140–168). New York, NY: Guilford Press.

Polanczyk, G., de Lima, M. S., Horta, B. L., Biederman, J., & Rohde, L. A. (2007). The worldwide prevalence of ADHD: A systematic review and meta regression analysis. *American Journal of Psychiatry, 164,* 942–948.

Spruyt, K., & Gozal, D. (2011, April). Sleep disturbances in children with attention-deficit/hyperactivity disorder. *Expert Review of Neurotherapeutics, 11*(4), 65–577.

Stanford Medicine. (2015, December 15). *Interactions between attention-grabbing brain networks weak in ADHD.* Retrieved from https://med.stanford.edu/news/all-news/2015/12/attention-networks-different-in-kids-with-adhd.html

Tannock, R., & Brown, T. E. (2009). ADHD with language and/or learning disorders in children and adolescents. In T. E. Brown (Ed.), *ADHD comorbidities: Handbook for ADHD complications in children and adults* (pp. 189-231). Arlington, VA: American Psychiatric Publishing, Inc.

Tarver, J., Daley, D., & Sayal, K. (2014, November). Attention-deficit hyperactivity disorder (ADHD): An updated review of the essential facts. *Child: Care, Health, and Development, 40*(6), 762–774.

Visser, S. N., Danielson, M. L., Bitsko, R. H., Kogan, M. D., Ghandour, R. M., Perou, R., & Blumberg, S. J. (2014, January). Trends in the parent-report of health care provider-diagnosed and medicated attention-deficit/hyperactivity disorder: United States, 2003–2011. *Journal of the American Academy of Child & Adolescent Psychiatry, 53*(1), 34–46.e2

Yang, X., Carrey, N., Bernier, D., & MacMaster, F. P. (2015). Cortical thickness in young treatment-naive children with ADHD. *Journal of Attention Disorders, 19*(11), 925–930.

Chapter 2

OVERVIEW OF THE ADHD*OLOGY* TREATMENT APPROACH

THE SIX PHASES OF ADHD TREATMENT

The most comprehensive and effective treatment for ADHD involves a long-term management perspective that utilizes a number of approaches and interventions. The ADHD*ology* treatment model for children and adolescents involves six phases:

1. **Evaluate ADHD and Other Co-Existing Conditions**
    a. Obtain a comprehensive ADHD evaluation or full neurodevelopmental assessment
    b. Explore other possible co-existing medical, sleep, psychological, and neurodevelopmental conditions and disorders
    c. If other conditions are suspected or detected, obtain additional evaluations and treatment from appropriate providers
2. **Education About ADHD**
    a. Receive accurate information about ADHD
    b. Learn about grieving issues concerning ADHD to move towards acceptance
3. **Address and Manage ADHD at Home**
    a. Learn and use effective behavior management perspectives and methods, and maximize parental effectiveness at home
    b. Utilize additional services and management approaches to address various ADHD challenges
    c. Address sleep problems
4. **Address and Manage ADHD School Issues**
    a. Address homework and school behavioral problems through the use of the notebook systems

    b. Obtain 504 Plans or Individual Education Plans at school
    c. Utilize additional ways to address and manage school issues
5. **Medication Treatment for ADHD**
6. **Additional and Alternative ADHD Approaches and Treatment**
    a. Utilize additional approaches including diets, fish oil supplements, increasing sleep, increasing physical activity, green time, limiting screen time and video games, and mind-body therapies
    b. Utilize alternative treatments including neurofeedback, correcting vitamin and mineral deficiencies, Walsh's Biochemical Imbalances Approach and Advanced Nutrient Therapy, Brain Gym® and Bal-A-Vis-X

1. Comprehensive Evaluations and Assessments of ADHD

The first step for any parent concerned that their child may have ADHD or any other behavioral or psychological condition is to obtain diagnostic services. Identifying the problems and conditions should occur before treatment. Families with children and teens who still have suspected behavioral health diagnoses, or if their physicians or other providers are still unclear about what conditions exist, should receive a psychological or ADHD evaluation or a comprehensive assessment. Schools often do not diagnose ADHD in their evaluations, and they may or may not be helpful in directing parents to obtain diagnostic services outside school.

If ADHD is suspected, it is essential that families obtain ADHD evaluations or testing assessments from qualified and experienced providers. This diagnostic process should include exploring other possible co-existing conditions and disorders. Children and teens with true ADHD commonly have other conditions, so it is important to identify and treat these along with the ADHD. Parents should ensure that assessing providers are screening for a number of specific medical, sleep, psychological, and neurodevelopmental disorders. These other conditions can look like ADHD when it does not exist, so a thorough diagnostic approach should be the first step. These topics will be discussed in the next chapter.

2. Education about ADHD

One of the most important treatment approaches is accurate information about ADHD. When families and important others properly understand ADHD, they can be more effective with greater patience and acceptance. Additionally, grieving and disability perspectives can be helpful once ADHD is confirmed. Chapter 4 will address these topics.

3. Addressing and Managing ADHD at Home

A critical aspect of treating ADHD at home is to learn behavior management principles and practices that maximize parental effectiveness. Because ADHD is a brain functioning condition, ADHD is generally managed and not cured. This phase of the model also addresses a range of issues at home, including oppositional defiant disorder (ODD), sibling issues, and using emotional management skills for children and teens. Parents will learn effective ADHD management skills to become master parent wizards to help their children meet their true potentials.

Parents need to be coaches, managers, advocates, and motivators who maintain consistency, understanding, and structure. Caregivers need training to use these approaches to address daily ADHD problems. Using standard daily expectations for behaviors, such as morning routines, after school homework, chore, and bedtime routines, are critical if these are problematic. Chapters 5, 6, and 7 will teach these and other skills, as well as how to parent more effectively. Information about family therapy, individual therapy, and ADHD coaching will also be presented in Chapter 7.

Another important issue during this phase involves addressing sleep difficulties. Those with ADHD have higher rates of sleeping problems, and these can also worsen ADHD symptoms. Parents can improve sleep insomnia, inadequate sleep duration, and other sleep issues by using sleep hygiene and behavioral interventions. Chapter 8 will address these topics.

4. Addressing and Managing ADHD School Issues

Parents should be actively involved with the child or teen's school and inform the school staff of the child's conditions. Parents who avoid informing schools about their children's conditions may not have fully understood, accepted and grieved the diagnosis. While some parents may believe that "it's none of the school's business," this can make the school situation worse, particularly if the child has serious learning and behavioral problems at school. Parents need to be advocates for their school needs, and actively work with the school staff. While every family's situation is unique, generally a partnership approach is best.

Individual Education Programs (IEPs) and 504 plans can be created with the school staff to formally provide school services and accommodations that address and manage school problems. Parents may also utilize effective behavioral management approaches to manage homework and behavioral difficulties at school, including the use of the homework and school behavioral notebook systems. These involve applying daily consequences for school issues at home where the consequences tend to motivate children more effectively. Other school management topics include methods to enhance parent and school staff collaboration, becoming a detective when grades decrease, teaching study skills, ways to encourage reading at home, use of tutoring and educational therapist services, and ADHD classroom teaching approaches. Please refer to Chapters 9, 10, and 11 for more information on these school topics.

5. Medication Treatment for ADHD

Research has shown that medication can be one of the most effective and critical elements in the treatment of school-aged children and adolescents. especially for more moderate to severe ADHD. Studies show that 70 to 80 percent of individuals respond positively to stimulant medication treatments (Barkley, 2015), while medication along with psychological treatments and educational interventions produce the greatest ADHD improvements (Barkley, 2013). Medication works by temporarily correcting the brain-functioning problems by increasing the availability of the special brain chemicals, or neurotransmitters, dopamine and norepinephrine. Chapter 12 will address this topic.

6. Additional and Alternative ADHD Treatment Options and Approaches

In addition to the more traditional ADHD approaches, there are a number of promising research-based ways to reduce symptoms which can be used with or without medications. These approaches include improving the quality of diets (eating healthier foods, avoiding foods with artificial colors and additives, and consuming more protein and lower carbohydrates), detecting and managing food sensitivities and allergies, taking omega-3 fatty acids, increasing the amount of sleep and addressing sleep problems, utilizing regular and consistent physical exercise, obtaining more "green" time outside with grass and trees, limiting screen time and video games, and using mind-body therapies. Chapter 13 provides more information on these additional approaches.

There are also special providers who can offer other alternative treatments. Neurofeedback is a powerful type of biofeedback where practitioners use a computer with special video games or screen activities that can enhance brain functioning over time. Neurofeedback stimulates the brain by creating and strengthening new neural pathways. These changes can actually improve ADHD permanently, with progress ranging from minimal to dramatic. Neurofeedback can also treat a number of other conditions, such as learning disorders, anxiety, depression, and autism. Some may even be able to reduce or end their ADHD medication.

Another treatment involves using supplements. Research has shown that deficiencies in iron, zinc, magnesium, and vitamins B and D have all been found to cause ADHD-like symptoms. Families can obtain testing to see if their child or teen has these deficiencies and may benefit from appropriate supplementation.

The Walsh Biochemical Approach and Advanced Nutrient Therapy is an innovative way of treating ADHD. This approach utilizes specialized biochemical urine and blood testing to explore if a person has a number of certain biochemical imbalances that can cause ADHD and/or other psychological conditions. Based on the imbalances, individualized blends of vitamins, minerals, and amino acids are created by special pharmacies. This approach is supervised by professionals and can be quite effective and without the side effects of psychiatric medications.

Lastly, the practices of Brain Gym® and Bal-A-Vis-X can help as well. Chapter 14 presents information on all of these approaches.

REFERENCES

Barkley, R. (2013). *Taking charge of ADHD* (3rd ed.). New York, NY: The Guilford Press.

Barkley, R. (2015, March 19). *Treating children and adolescents with ADHD: An overview of empirically-based treatments.* Retrieved from www.continuingedcourses.net/active/courses/course068.php

Chapter 3

EVALUATING ADHD AND OTHER CO-EXISTING CONDITIONS

ADHD EVALUATION AND ASSESSMENT PROVIDERS

The first step of treating ADHD is to determine that a child or teen truly has ADHD, and are there any other co-existing medical, sleep, psychological, or neurodevelopmental conditions. ADHD can be evaluated by clinical psychologists, experienced mental or behavioral health therapists (who should have a master's degree or doctorate in psychology, counseling, social work, or education), child or adolescent psychiatrists, school psychologists at school settings (who should have a master's degree or doctorate), primary care physicians, and nurse practitioners who have experience diagnosing ADHD.

Although some providers use the terms "evaluation" and "assessment" interchangeably, others distinguish these as similar but separate services. Both can effectively diagnosis ADHD. An evaluation is a more limited diagnostic process that does not use psychological testing and may not produce a report, while an assessment is a more extensive psychological testing process that uses a range of tests and measures that includes a report.

While their licenses permit them to diagnose ADHD, primary care physicians (including pediatricians and family practice physicians) may or may not accurately diagnose this condition. Because they typically treat children before other providers and parents often discuss behavioral problems with them first, these physicians may be the first provider to learn about a child's ADHD-like symptoms. While some primary care physicians may refer ADHD evaluations out to behavioral health specialists, others may evaluate it. In more rural or limited areas, they may be the only accessible clinicians available. While some are competent and effective in diagnosing ADHD, others may not provide adequate and comprehensive evaluations. A proper ADHD evaluation will take a number of office visits, and primary care physicians may not have the time or proper training to provide these diagnostic services.

Because these physicians are generalists, families can consider obtaining evaluations or assessments from behavioral health providers while involving their physician in this process. Primary care physicians do have an important role in the ADHD evaluation process because they should ensure that the child or teen does not have any contributing medical conditions (which will be addressed later). Parents can discuss with physicians if they will provide the thorough ADHD evaluation, or if they prefer to refer these out to other behavioral health providers.

There are too many incorrectly diagnosed children and teens who have false negative and false positive ADHD diagnoses. False negatives occur when individuals receive clinical services yet are not diagnosed with ADHD, even though they have true ADHD. These are children or teens who have been told that they will "grow out" of their behavioral or school problems, and/or they have been improperly diagnosed with other conditions. False positives occur when children and teens have been incorrectly diagnosed with ADHD, when they really have other conditions that mimic ADHD. They may also receive ADHD treatments that do not help or make them worse. With both of these scenarios, families will suffer and continue to struggle. They may also give up hope and turn away from further treatment and services because they are not improving.

To avoid these mistakes, accuracy can increase when children and teens are evaluated or assessed properly by experienced behavioral health providers. Properly determined diagnoses should inform treatment. Many parents do not know what they are looking for when they seek behavioral health services, and thus may not locate the right provider. Parents should obtain services from experienced and qualified providers, rather than those who will see them the soonest. When looking for providers, some will permit parents to interview them on the phone, and ask how they specifically evaluate and treat ADHD in children and adolescents. Parents can inquire about their credentials, experience working with children and teens with ADHD, and their diagnostic and therapeutic approaches. Many parents do not realize they can be assertive with their questioning during these initial calls to find a provider that best meets their needs.

There are two main ways to receive diagnostic services to address suspected ADHD. For the most comprehensive approach, children and teens can receive a specialized psychological testing assessment. These are called neurodevelopmental, neuropsychological, or neurobehavioral assessments. They are conducted by a clinical psychologist, often called a neuropsychologist, who works with children and adolescents. They will typically assess intellectual levels with IQ testing, ADHD-like symptoms and attentional abilities, possible learning disorders, processing deficits, and other psychological and neurodevelopmental conditions. The neuropsychological assessment typically produces a report with the findings, diagnoses, and recommendations. This report should be given to the parents at the end of the testing process. The downside to these assessments is there are fewer neuropsychologists, they may have waiting lists, the testing process can take a number of weeks to months to complete, and are costly (about $1,000 to $3,500, or more). Finally, health insurance plans may or may not cover this testing. Children and teens who have "uncomplicated ADHD," meaning they have no other co-existing psychological or neurodevelopmental diagnoses, may not be covered for neurodevelopmental testing unless they have a PPO health insurance plan.

Many people confuse neuropsychologists and neurologists. Neuropsychologists are clinical psychologists with special training and experience assessing children or adults with brain functioning difficulties, cognitive deficits, and other neurodevelopmental conditions. A neurologist is a medical doctor that specializes in treating disorders that affect the nervous system, brain, and spinal cord. While pediatric neurologists and psychiatrists can diagnose and treat ADHD with medication, they do not provide comprehensive psychological testing.

The second main way is to obtain an ADHD evaluation. Although this can be effective and easier to obtain, it may not be as accurate as the first method. These evaluations do not provide full psychological testing and are less comprehensive. However, they can still be helpful in diagnosing ADHD and screening for other conditions. In many cases, full neuropsychological testing is not necessary for evaluating ADHD, unless the child or teen has suspected learning disorders, other possible conditions, or a more complex diagnostic presentation. ADHD evaluations can be conducted during the initial phase of outpatient therapy by behavioral health therapists, as well as conducted by pediatricians or other physicians, school psychologists at schools, and psychiatrists.

Parents should ask ADHD evaluation providers how comprehensive their services will be. ADHD evaluations typically do not include extensive testing, but should utilize thorough clinical interviews with parents and children and teens to rule out other conditions and disorders that may be causing or contributing to the ADHD-like difficulties. These evaluations should also incorporate ADHD behavior rating measures completed by parent/s and teachers. A report may or may not be produced from these evaluations, but some clinicians may write a letter with their findings that can be shared with other health care providers and schools. Testing providers and evaluators should include relevant cultural issues and factors in their diagnostic formulations and conceptualizations of ADHD and behavioral challenges as well.

CHECK FOR CONDITIONS THAT MAY CAUSE ADHD-LIKE SYMPTOMS AND/OR CO-EXIST WITH ADHD

Although stated previously, during the diagnostic ADHD process, it is essential that providers screen for and review a number of specific possible medical, sleep, psychological, and neurodevelopmental conditions. The American Academy of Pediatrics' (2011) clinical practice guidelines state that ADHD evaluations should include assessments of other co-existing conditions. Unfortunately, providers often miss these other conditions. Because ADHD can be a diagnosis of exclusion, the other potential causes of ADHD-like symptoms should be explored. Additionally, because ADHD commonly presents along with other psychological conditions, families should not be surprised if their child with true ADHD has other disorders. As stated previously, as many as 67 to 80 percent of clinic-referred children with ADHD also have at least one other psychological disorder, as many as 50 percent have two or more other disorders (Pliszka, 2015), and 20 percent have three or more co-existing conditions or disorders (Spruyt & Gozal, 2011). If or when any other conditions are identified, these should be addressed in the overall treatment plan and approach. When co-existing conditions are not treated, the ADHD can worsen and will not be as effectively managed. Sometimes treatment is abandoned entirely when families do not believe their efforts are worthwhile due to lack of progress. These other conditions can be the missing piece of information to explain why progress was partial or to better understand a child's difficulties.

The various conditions listed below should be reviewed during ADHD assessments and evaluations. Parents should ask clinicians to specifically screen for these conditions. Because this list is comprehensive, ADHD evaluators and assessment providers may not be aware of these conditions. Parents may request that specialist providers screen for specific conditions while working with their evaluating clinicians. Additionally, if children and teens have been diagnosed with ADHD and are receiving treatment, but they are not progressing or are only partially progressing, it is possible that they may have other undetected conditions with or without true ADHD. Second opinion evaluations or neurodevelopmental assessments may be helpful or necessary for further diagnostic clarity.

Medical Conditions That Can Cause ADHD-Like Presentations Without True ADHD, Can Co-Exist with True ADHD, or Worsen True ADHD: Vision difficulties, hearing difficulties, nasal allergies and allergy medication use, chronic sinus problems, asthma and related medications, enlarged tonsils and adenoids, hypoglycemia, diabetes, anemia, thyroid disorders, food sensitivities and allergies, persistent/recurring childhood ear infections, seizure conditions, conditions causing chronic bodily pain or discomfort, the use of certain prescription or over-the-counter medications. The following may cause or is associated with higher risks of ADHD or ADHD-like presentations, including: phenylketonuria, strokes, meningitis, encephalitis, other brain diseases/infections/tumors, Lyme disease, celiac disease, and leukemia/head/neck cancer treatments.

Sleep Problems, Disorders, and Conditions That Can Cause ADHD-Like Presentations Without True ADHD, Can Co-Exist with True ADHD, or Worsen True ADHD: Sleep-disordered breathing (snoring, persistent mouth-breathing, obstructive sleep apnea), increased nocturnal motor activity, periodic limb movement disorder, restless legs syndrome, insomnia and sleep initiation difficulties, inadequate hours of sleep/ chronic inadequate sleep duration, delayed sleep-phase disorder, and parasomnias.

Psychological Conditions That Can Cause ADHD-Like Presentations Without True ADHD, Can Co-Exist with True ADHD, or Worsen True ADHD: Anxiety, social anxiety disorder, obsessive compulsive disorder, younger children with school transitions and naps, depression, bipolar disorder, intermittent explosive disorder, substance abuse, conduct disorder, psychological trauma (including physical abuse, sexual abuse, emotional abuse, significant bullying, medical trauma, traumatic parental separations or divorce, unstable or highly dysfunctional family environments, significant traumatic family stressors and experiences, traumatic grief, community and school violence, natural disasters, terrorism, war and refugee traumas), neglect experiences, dissociation, and attachment disorders.

Neurodevelopmental Conditions and Prenatal Substance Exposure That Can Cause ADHD-Like Presentations Without True ADHD, Can Co-Exist with True ADHD, or Worsen True ADHD: Sluggish cognitive tempo, reading learning disorder, math learning disorder, dysgraphia (handwriting difficulties), written expression learning disorder, non-verbal learning disorder, expressive language disorder, slow processing speed and deficits, speech and articulation deficits, Tourette's disorder and tic disorders, giftedness, intellectual disorders, autism spectrum disorder - level 1 (Asperger's syndrome), and fetal exposure during pregnancy to alcohol, nicotine, marijuana, cocaine, opioids, and methamphetamine.

Sensory Processing and Motor Disorders That Can Cause ADHD-Like Presentations Without True ADHD, Can Co-Exist with True ADHD, or Worsen True ADHD: Auditory processing disorder, visual processing disorder, tactile sensory processing disorder, olfactory sensory processing disorder, vestibular sensory processing disorder, proprioceptive sensory processing disorder, dyspraxia, sensory based motor disorder - postural disorder, and immature symmetric tonic neck reflex.

Factors and Conditions That May Have Caused ADHD and Suggest ADHD May Exist: Family history of ADHD, certain pregnancy or birth complications, situations before, during, or just after birth that cause deprivation of oxygen in brain (ischemic-hypoxic conditions), premature birth, low birth weight, moderate to severe jaundice in newborn infants, near drowning experiences-severe smoke inhalation-carbon monoxide poisoning, previous head injury or injuries, childhood neurotoxic exposure (such as mercury, cadmium), certain mineral and vitamin deficiencies (zinc, magnesium, iron and B and D vitamins), and Walsh biochemical imbalances (please refer to Chapter 14 for more information on this).

Evaluations for Vision Deficits, Visual Processing Disorders, Hearing Deficits, and Auditory Processing Disorders

As a general rule, it is suggested that parents obtain vision and hearing tests for any child or teen suspected of having ADHD, and for students with academic, reading, or math concerns. These tests should be standard and are basic rule outs during ADHD evaluations because undetected and untreated vision and/or hearing difficulties can cause learning, ADHD-like, and behavioral difficulties. When asked if the child has had vision and hearing examinations, some parents may say that their child had this testing at school, and there were no negative findings. However, because many school screenings lack sensitivities and may detect only certain moderate to higher-level difficulties, families should obtain more comprehensive assessments.

In addition to exploring vision deficits, parents should be aware of visual processing disorders (VPDs). In this sensory processing disorder, the eyes function adequately, but the communication between the brain and eyes is not working properly and visual information is not interpreted correctly. VPDs can cause significant learning, reading, math, homework, and handwriting problems. It can also cause a range of visual perception difficulties at home, such as discomfort during reading or screen use, and difficulties judging distances, playing with balls, or searching for things. VPDs are often "hidden," and those with this condition will often pass vision tests. These are commonly undetected by primary care physicians, school screenings, and even regular eye exams by optometrists and ophthalmologists because they are visual perceptual difficulties and not eye deficiencies. Unfortunately, these visual processing problems cannot be determined with brief vision screenings or eye charts, and require special visual processing assessments.

VPDs are often mistaken as learning disorders, and can be a lifelong condition without treatment. For children and teens with suspected learning disorders, it is recommended that most receive VPD testing before neurodevelopmental testing. Because ADHD can also cause learning and reading difficulties, it will be important to obtain these assessments to determine if their learning challenges are related to ADHD, a learning disorder, and/or VPDs.

Regular but more extensive vision evaluations can be obtained from pediatric optometrists and ophthalmologists. Ophthalmologists are medical doctors that specialize in eye conditions and diseases but do not provide visual processing assessments. Optometrists are doctors of optometry who specialize in eye exams and care, do not provide surgeries, and typically addresses less complex conditions. However, certain specialist optometrists, called developmental or behavioral optometrists, do provide visual processing deficits assessments, and they would be an excellent option because they can provide both vision exams and VPD testing. VPD cannot be treated with corrective lens or surgery, but can be improved from vison therapy, which only these special optometrists provide. Vision therapy is like physical therapy for the eye-brain connection, and involves doing special eye exercises, using special lens and instruments, and use of visual computer activities. For additional information, parents can perform internet searches on VPD and VPD screening questions as well.

Auditory processing disorder (APD) is another type of sensory processing disorder that can also produce symptoms that are very similar to ADHD, as well as cause reading and academic problems. While the ears function adequately with APDs, the communication between the brain and ears is not working properly. As a result, spoken information and other sounds are not processed and interpreted correctly. This can cause ADHD-like, focusing, reading, academic, social, expressive language, and behavioral difficulties. Individuals with APD can misperceive spoken words and sentences, and may not properly understand others when they speak to them. They can misperceive or be highly sensitive to sounds as well. Similar to VPDs, it is often a "hidden" condition that is typically not detected by primary physicians, schools, and behavioral health providers. APD is commonly misdiagnosed as ADHD, and can be difficult to distinguish at times without auditory processing testing.

Hearing testing can be obtained from audiologists and Ears-Nose-Throat (ENT) or otolaryngologist physicians. ENTs can address hearing concerns, particularly if these are related to medical conditions. They are medical doctors who specialize in ear conditions and diseases but usually do not provide hearing assessments or auditory processing disorder assessments or treatments. It is important to know that routine hearing tests will not detect APD because it is not a hearing problem with the ears, but an auditory perceptual difficulty. Quick hearing screenings at schools typically identify basic sound detection difficulties. Only audiologists provide comprehensive hearing and auditory processing assessments. APD is not treated with surgeries or hearing aids. However, certain audiologists provide listening therapy, which is believed to be the most effective treatment for auditory processing disorders. For more information, parents can perform internet searches on APD and APD screening questions as well.

Referrals to Occupational Therapists for Higher Levels of Hyperactivity in Young Children

All young children (ages six or seven and under) who have high or very high levels of hyperactivity, excessive motor activity levels, and impulsivity should be considered for a referral to an occupational therapist (OT). The OT should evaluate them for certain sensory processing disorders or deficits, particularly vestibular sensory processing disorder and/or proprioceptive sensory processing disorder, since they can cause ADHD-like hyperactivity and impulsivity problems. Also, vestibular intolerance to movement and vestibular underresponsivity conditions can mimic inattentiveness. Hyperactivity can result from children with hypo or underarousal because they excessively seek stimuli and sensory input. Hyperactivity can also result from hyper or overarousal conditions where the child is seeking excessive sensory inputs or stimuli to calm down their imbalanced nervous system. Paradoxically, children can experience hyperactivity from both under and over arousals sensory conditions as well.

Unfortunately, these two sensory processing conditions will be very difficult to differentiate from ADHD in brief evaluations, and most psychologists and other providers will not be able to tell the difference without an OT evaluation. An OT evaluation should also be especially considered if a child with higher hyperactivity levels is not progressing with more traditional ADHD treatment. Lastly, if these sensory processing disorders exist, occupational therapists can provide the main treatment.

Sluggish Cognitive Tempo (SCT)

This condition appears similar to Inattentive ADHD and frequently has been mistakenly diagnosed as this. Few clinicians seem to know about Sluggish Cognitive Tempo (SCT), also called Concentration Deficit Disorder. Some research has determined that while it is similar to ADHD-Inattentive, it is a separate and distinct disorder (Barkley, 2015). It is estimated that 30 to 50 percent of individuals who appear to have Inattentive ADHD really have SCT (Barkley, 2010). In one survey, 59 percent of children that met the criteria for ADHD (mostly the Inattentive type) also met the criteria for SCT. Additionally, they exhibited little to no oppositional and defiant difficulties, but had greater depression and anxiety (Barkley, 2015).

Because SCT is less researched and understood, it is more controversial. It has some overlap with slow processing speed, but not everyone with SCT will have slow processing deficits. SCT impacts children and teens more broadly than just processing speed. Symptoms include frequent lethargy, moving more slowly, an overall mentally foggy or spacey presentation

(Braaten, 2014–2017), trouble staying awake, confusion, sluggishness, being withdrawn, inactivity, starring and daydreaming. It is important to identify SCT because this can impact treatment. Fewer treatment studies exist for this condition. While it is unclear if stimulants are helpful, one study showed that atomoxetine (Strattera) was effective. Behavioral management approaches can be utilized (Barkley, 2015). Clearly more research is needed on this condition. Parents should specifically ask ADHD evaluators and assessors to explore SCT if their children and teens have Inattentive ADHD-like presentations. Neuropsychologists who are aware of this condition will probably be the best evaluators.

SLEEP PROBLEMS AND DISORDERS

Understanding Sleep Problems and Disorders

The association of ADHD and sleep is complex and multifaceted. Sleep difficulties may be an inherent feature of ADHD, and/or may worsen from ADHD. The effects of disordered or inadequate sleep can mimic behaviors and symptoms remarkably like those of true ADHD (Hvolby, 2015). Primary sleep problems can cause ADHD-like symptoms when true ADHD does not exist, and sleep difficulties can exacerbate and worsen true ADHD conditions. It can be diagnostically challenging sometimes to determine whether sleep problems are causing the ADHD-like symptoms or are a result of true ADHD. This dilemma is compounded because children with true ADHD have significantly more sleeping problems than children without ADHD, so we have a "which came first" situation. Any conditions that impact a child's amount and/or quality of sleep should be explored carefully, including medical conditions such as asthma and allergies.

When sleep is disrupted or reduced either acutely or chronically, there are brain and behavior changes. Collective evidence shows sleeps plays a vital role in brain development and performance (Spruyt & Gozal, 2011). Any problems or disorders that cause disrupted or fragmented sleep, lack of adequate duration of sleep, or higher levels of daytime sleepiness can cause or contribute to difficulties with attention, behavior, and mood. One group of researchers found that those with sleep conditions and ADHD symptoms had improvements or an elimination of ADHD-like problems after treatment of their primary sleep disorder (Konofal, Lecendreux, & Cortese, 2010).

A number of researchers and authors have reported the growing awareness and importance of screening and evaluating sleep problems for children and adolescents as a routine part of ADHD evaluations, as well as when exploring ADHD-like symptoms, mood, and behavioral difficulties

(Spruyt & Gozal, 2011; Owens, 2009; Konofal, Lecendreux, & Cortese, 2010; Hvolby, 2015). Unfortunately, many mental health clinicians, pediatricians, and other health care providers often fail to appreciate the tremendous impact that sleep problems, disorders, and sleep-disordered breathing can have on psychological, behavioral, and medical conditions, including ADHD.

Specifically, ADHD can cause significant sleep difficulties by increasing the likelihood of bedtime resistance, inadequate sleep hygiene, insufficient hours of sleep, and poor sleep quality. In contrast to sleepy adults that will appear tired and fatigued, sleep deprived children can exhibit disruptive behaviors, inattention, hyperactivity and impulsivity.

Sleep difficulties reported by parents have been estimated at 25 to 50 percent of children and teens with ADHD. The two most common sleep difficulties are bedtime resistance and delayed sleep onset (or how long it takes to fall asleep when in bed). Some younger children may exhibit protest behavior when going to bed due to trouble falling asleep. Older children and teens may stay in bed quietly while struggling to sleep with parents unaware of this (Owens, 2009), and can suffer from difficulties arising and functioning in the morning.

Chronic partial sleep deprivation and inadequate sleep is a serious growing problem that is frequently underestimated and minimized, and should be addressed. Children ages 3 to 5 should consistently obtain 10 to 13 hours of sleep per 24 hours (including naps), and most do not require a nap after age 5. Children ages 6 to 12 consistently require 9 to 12 hours of sleep per night. Adolescents ages 13 to 18 consistently require 8 to 10 hours of sleep per night (American Academic of Pediatrics, 2016).

Child and adolescent sleep problems can result from a number of sources. Insomnia can cause a chronic lack of adequate sleep. Sleep disordered breathing consisting of snoring, mouth breathing, and obstructive sleep apnea can cause significant sleep and health difficulties. Excessive use of electronic screen devices, overscheduled and long days can also create challenges. ADHD stimulant medications can linger in the body and delay falling asleep. Additionally, sleep problems can result from poor sleep hygiene and behavioral resistance at bedtime, particularly for those with ODD or conduct disorder. Delayed sleep phase disorder can cause older children and adolescents to go to bed late and sleep later in the morning, causing decreased sleep duration and difficulties waking and performing the next day (Owens, 2009). Environmental issues may also impact sleep, such as uncomfortable temperatures, excessive light, and noise. Finally, periodic limb movement disorder and restless legs syndrome can cause serious sleep impairments.

Screen and Evaluate for Sleep Conditions

Identifying sleep difficulties is an important part of ADHD evaluations and testing assessments. Parents should request that clinicians screen for a number of possible sleep issues when they evaluate ADHD. Additionally, working with clinical psychologists and psychiatrists who treat sleep difficulties can be an important contribution to the overall treatment approach for ADHD. Sleep studies at sleep centers will provide more comprehensive assessments of sleep problems and disorders and may be necessary for severe sleep conditions. To help providers identify, explore, and track sleep patterns and difficulties, parents can use nightly sleep journals or notebooks. These can be used to document before bed routines, the times the child went to bed and arose, mouth breathing, activity levels while sleeping, and other sleep issues. Please refer to Chapter 8 for information on how to address sleep problems.

Sleep-Disordered Breathing (SDB)

Sleep-disordered breathing (SDB) is its own special category of sleep conditions, and can cause significant health, ADHD-like, behavioral, and academic difficulties. While awareness is slowly growing about these serious health issues, many healthcare providers and parents lack awareness and understanding of these conditions. SDB is an umbrella term for a spectrum of different types of breathing difficulties during sleep, including frequent or loud snoring, trouble breathing or loud noisy breathing during sleep, open mouth breathing during the day and/or night, upper airway resistance syndrome, and obstructive sleep apnea. SDB is estimated to occur in 4 to 11 percent of children who are school-aged. Because SDB in children can have nonspecific and varied presentations, it can easily be missed and underdetected (Bauer, Lee, & Campbell, 2016).

Children and teens who snore should be evaluated for SDBs because snoring can have a number of underlying causes. It is associated with sleep impairments, as well as various behavioral and academic difficulties. Only about 10 percent of children who snore do not have underlying health concerns. Additionally, snoring may be related to obstructive sleep apnea, a serious condition where a child or adult will stop and start breathing while sleeping, often with pauses in breathing with snorting and gasping. Obstructive sleep apnea can significantly impair the quality of sleep and can cause a number of behavioral and learning problems (O'Brien, 2000–2012).

Mouth breathing occurs when children and teens persistently breathe with their mouths open during the day and/or night. It can be a serious condition, associated with underlying causal issues and can create growth problems, the development of a long narrow face, a number of dental issues, and behavioral, mood, and learning challenges.

Since the 1990s, there is a large body of literature that has found neurocognitive, executive functioning, memory, attention, hyperactivity, and behavioral difficulties resulting from SDB. Research has consistently associated SDB-related neurocognitive deficits with lower academic achievement across cultural contexts. Because academic underperformance is so prevalent with children and adolescents with SDBs, screening for SDB has been recommended in the assessment of children's learning problems (Galland et al., 2015), as well as ADHD. SDB conditions can easily be misdiagnosed with ADHD because the symptoms can be so similar. One researcher stated that 25 percent of all children with ADHD could experience an elimination of their ADHD if their SDB was treated effectively (Fischman, Kuffler, & Bloch, 2015).

If there are concerns about the presence of possible SDB conditions, the family should first obtain an evaluation from an otolaryngologist (or Ears, Nose, Throat physician). This doctor can explore potential medical factors, including enlarged tonsils and adenoids, asthma, allergies, gastroesophageal reflux (Breus, 2005), narrower nasal passages, sinus problems and smaller jaw structures. They may be able to address some of these difficulties with surgeries or other treatments. A sleep study at a sleep center may then be recommended for suspected sleep apnea and potentially for mouth breathing.

After an ENT evaluation and a possible sleep study, children and teens with mouth breathing difficulties should visit orthodontists experienced with detecting and addressing mouth breathing difficulties and their co-occurring related dental issues. Fewer health care providers are aware of diagnosing and treating mouth breathing, so this may be a challenge. Finally, Thome Pacheco et al. (2015, July/August) shared that after the causes of the mouth breathing are addressed, the habit of nose breathing should be taught.

PHYSICIANS SHOULD RULE OUT POSSIBLE MEDICAL CONDITIONS

As part of a standard ADHD evaluation, children or teens should be referred to their pediatrician or family practice physician to rule out certain potential medical conditions causing ADHD-like behaviors, or any undetected medical conditions that may worsen a true ADHD condition. Clinicians providing ADHD evaluations can write a letter to the primary care physician with their findings, and suggest specific medical conditions be explored. Parents can also request that physicians evaluate these conditions which include:

- Vision difficulties
- Hearing difficulties
- Hypoglycemia
- Asthma
- Allergy and related medications use
- Diabetes
- Anemia
- Thyroid disorders
- Toxic heavy metals exposure (such as lead, mercury, cadmium)
- Deficiencies in iron, zinc, magnesium, B vitamins (including B6, and not just B12 which is the easiest to test for) and vitamin D
- Additionally, discuss the possibility of:
  - food allergies and sensitivities
  - seizures
  - conditions causing chronic pain or bodily discomfort
  - head injuries

Parents and clinicians should know that some physicians may be reluctant to explore all of these suggested medical conditions as a routine part of the diagnostic ADHD process. Even though physicians may be uncomfortable with this testing or reluctant to provide related referrals for other evaluations, parents can be assertive to meet their children's needs. Although only a minority of children and teens have undetected medical conditions that cause ADHD-like difficulties, ruling out potential medical causes is the most thorough approach.

A physician's potential reluctance for this medical testing may be related to health insurance company approvals. They may not approve some of the suggested diagnostic approaches for ADHD evaluations unless there are other medical concerns for the testing. Additionally, at this time, neuroimaging, such as SPECT, CT, PET, or MRS imaging, is typically not utilized by clinicians for more routine ADHD evaluations, and is most likely not covered by health insurance companies even if an imagining provider could be located. Families should discuss with their physicians which services may be covered by their insurance and what are the out-of-pocket expenses.

Parents can also request that primary care physicians test for deficiencies or imbalances in iron, zinc, magnesium, and B (particularly B6) and D vitamins since research has shown that these deficiencies and imbalances can cause ADHD-like symptoms (Harvard Medical School, 2009). Serum ferritin tests assess iron deficiency, and 25(OH)D tests for vitamin D deficiency are the most accurate. Both can be ordered by physicians. While testing vitamin B12 levels is not difficult, assessing all the B vitamins can be more challenging, and other health care practitioners may be needed. While controversial and less common, zinc and magnesium deficiencies can be assessed with blood testing (Laake & Compart, 2013). However, some believe blood testing for magnesium does not provide accurate or helpful results (Stevens, 2016). After testing is completed and if deficiencies are determined, supplements can be considered. Qualified health professionals should supervise and direct this supplementation approach. Be aware that many physicians may be reluctant to do this or may not even believe in this approach. These tests may not be covered by health insurance plans as well. Please refer to Chapter 14 for more information on these approaches.

SUMMARY POINTS

- To properly determine if ADHD exists or not, a brief ADHD evaluation can be conducted, or a more comprehensive ADHD assessment and report can be obtained.
- Children and teens with ADHD frequently have one or more co-existing conditions. Evaluators or assessors should explore specific medical, sleep, psychological and neurodevelopmental conditions to determine if these are causing ADHD-like difficulties when true ADHD does not exist, or if they occur along with true ADHD.
- If identified, these other conditions should be properly evaluated and treated by appropriate providers.
- Children and teens suspected of ADHD should obtain vision and hearing tests outside of the school because they can cause ADHD-like difficulties.
- Visual processing testing should be obtained for those with significant learning and reading difficulties.
- Auditory processing disorder can closely mimic ADHD and may need to be evaluated.
- Children under age seven with high hyperactivity levels may have a sensory processing disorder and can receive an occupational therapist evaluation to explore this.
- Significant inattention difficulties can be misdiagnosed as Inattentive ADHD when it may be Sluggish Cognitive Tempo, a lesser-known condition.
- Sleep conditions, including sleep disordered breathing (snoring, mouth breathing, and sleep apnea) and insufficient sleep, can cause ADHD-like difficulties and should be evaluated.
- Primary care or family practice physicians should evaluate specific medical conditions as part of ADHD evaluations.

REFERENCES

American Academy of Pediatrics. (2011, November). Clinical practice guideline—ADHD: Clinical practice guideline for the diagnosis, evaluation, and treatment of attention-deficit/hyperactivity disorder in children and adolescents. *Pediatrics, 128*(5).

American Academic of Pediatrics (2016, June 13). *American Academy of Pediatrics supports childhood sleep guidelines.* Retrieved from https://www.aap.org/en-us /about-the-aap/aap-press-room/pages/American-Academy-of-Pediatrics-Supports -Childhood-Sleep-Guidelines.aspx

Barkley, R. (2010). *Taking charge of adult ADHD.* New York, NY: The Guilford Press.

Barkley, R. (2015). Concentration deficit disorder (sluggish cognitive tempo). In R. Barkley (Ed.), *Attention deficit hyperactivity disorder: A handbook for diagnosis and treatment* (4th ed., pp. 435–454). New York, NY: Guilford Press.

Bauer, E. E., Lee, R., & Campbell, Y. N. (2016, December). Preoperative screening for sleep-disordered breathing in children: A systematic literature review. *Association of Perioperative Registered Nurses, 104*(6), 541–553.

Braaten, E. (2014–2017). *What's the difference between sluggish cognitive tempo and slow processing speed?* Retrieved from https://www.understood.org/en /learning-attention-issues/child-learning-disabilities/information-processing-issues/whats-the -difference-between-sluggish-cognitive-tempo-and-slow-processing -speed

Breus, M. J. (2005). *Back to school, back to sleep.* Retrieved from www.webmd .com/sleep-disorders/features/fixing-sleep-problems-may-improve-child-grades -and-behavior?print=true

Fischman, S., Kuffler, D. P., & Bloch, C. (2015). Disordered sleep as a cause of attention deficit/hyperactivity disorder: Recognition and management. *Clinical Pediatrics, 54*(8), 713–722.

Galland, B., Spruyt, K., Dawes, P., McDowall, P. S., Elder, D., & Schaughency, E. (2015, October). Sleep disordered breathing and academic performance: A meta-analysis. *Pediatrics, 136*(4), e934–e946. Retrieved from http://pedatrics .aapublications.org/content/136/4/e934

Harvard Medical School. (2009, June). *Diet and attention deficit hyperactivity disorder. Harvard Mental Health Letter, Harvard Health Publications.* Retrieved from https: //www.health.harvard.edu/newsletter_article/Diet-and-attenttion-deficit-hyper activity disorder

Hvolby, A. (2015). Associations of sleep disturbance with ADD: Implications for treatment. *Attention Deficit and Hyperactivity Disorders, 7*(1), 1–18. Retrieved from https://www.ncbi.nlm.nih.gov/pmc/articles/PMC4340974/

Konofal, E., Lecendreux, M., & Cortese, S. (2010). Sleep and ADHD. S*leep Medicine, 1*(7), 652–658. Retrieved from https://www.ncbi.nlm.nih.gov/pubmed/20620109

Laake, D. G., & Compart, P. J. (2013). *The ADHD and autism nutritional supplement handbook.* Beverly, MA: Fair Winds Press.

O'Brien, L. M. (2000-2012). *Snoring in children.* Retrieved on 07/11/12 from http: //www.pedsforparents.com/articles/2785.shtml

Owens, J. A. (2009, May). A clinical overview of sleep and attention-deficit/hyperactivity disorder in children and adolescents. *Journal of the Canadian Academy of Child & Adolescent Psychiatry, 18*(2), 92–102.

Pliszka, S. (2015). Comorbid psychiatric disorders in children with ADHD. In R. Barkley (Ed.), *Attention deficit hyperactivity disorder: A handbook for diagnosis and treatment* (4th ed., pp. 140-168). New York, NY: Guilford Press.

Spruyt, K., & Gozal, D. (2011, April). Sleep disturbances in children with attention-deficit/hyperactivity disorder. *Expert Review of Neurotherapeutics, 11*(4), 565–577.

Stevens, L. J. (2016). *Solving the puzzle of your ADD/ADHD child.* Springfield, IL: Charles C Thomas, Publisher, Ltd.

Thome Pacheco, M. C., Casagrande, C. F., Teixeira, L. P., Finck, N. S., & Martins de Araujo, M. T. (2015, July/August). Guidelines proposal for clinical recognition of mouth breathing children. *Dental Press Journal of Orthodontics, 20*(4), 39–44. Retrieved from https://www.ncbi.nlm.nih.gov/pmc/articles/PMC4593528/

Chapter 4

EDUCATION ABOUT ADHD

After a child or teen receives the diagnosis of ADHD and/or other conditions, the second treatment phase should be education. This is one of the most important aspects of ADHD treatment. It is critical for parents and children to firmly understand that ADHD is a brain-functioning condition that impacts individuals in specific ways. It is a chronic neurobiological disorder that is generally managed and not cured. Therefore, families need to understand and accept the condition so that they can live with it most effectively. If parents and others lack the correct perspectives, these problems often continue or worsen. When parents and others truly understand what ADHD is and its impact on a daily basis, then they can better understand the challenges and stop taking the difficulties personally.

Families can learn about ADHD and other conditions through clinicians and various information sources. The first chapter of this book should help readers better understand ADHD. There are a number of informative books and websites on this topic as well. Websites include chadd.org, add.org, additudemag.com, addresources.org, and russellbarkley.org. Other helpful books include *Taking Charge of ADHD* by Russell Barkley (for parents of children and teens); *Healing ADD* by Daniel Amen (for parents of children and teens, as well as adults with ADHD); *1-2-3 Magic* by Thomas Phelan (for parents to learn effective discipline of children); *Putting on the Brakes: Young People's Guide to Understanding ADHD* by Patricia Quinn and Judith Stern (for children ages 8 to 13); and *Teenagers with ADD and ADHD* by Chris Dendy (for parents and teens). Additionally, it can be helpful for parents and adults with ADHD to attend local ADHD support groups (chadd.org has these listings). Parents can share this information on ADHD and other conditions with family members, teachers, and important adults in the child's life as well.

Because parents of children with ADHD often have ADHD themselves, awareness and education about their own adult ADHD can be critical. Parents who suspect they may have ADHD should be evaluated and treated to maximize the functioning of the entire family. Besides medication, adult ADHD is best managed by understanding the condition, accepting it as a disability, and actively working on managing the various specific daily and long-term challenges and problems it causes ADHD psychotherapy and coaching can help with these tasks.

GRIEVING PROCESS AFTER DIAGNOSIS

Various authors have discussed that there can be a grieving process for parents after they first receive their child or teen's diagnosis of a disability (Bellis, 2002; Silver, 2006). Caregivers may have mixed reactions to the ADHD diagnosis initially. They may be relieved or even thrilled that the child's problem was finally identified and diagnosed with an actual condition to explain the confusing and frustrating difficulties. However, they may also feel anger and sadness that their child has a brain-functioning disorder that they may not outgrow. While not every parent experiences grieving, it can be helpful for some caregivers to identify and experience the grieving stages so that they can hopefully move towards acceptance.

Since grieving is a process, it can be helpful for caregivers to give themselves time to understand and work towards accepting their child's ADHD. The classic stages of grief are denial, anger, bargaining, depression, and finally acceptance, which is the goal. Caregivers can struggle with any stage or stages, and everyone's process can be different. While ADHD often persists lifelong in various ways, people with ADHD can be quite successful in their lives. However, because it is a disability that touches many areas of life, children and teens often need to work harder at certain things. They will also need extra support, such as medication, parent's extra assistance, behavioral systems, school accommodations and services, organizational routines, and other approaches and services. Older children and particularly adolescents can also experience grieving reactions in accepting this diagnosis and committing to the long-term interventions ADHD often requires. Parents and children need to know that ADHD does not make a person "crazy." Proper education about what it is and what it is not should help with these misunderstandings.

Part of healthy acceptance can be taking a disability perspective for ADHD, as well as other conditions (Barkley, 2013). Individuals with ADHD, particularly more moderate to severe ADHD, with or without ODD, can have serious behavioral and self-control problems that make them different. Parents should understand and accept that they are not an average or neurotypical child, and have a serious behavioral condition that can limit their ability to act in normal ways at times, particularly without effective treatment. While initially difficult or distasteful to some parents, over time a disability perspective can be quite helpful in appreciating a child or teen's limitations and lowering expectations in certain appropriate ways.

Many parents may initially cringe when the topics of diagnosis and disability are discussed. No parent wants to believe their child has something wrong with them. However, accepting the reality of the condition while not giving up on the child and hoping for the best is an aspect of grieving. Most parents of children with handicaps can be challenged to accept the limitations while helping their child strive to be their best. Fortunately for those who receive effective treatment, they can have successful or even amazing lives. Accepting the condition does not mean that the child or teen will never achieve anything. Taking a disability perspective can help parents to lower unrealistic expectations they may have for the child or teen, but not release all expectations for everything or any accomplishments. A child's abilities and future are not black or white. This is an important distinction. Some fathers tend to struggle with this concept more than mothers, but each family is different.

It rains a lot in England and Seattle. Most people who live there have accepted the wet climate because they cannot change it. When it rains, residents do not run outside, cursing and screaming "Can you believe this rain? Why is it raining so much? I hate this weather! This is so unfair!" They may not like the rain, but most have accepted it and work around it. This is acceptance and a healthier way to live with the wet environment. Similarly, parents should work on accepting their child's problems and limitations, while doing what they can to improve the ADHD. Acceptance does not mean that parents like the problems or just take whatever happens. Parents should focus on the things they have control over (such as their attitudes, parenting behaviors, and ability to engage effective treatments), and accept and manage what they do not have control over as much as possible. If parents are struggling with this, they should work with psychotherapists about what is fair and realistic to expect from their children and teens in the short and long term. Therapists may also help parents and families in navigating the grieving process, which may be more extended and complicated for some.

When caregivers work on accepting and not "fixing" the child's problems, they can begin to experience less bitterness and stress. This can improve their relationships with their children, and improve their mood and perspectives. Lowering expectations does not mean that the child will not succeed in life or will never meet their potential. It means each parent should be fair and realistic as to what they should expect from their unique child or teen. Parents should continue to read about ADHD and keep discussing the topic to help with their ongoing acceptance process.

Finally, some parents may wish to take a spiritual perspective in raising a child or adolescent with ADHD and other disabilities. This may help some with their acceptance and provide a sense of purpose regarding the daily struggles and long-term challenges. Some may pray, reflect, or meditate upon the reasons why ADHD has appeared in their life, as difficult as it is. Others may believe there are certain spiritual lessons to be learned from these conditions and situations, such as learning how to persevere despite adversity, patience, selflessness, being present in the moment (mindfulness), gratitude, not reacting emotionally to negative experiences, empathy for others with hardships, as well as other personal lessons.

INFORM CHILDREN AND TEENS ABOUT THEIR CONDITIONS

Children and teens should be informed that they have ADHD. They should participate in discussions about their condition and how it affects them. Some parents may believe if they discuss ADHD they will harm their child, give them permission to not succeed, or will give their children excuses not to work hard. However, for most children, it can cause difficulties if they are not told why they are having struggles. It is better for a child to have a realistic understanding of their challenges so they do not internalize their problems or blame themselves for being "dumb" or "stupid." Children should be taught that ADHD is brain-functioning condition, and does not mean they are crazy. A developmentally-appropriate explanation of ADHD should be given to the child or teen so they understand why they have their difficulties. Therapists may be able to facilitate and assist parents with these conversations, as well.

Here is a sample explanation that can be given to children and teens. The content should be adjusted to their age and developmental level.

> *I'd like to tell you some important things that we have learned about you. You have a condition called Attention-Deficit/Hyperactivity Disorder or ADHD. Your brain works a bit differently from others, but this does not mean you are dumb, stupid, lazy, or crazy. Millions and millions of people from little kids to older adults have ADHD, so it is not a rare or weird condition. About one out of every ten kids have ADHD, or about two in every classroom. There are certain parts of your brain and brain chemicals called neurotransmitters that are working slightly differently than they should. This causes you to have a harder time focusing, staying motivated to complete things, and getting things done, (and for those with hyperactivity and impulsivity, problems with moving and talking too much and controlling yourself). People with ADHD often have more trouble with reading, homework, school grades, following rules, doing chores, and getting along with other people. As a result of these problems, many kids with ADHD wind up not liking themselves or even feeling down and nervous about their problems. I want*

you to know that it is not your fault that you have ADHD and these problems that go with it. You should also know that you are responsible for your actions and behaviors even though you have ADHD.

People with ADHD have to do some things differently and sometimes have to work harder in certain ways to deal with their challenges. Parents need to do some things differently to help kids too, such as not yell and use consequences and behavior routines. Sometimes kids get extra help at school as well. People with ADHD can be successful and do fantastic things, like the unbelievable Olympic swimmer Michael Phelps and actor Jim Carrey. Even some famous people from the past are believed to have had ADHD, like the musical composer Mozart, the genius inventor Thomas Edison, and the amazing scientist Albert Einstein! There are books and websites we can look at to learn more about ADHD as well. Together we can work on these challenges and you don't have to do it alone. We are here to help you.

Despite the difficulties and challenges presented by ADHD (and other conditions), children and adolescents should know that with proper treatment and management, they can achieve their dreams and ambitions. Adults with ADHD can be physicians, lawyers, professors, and any number of successful professionals. Also, there can be positive aspects to having ADHD or learning disorders. Those with ADHD can be very creative and generate novel thinking which can produce new approaches and products. They can be good "idea" generating people with high energy and enthusiasm, or may be successful entrepreneurs by pursuing unconventional approaches to businesses or other professions. They can be original and innovative dreamers to create and achieve new things while not being limited by old ways of thinking. Additionally, people with Combined ADHD can be very fun, spontaneous, and enjoyable people who can have much charisma and personality. Those with ADHD may also have a gift for sales, and may become successful in this field. Indeed, these and other "upsides" of ADHD can be powerful and inspiring.

SUMMARY POINTS

- After receiving a diagnosis of ADHD, an initial important treatment component will be for families and others to receive specific information about this disability.
- There is a grieving process that parents, children, and adolescents may experience after ADHD is identified, and acceptance can significantly improve its management.

REFERENCES

Barkley, R. (2013). *Taking charge of ADHD* (3rd ed.). New York, NY: The Guilford Press.
Bellis, T. J. (2002). *When the brain can't hear.* New York, NY: Pocket Books.
Silver, L. (2006). *The misunderstood child: Understanding and coping with your child's learning disabilities* (4th ed.). New York, NY: Three Rivers Press.

Chapter 5

ADHD BEHAVIOR MANAGEMENT ESSENTIALS

OVERVIEW

It is difficult for an entire family when a member has ADHD. Untreated ADHD can generate tremendous stress and frustration not only for the children and teens, but also for their parents, siblings and extended family members. ADHD can bring out the worst in the entire family. Children and teens with ADHD can persist with arguing, lying, and disruptive behavior. When ADHD is untreated, grades often drop. Homework is forgotten or becomes a battleground taking hours to complete. Chores are avoided or poorly done after much yelling. Children and teens with ADHD may feel unloved and misunderstood because their difficult behaviors and conflicts with parents persist. When asked, they may honestly say that they just don't know why they act the way they do. Parents and siblings can get depressed and disheartened as the struggles continue, and negativity can seep into many aspects of the family's lives. Each new day, the problems continue and even worsen.

Indeed, in these situations parents often become desperate to get the ADHD problems stabilized. Untreated conditions can cause parents to lose control of themselves and the home. This powerlessness can be painful and overwhelming, resulting in a great amount of ineffective parenting and toxic interactions. The issues may become even more pronounced in single parent families, especially with mothers. Multiple researchers have found that adverse parenting practices and difficult family environments are common in families with children and teens with ADHD (Tarver, Daley, & Sayal, 2014). This stress can impact the entire family environment. When parents strongly disagree with each other on how to handle these problems, additional conflicts can accumulate. The negativity, fallout, and grudges between family members can linger in the house like gloomy storm clouds, and make the home a most miserable place.

Fortunately, parents can learn to better manage challenging behaviors at home. Because ineffective disciplinary habits surround many families with ADHD, structure and order is necessary in the home. This is achieved through parent behavioral management training, which is an essential part of effective ADHD treatment. The more severe the ADHD, the more critical the parental management efforts need to be. Using behavioral management approaches can help families to become more balanced, effective, and emotionally safe. These can help restore imbalances that may result from behavioral disorders, and provide a focused way to address unwanted behaviors. Once this occurs, the relationships between parents and children often improve. Parents may no longer feel bitter, disrespected, and ineffective, and can start enjoying and connecting with their children and teens more. Effective behavioral management approaches are not just for children or teens with ADHD; these approaches are healthy and effective for almost all children and teens.

This ADHD behavior management initially focuses on changing the parenting perspectives and behaviors first, not the child's or teen's. Parents are often confused initially by their need to change first. They may say, "Why do I have to change? My child has the problem, not me!" However, it is not just the child's problem because all the members are part of the family system and environment. Once parents understand their ineffective approaches and change their unproductive interactions, then children and teens often change.

Parents should have structured and consistent approaches to their children's daily ADHD problems and difficult behaviors. Using standard daily expectations for morning routines, after-school homework routines, and bedtime routines are critical, if these are problematic. An essential part of these routines is using consequences, such as rewards or praise for desired behavior, as well as loss of privileges or writing assignments for unwanted behaviors. While using these skills, parents should take a firm but neutral attitude when addressing behavior problems. Additionally, these behavior management approaches only work when used and enforced consistently.

At its simplest, parent behavioral training involves two parts. First, learning and consistently utilizing the foundational principles of behavior management, and second creating and enforcing specific, written, solution-focused plans to target the unwanted home and school behaviors with positive and negative consequences. If parents wish to jump to targeting unwanted behaviors without first understanding and using the fundamental principles, the desired results often do not occur and families may feel more hopeless and avoid future efforts for change.

When there are home and school problems, it is suggested that parents first work on addressing the home difficulties. It can be tempting to address all of the child's problems right away, but if the parents cannot manage the home behaviors, they will not be able to manage the school issues. Also, it is important to prioritize the initial focus to address only a few specific problems. An initial goal should be to create a written behavior plan for several targeted unwanted behaviors at home with specific consequences. These should be posted on the refrigerator for all to see and review over time.

Many parents are on survival mode and simply react to their children with behavior problems. However, once parents change the way they respond to their children, these powerful tools can help the entire family live more productively and happily. While this book is not designed to replace treatment, it can help to accelerate the learning process and improve the skills to effectively manage ADHD.

Ideally, this behavioral management approach should be used by both parents. Depending on the situation, step-parents may also administer some of these skills, but this can be tricky if the child has a negative relationship with the step-parent. If a child's parents do not live together, then this behavioral management approach will work if only one parent uses these skills, but it is better if both are "on board." Similarly, if parents live together but only one parent applies these methods, this approach can still be effective, as long as the other parent doesn't sabotage or interfere with the behavioral expectations and systems.

Effective behavior management is a set of skills that require practice. Many parents of children with ADHD feel like failures, but managing children with ADHD and other psychological conditions is not normal parenting. These conditions require different parenting approaches. Parents may need to grieve and understand disability perspectives to fully accept and practice these new skills.

Learning and living the focused behavior management principles is like "master parent wizard" training. Parents can envision themselves as becoming highly skilled wizards, wielding these abilities to achieve successful results. However, master wizards do not learn their craft overnight. While they have magic, it takes time, dedication, and energy to absorb the principles and use them effectively. Master parent wizards have to unlearn their ineffective and faulty parenting spells, and practice interacting differently.

USE CONSEQUENCES

Utilizing an effective system of consequences is one of the most essential keys to the behavioral management of ADHD. Consequences are reinforcers used by parents to modify behavior. They are given after desired or unwanted behaviors occur. Positive consequences are praise, rewards, or privileges that are given after a desired or positive behavior occurs. Negative consequences are loss of privileges, time-outs, chores, or writing assignments that are delivered after unwanted behaviors occur. Consequences must be effective and meaningful to the child, as well as enforceable, realistic, and something that the caregiver has control over. Consequences should be changed when they are less effective, and this will happen over time. Additionally, these should reflect the importance and severity of the desired and unwanted behaviors.

Consequences utilize the psychology principle of behavior modification. Reinforcement is a consequence that increases the likelihood of future behavior. Consequences should help increase desired behaviors, and decrease unwanted behaviors. They are behavioral modifiers that provide motivation for the child to follow parental expectations. ADHD is a motivation disorder that causes difficulties with compliance. Because of this, children and teens with ADHD need strong consequences to activate them to follow the rules and meet expectations.

Structure, Structure, Structure. Expectations and consequences provide structure and direction. Due to their brain-functioning challenges, children and teens with ADHD require a tremendous amount of structure, even though they may not like it. Because ADHD causes them to be disorganized and unfocused, they need structure in the form of clear consequences for expectations, routines, and lists to help them perform activities consistently.

Desperate or highly aggravated caregivers sometimes resort to using corporeal punishments or physical consequences to control the situation. Often, these will only make the child angrier, cause them to act out worse, and sour the parent-child relationship with bitterness. Years of consistent and strong research has indicated that spanking and physical punishment increases the risk of detrimental outcomes for children, and this is encountered equally across neighborhoods and cultural groups (Gershoff et al., 2018).

The entire concept of giving consequences involves providing children and teens with choices for their behaviors. The choice is theirs. They will either choose to follow specific expectations, such as doing homework soon after they come home, or they will cause themselves to experience a negative consequence, such as no screen time until homework is completed.

Parents can also use logical consequences. These are negative consequences that are connected to the misbehavior, and help increase the association between their poor choice and the unpleasant result of the reinforcer. Examples include parents taking away toys left on the floor after they asked children to pick these up, losing days of bike privileges after not wearing a helmet when they are expected to do so, and children and teens doing extra chores to earn money to repay what they stole at home. Writing assignments about unwanted behaviors after these occur could be considered logical consequences as well. These could be on paper or electronic. If they hurt someone's feelings with their actions they could write an apology letter, or write about how an impacted sibling or other may feel about their upsetting behaviors. They can also write about the topic in more general ways, or discuss why it's important not to do the behavior. They can even be required to incorporate information from the internet on the topic. Additionally, specifying the length of the assignment will be important, such as one paragraph or three one-sided pages. The length should vary based on the age of child, their writing or typing abilities, and the severity of their actions.

When caregivers first begin to use consistent and structured consequences, the behaviors of children and teens may become worse before they get better. The behavior may deteriorate temporarily as a way of testing parents to see if they will persist with these new approaches. When new music is played to the old dance, the dance changes. Parents have to resist the urge to return to the old music and should keep playing the new tunes. With time and consistency, this testing phase often ends when children and teens witness parents' commitment to this approach.

CONSISTENCY AND TIMELINESS WITH CONSEQUENCES

This behavioral management parenting approach only works if caregivers are consistent in providing consequences to specific behaviors almost all of the time. This means that if parents give a negative consequence of no screen time for the rest of the day, they must enforce this. If parents say a reward will be given, they must do this. Parents should teach their child that if they give a consequence, it is written in STONE. When parents only enforce consequences sporadically, the child will not believe the parents are serious. What would a parent think of a boss who did not give pay checks consistently, threatened to fire employees when they were angry but never did, or did not give raises when promised? Most parents would resent this boss, not be motivated to work hard, and would not believe what was said. Further, their productivity would be poor and the morale would be terrible. Why would anyone want to work for that type of boss? The same is true for children and teens with inconsistent parents.

Many children simply do not take the threats seriously that parents make because they know the parent will not follow through. When parents are not consistent, they will automatically condition the child to not believe their threats. Even very young children will test limits and know which adults enforce consequences and which do not. Therefore, difficult behavior can continue because they know they may not have consequences at all times. Some parents are too lenient and do not follow through on enforcing consequences. Sometimes caregivers feel sorry for the child or don't have enough energy to follow through with the consequence. Those who are inconsistent should reflect on the reasons for this. Quiet reflection, journaling, or talking with close friends about this topic can help uncover insights.

Energy and focus are required for being consistent when applying negative consequences. Some parents can feel like "the bad guy," particularly at first. Due to their poor frustration tolerance, children and teens with ADHD and ODD can have meltdowns, tantrums, and even aggressive outbursts when they do not like something or do not get their way. Parents many times may not want to deal with these reactions, and simply avoid delivering negative consequences. Parents may have a history of just giving in to the child to prevent these episodes. However, this can reinforce the exact behavior parents do not want. Children and teens must be taught that negative consequences will be enforced every time. Those with more dangerous or higher risk behaviors may require somewhat different approaches, and this will be addressed at the end of this chapter.

In addition to being consistent, consequences should be swift and timely to be effective. Consequences are most effective when they are given immediately or on the same day as the behaviors. This will create a stronger link or association between the behavior and the outcome. If caregivers cannot deliver consequences when they are out of the house, they can inform the child they will receive them as soon as they return home. Rewards that are promised months into the future or loss of privileges that last too long will not be effective. Also, if consequences or groundings last too long, they can lose their effectiveness and will not motivate the child sufficiently.

REWARDS AND PRAISE FOR POSITIVE BEHAVIORS

Parents should use the reinforcers of rewards and praise as behavioral tools for increasing desired behaviors as much as possible, instead of relying upon negative consequences to decrease undesired behaviors. Praise can go a long way, particularly if parents are not in the habit of using it. For most parents, it is easier to give negative consequences for unwanted behaviors because they work more quickly and it can feel more satisfying when they are frustrated in the moment. Most people automatically focus more on almost anything that is negative. Negatives simply seem to be more captivating and powerful. Consequently, parents can get stuck in relying only on using negative consequences, such as time-outs or withholding privileges.

Parents should utilize more positive consequences for desired behaviors than negative consequences for unwanted ones. This can take time. Creating a predetermined plan for using more positives can help change this habit. Also, children and teens will be more cooperative and it will be more pleasant for the caregiver if positive consequences are given for desired behaviors.

To help break the cycle of focusing only on negative behaviors, one approach is to acknowledge compliance for little tasks. Parents can make small requests and then give praise, such as "Please pick up my shoes for me," and then a warm "thank you!" after completion. Parents can make several daily requests to practice compliance (Barkley, 1997).

Some parents may struggle with these new parenting behaviors and may not feel genuine. They may feel like they are being "fake" in their interactions and use of rewards and praise. It can take time to get into the habit of focusing upon and reinforcing positive behaviors. Some parents have found a "fake it till you make it" attitude helps them transition. Becoming a master parent wizard takes time.

WAYS TO IMPROVE COMPLIANCE

Expectations for children with ADHD must be clear, specific, and applied consistently. Instructions and directions should be brief and focus on one task at a time (Barkley, 1997). Because those with ADHD have working memory deficits, it can be hard for them to keep several items in their mind at the same time. Parents should not give lengthy explanations or lectures when making requests.

When making requests, parents should use commands ("James, please pick up that towel"), not questions ("Would you do me a super big favor and grab the towel?"). Also, parents should utilize positive or negative consequences when making requests or commands. If the task has several steps, use written lists or break these into smaller ones. Ask that the first part be completed, then request they come back for the next (Barkley, 1997). Also, setting time limits for tasks and using a timer can be helpful (Barkley, 2013).

To improve attention to directions, ask the child to make eye contact ("Let me see your eyes") and repeat the directions. Parents should also routinely check to see if they understood what was said (Barkley, 1997). Parents can also praise when they start complying with the request, praise throughout the task, and can reward when the task is completed.

Parents should give reprimands for off-task and unwanted behaviors in a firm voice after getting the child's eye contact. Comment on specific behaviors, such as "Stop teasing your brother and do your homework now!" (Barkley, 2013). When parents are done reprimanding, they should not hold a grudge, linger on the topic, or lecture the child.

Another way to increase compliance involves giving random "bonus" rewards when children perform desired behaviors. This should increase the reinforcement of the wanted behaviors even more. This practice uses the principle of intermittent reinforcement. Slot machines utilize this. When people do not know when they will be rewarded, they will persist with their efforts because they do not know when the extra payoff is coming (as long as it occurs with some frequency and is not rare). These bonus rewards should be in addition to the standard positive consequences or rewards that are earned for the desired behaviors. Most children and teens love these bonuses and they are fun to give.

USE BEHAVIORAL EXPECTATIONS WITH CONSEQUENCES

To motivate children and teens to perform desired behaviors, parents can use written behavioral expectations along with specific reinforcers. This utilizes a clear and practical written plan that allows parents to proactively transform ongoing behavioral problems. Targeted behaviors should be significant and worth the energy to create a routine that parents will have to enforce. This list of daily or weekly expected behaviors can contain specific and regular positive and negative consequences for doing or not doing the behaviors. As mentioned previously, positive consequences or rewards include earning electronic screen time, money, spending time with friends, going outside, or other privileges and should be given if the expected behavior is completed. Negative consequences could be time-outs, loss of screen time, monetary fines when allowances are used, loss of time with friends or playing outside, or writing assignments. These should be given if the expected behavior is not completed or done in a timely manner. Examples of writing assignments include copying a page of a dictionary, a one- or two-page essay about an unwanted behavior, or completing a page of math problems.

These expectation systems can be used to address large and small behaviors. More complex problems, such as chore and homework compliance, as well as school behavioral problems, will be discussed later in this chapter and in following chapters. Parents should start with two or three unwanted behaviors. Some families may initially target too many behaviors before they are effective with this approach, which can be unproductive and overwhelming. To use this approach, parents should state what desired behavior is expected and its resulting positive consequence, and which unwanted behaviors will earn negative consequences. These should target recurrent problems, such as whining, nagging, screaming, defiance, aggression, or other unwanted behaviors. Certain behaviors, such as aggression, can receive automatic standard negative consequences without positive consequences, such as writing assignments or time-outs.

As an example, if a ten-year-old refuses to consistently brush her teeth, parents can put on their expectations list "Larissa will brush her teeth twice a day, and will earn screen time the following day from 5 to 5:30 p.m. daily when she does this. If she does not brush her teeth, she will copy one half-page of the dictionary and will receive no privileges until this is done."

The attitude that parents take when using behavioral management approaches is important. Acting neutrally when giving negative consequences and being enthused and congratulatory ("Give me a high five for doing that! That's awesome! Thank you!") when desired behaviors occur can contribute to the success of the program. Parents should practice neutrality and not lecture, become upset, or yell when unwanted behaviors occur. Some parents may need to work on this, and this will be addressed further in the next chapter.

When implementing new behavioral systems, parents should discuss these first with the child or teen. They should explain what the system is, and how it will work. Parents can share that the family will be doing things differently, and this means that there will be much less yelling, screaming, and arguing. This should help everyone's stress levels at home. Also, the child or teen will get the chance to make choices about how they will behave and can earn rewards. They may even get more privileges than they are getting now, such as money or more electronic screen time. However, if they do not make good choices and do not meet the written expectations, then they will be losing privileges and the things they want. The choice will be theirs every day.

When possible, and particularly for older children and adolescents, parents should also try to include the child in deciding which consequences will be given for the wanted and undesired behaviors. A menu can be created so there are more options for consequences, and children and teens can have the option of selecting a reward or privilege when meeting an expectation. While behavioral management generally works whether the child likes it or not, it can be more effective when the child or teen has some level of input and agrees to the program. This can be a fun way to involve them. Curiously, many children and adolescents can be surprisingly hard on themselves regarding negative consequences. However, some parents should be careful not to be too permissive in agreeing to excessively weak expectations or consequences suggested by children. Children and teens should know that they will not always be given the privilege to participate in all of these decisions.

Expectations should be posted on the refrigerator or in main areas within the home. In the beginning, they can be reviewed each day briefly with the child, but parents should not nag or have a negative attitude while doing this. Additionally, if children or teens have sleeping difficulties, parents should enforce negative consequences outside of children's bedrooms so that there is a positive association maintained between their bedroom and sleep. This would include no time-outs or writing assignments in their room. If parents find that the behaviors aren't improving, the reinforcers may be too weak, and should be increased. Parents may also be talking and lecturing too much when administering negative consequences (these undesirable parenting behaviors will be addressed in the next chapter). Bonus rewards can be given occasionally for good attitudes and efforts. Finally, once there is success and experience modifying the initial targeted behaviors, families can move on to adding new ones.

If negative or positive consequences will persist for two or more days for older children and teens, parents should use a calendar. This makes it clear for everyone, and all can track when the consequences expire. It is suggested that parents obtain a large single-family paper calendar to record the consequence start and stop dates. Of course, calendars on everyone's phones can be used as well, but be prepared for the possibility that children and teens may alter these dates.

If possible, parents can create and save these behavior expectation lists as documents on their computers so they can print out multiple copies. Typed and printed lists can look more "official," and reflects their importance. This system can be used for years and should be altered as the child ages and unwanted behaviors and consequences change. Having these on a computer makes it easy to modify them over time and print more if the child rips them up.

If there are frequent requests for a child to do a specific activity with which they are inconsistent, such as cleaning up after eating snacks, parents can create a behavioral expectation for this. This would be an example of addressing a more minor unwanted behavior. Parents can first list and number the steps of how to clean up after messy snacks, and then post them in a location where that activity occurs. Parents can review the routine regularly with the child and clearly state what specific consequences will occur if the routine is followed (such as praise or a small reward) or is not followed (writing assignment about the routine, time-outs, or loss of privileges).

Another example of a minor unwanted behavior could be addressing a book bag that is repeatedly left on the floor. Assume that the book bag is typically thrown on the floor near the front door when the child comes home from school. They refuse to hang it up at the designated spot, despite parental complaints. The parents are continually frustrated by this and are tired of tripping over the book bag and picking it up themselves. Over time the parents have escalated to threatening and yelling about this annoying behavior.

To stop being reactive and to alter this unwanted behavior, the parents could create a simple plan. The expectation would be for the child to hang up the book bag as soon as they walk in the door after school. The child will receive one daily reminder for the first two weeks. If the book bag is left on the floor, a negative consequence of a two-paragraph writing assignment about why items should not be left on the floor is given. Alternatively, 15 minutes of additional screen time is earned the day the book bag is hung up without a second reminder. If the writing assignment is refused, screen time will be lost indefinitely until the writing assignment is completed. This expectation with both consequences would be written down and put on the refrigerator and/or in the child's room.

The expectation can remain in place for as long as necessary and until the unwanted behavior consistently ends. Praise is given when the bag is hung ("Great job! I really appreciate you remembering to do this."). As the book bag is consistently hung up after school over weeks or months, the positive consequences can be reduced, or the expectation can be re-written and changed. It can be adjusted so that it must be hung up each day for one week to earn additional screen time on Saturday (whatever time and amount is determined). However, the daily negative consequence should remain until the desired behavior occurs consistently. Bonuses can be given over time when the rewards are phased down as well.

Some parents make the mistake of expecting behaviors that are too vague. They are not specific enough and have not defined the behavior well, and so the behavioral management isn't effective. They may expect the child to "be good" for the week at home or "do well" in school so they can earn a treat on the weekend. "Being good" and "doing well" are too vague. Instead they should list what specific behaviors they expect. Broad expectations should be broken down into smaller and clearer ones, and the reward should be specific as well. Also, those with ADHD require more immediate consequences because their concept of time is different. They live in the moment, and waiting for a reward they will earn on the weekend can seem like a year.

Some parents make another error of saying that a child or teen can earn a large reward (like a bike or expensive video game system) if they get on the honor roll or some other challenging longer-term goal. These types of rewards often fail because children and teens with ADHD struggle on a daily basis to consistently complete the small academic tasks required for good grades, like daily homework and effectively studying for quizzes and tests. Waiting weeks and months can be too hard for most children and teens with ADHD. Generally, they should receive more daily consequences focused on accomplishing the small tasks. If certain teens can tolerate consequences that extend farther into the future, then that is fine. Typically, however, the younger the child, the more day by day expectations and consequences are required.

Create Behavioral Expectations for Mornings, After School and Bedtimes

If mornings are challenging due to lateness, lack of focus, excessive slowness, defiance with getting ready or other difficulties, parents can create a morning routine with consequences using specific posted times for expected morning behaviors. A schedule can be created with specific times for waking up, bathing, dressing, eating breakfast, and walking out the door. Regular rewards or a selection from the reinforcer menu can be given for completing all of the tasks on the schedule by a certain time, and negative consequences for not following this. As an example, a parent can say "If you are completely ready by 7:15 a.m., you may have electronic screen time for 15 minutes until we have to go." They can also earn rewards as soon as they come home from school for achieving the morning expectations, as well as receiving negative consequences for not meeting this morning schedule when they come home (as long as this does not impact other expectation systems).

If mornings are difficult, parents can make a list of all the bathroom hygiene expectations and tape this on the bathroom wall. Similarly, a list can be made of the steps to get dressed in the morning, and this can be posted on the back of the bedroom door. Digital clocks should be placed in the bathroom and bedroom with a list of specific times for each step that are posted on the walls (6:35 a.m.—brush teeth, 6:38 a.m.—wash face, etc.). Parents can then say, "It is 6:45 a.m. Look on the list, what should you be doing now?" Pictures or stick figures can be attached to each of the steps to provide more robust visual cues as well.

Caregivers should adopt a coaching attitude each morning, using praise and encouragement. They can also remind children of their morning rewards for completing expectations. Finally, if the child continues to struggle with morning activities, consider exploring if there is an undetected and untreated sleep problems or conditions. Please refer to Chapter 8 for more information on sleep issues.

If behavioral difficulties occur after school, parents can also create after-school routines. These can consist of a list of daily expectations that should be completed each day after school, and these should be posted on the refrigerator too. Generally, it is best for students to come home and do homework first, then do chores (if parents expect these), and then earn privileges to watch TV, play video games, go on the computer, use cell phone, go outside, or play with friends. Parents should teach children and teens that they must now earn these privileges after school by first doing homework and chores each day. After parents check their work, they can enjoy the privileges. If they refuse, they will not be permitted to receive the privileges for that day, and they can try again the next day.

This method uses the Premack reinforcement principle, which states that enjoyable behaviors can be used as reinforcements and rewards for less desirable behaviors. This will be a day-by-day routine, with each day presenting new chances and choices to comply or not with the parental expectations. Persistent homework problems are most effectively addressed with the Homework Notebook system, which will be explained in Chapter 9. Finally, if ADHD stimulant medications are used, they typically wear off soon after school. Therefore, students should take advantage of this enhanced brain-functioning window and should do homework soon after coming home.

Chores after school can be optional, and some parents may only wish to focus on homework, at least initially. However, if chores are desired, parents can create a list of specific chores that are expected to be completed each day after school and/or on weekends. These can include as many or little as desired, but initially only a few chores per day should be expected. However, an allowance system can be the most productive way of addressing chores. Parents should strongly consider using an allowance system to help with chore motivation and compliance. To help children learn exactly what is expected when doing the various chores, parents should write and post a list of steps of how to complete these. Parents should also review how to do the chores with their children so the chores are completed to the parents' standards. Certain larger chores can also be expected on weekends, such as cleaning bedrooms or pet cages on Saturday or Sunday morning before that day's privileges of electronics use or playing outside. Please refer to the section later in this chapter on implementing an allowance system for chores.

If going to bed is difficult, parents can create a specific bedtime routine with clear expectations. They can designate a regular specific bedtime and a pre-sleep "wind-down" period. A list for the bedtime schedule should include specific times for each item. For example: 8:00 p.m.—select and put on pajamas, 8:04 p.m.—brush teeth and go the bathroom, 8:10 p.m.—select story, get into bed, and read story, 8:30 p.m.—lights out and sleep time. Part of the evening routine should also include checking that their school book bag is ready to go for the next morning. Positive or negative consequences for this bedtime routine can be given on the next day.

USE OTHER EFFECTIVE BEHAVIORAL INTERVENTIONS

Time-Outs

Time-outs can be used for children that are about ages 3 to 12. They are very effective and relatively easy to use once parents learn how to utilize them properly. Time-outs are a humane and powerful tool for dealing with unwanted, unacceptable, and annoying behaviors. It is an excellent replacement for spanking, yelling, and threatening by parents. Time-outs are behavioral resets. When the child performs an unwanted behavior, they can receive a time-out, and once it is over, the parent and child can move on without over-focusing on what happened. Also, it will help many children stop undesired behaviors almost immediately once parents start their warning with counting, so that an actual time-out consequence may not even need to occur.

While time-outs have been used for decades, they have received criticism. Some have recommended other discipline approaches instead of time-outs, such as time-ins, which involves the parent connecting, talking, and empathizing with the child when they misbehave. However, many clinicians believe time-outs are a valuable parenting tool. When used along with praise, a variety of positive consequences, and loving interactions, they can greatly contribute to improved parent-child relationships. If time-outs are used excessively or incorrectly, they can become less effective. Time-outs can also help parents regain a healthy sense of control, without using verbal or physical aggression or threats. Ultimately, time-outs should help the child calm down and provide a break from their negative behavioral patterns.

While there are different approaches and versions of time-outs, the following are the steps suggested for parents to effectively use them. For more information on this topic refer to Thomas Phelan's excellent books *1-2-3 Magic* and *1-2-3 Magic Teen*.

1. Select only a few behaviors for which the child will be sent to time-out. Parents should state these in writing and post them around home. Explain these to the child and remind them periodically what behaviors earn time-outs. Parents should not use time-out for all unwanted behaviors because they will lose effectiveness. Time-outs can also be part of a larger written behavioral plan.
2. Choose an effective long-term time-out spot that will be used consistently. Pick a safe, boring location that will be the designated time-out location. This can be a chair in a corner of a mostly quiet room or on stairs. Do not use a time-out area that is near a kitchen, TV, or other room where others actively interact. Children's bedrooms can be acceptable for time-outs. Most children do not like the concept of time-out, so even though they may enjoy their bedroom, many will not like being required to go there when it's not their choice. However, they should not use electronics or screen time in their room during time-outs. If this is difficult to manage, other locations should be used. As stated previously, if the child has sleep difficulties, bedrooms

should not be a time-out location because it may create a negative association with the bedroom that can interfere with the positive connection bedrooms should have with sleep. This can be particularly true if the child is receiving frequent time-outs.
3. Keep time-outs brief. One rule is one minute per year of child, with a 5-year-old getting 5 minutes (Phelan, 2016a). Time-out lengths can be doubled for more serious behaviors, but the above guideline for most behaviors is adequate. It is vital to use a timer at the start of each time-out to indicate when they have started, and to signal when it is over. An inexpensive kitchen or egg timer or a timer on a stove will work fine. A cell phone timer is acceptable as well, as long as the child can clearly hear it. The timer should not be placed near the child to prevent them from shortening the time. Also, it can be helpful if the child can see the timer so they know how much time remains. This may be important to some children, and can reduce their asking "How much longer?"
4. In Phelan's version of time-outs, parents can hold up fingers to signal the warning counts. When the child misbehaves for the first time, parents can say "That's one," with one finger in the air. Additional misbehavior soon after the first should earn "That's two" with two fingers. The third earns the time-out. There should be five to ten seconds between counts. More serious misbehaviors can receive immediate time-outs. Additionally, counting should restart faster for young children. If a five-year-old child receives a one then two count for misbehavior, that child can go back to one if the unwanted behaviors stopped but then started again in about 15 minutes. However, for older children, counting for new misbehaviors can be after two to three hours (Phelan, 2016a).
5. If the child talks, asks questions, screams or attempts to leave the area while in time-out, tell the child that the time-out begins when they stay in the time-out area and are quiet. Parents should start the timer when they are silent. Parents should not discuss why the child received the time-out or talk to the child while they are in time out. Teach the child that time-out is over when the timer signals. Ignore their repeated questions about "how much longer?" or "when is it over?"
6. Do not restrain children if they resist taking the time-out. Some children will run away from or refuse to stay in time-out. Teach them that they lose all toys or privileges in the home until they do their time. If they say "I don't care" or act as if they are not affected by this, explain there is no screen time or any other privileges until they do the time, and their time-out will double its length when they decide to do the time-out. Parents can also go in their rooms and take away their

favorite electronics or toys and tell them they will receive these back once they do the time-out. This will be a power struggle, but parents hold the cards and have the power. If the child continues to say, "You can take everything away. It doesn't matter," then play the waiting game. In several hours or days, they will want their things and privileges. When they are ready to do the time-out, let them do the time, and then return their things. Do not lecture them about this while you are waiting for them to accept the time-out. Over time, the child should learn that their parents will take away their things, and that it is easier to just do the time. Once again, consistency is vital when using this approach.

7. Once the time-out is over, move on. Parents should not linger or review the behaviors during or after the time-out. If parents must discuss this, only address what occurred very briefly. Swift and consistent consequences given in a neutral manner without discussions is what motivates children to change, not lectures (Phelan, 2016a).

8. Parents should not be fooled if the child acts as if they enjoy or are not bothered while they are doing the time-out. For most children this is an act to try to sabotage and control the situation and influence their parents to stop using time-outs. Ignore their comments and proceed with giving the time-outs consistently. If children see parents are not influenced by their statements, then these comments should end in time. As mild as it is, most children do not like being "in trouble" and will seek to avoid time-outs.

9. If the child makes a mess in their room during the time out, parents can do nothing and let them live with it for days until they are ready to clean up (Phelan, 2016a), or can tell them they will lose all privileges until they clean their room.

10. For unwanted adolescent behaviors, parents can use teen versions of time-outs. These include warnings, then consequences of loss of cell phones, electronics screen devices, computers, going out of the home, and socializing with friends. Additional consequences can be paying fines, doing extra chores, community service, or writing assignments. These replace the time-outs in physical locations. More serious behaviors can generate in-home groundings and/or longer loss of electronic devices (Phelan, 2016b). See Chapter 7 for more on adolescent management approaches.

Ignoring Undesired Behavior

One of the most basic approaches is to withdraw the parent's attention to more minor unwanted behaviors. Attention from parents can be an essential component in the development and persistence of unwanted child behaviors. Many parents underestimate or are unaware of this. Parental attention is quite powerful, and children strongly desire and seek this. Parents may believe that they already give their focus on desired behaviors by their child. However, if attention is given to negative behaviors as well, there will be less or no change in the balance of the two. To generate a shift, parents can ignore the undesired behavior and focus on the appropriate behavior. For example, if parents wish to extinguish their child's yelling when they are upset, they can praise and reward when the child speaks more calmly. While not easy initially, this parental habit can be mastered with practice. Parents must be ready for children's intensified reactions when their behavior is ignored, and to continue with this approach until there is change (Flick, 1996). Once again, consistency will be critical in these master parent wizard efforts.

While practicing this disengagement, parents should create a plan of what they will do with themselves when the negative behaviors continue or increase. This can include withdrawal from the situation and use of coping skills (see the section on emotional management skills in Chapter 7). Finally, creating a private list of which behaviors the parent will consistently ignore, and which behaviors will generate standard positive and negative consequences can help with these efforts. Remember that giving praise and attention is a positive consequence.

Token Reinforcement and Point Systems

This is an effective but complicated behavioral currency system based on daily behaviors, where the child/teen will earn and spend chips or points for privileges they desire. This approach is comprehensive and involves giving tokens, poker chips, or points for a range of positive and negative behaviors. Second to ADHD medication, token and point systems can be the most powerful behavioral approach for managing behavior problems. While intensive and potentially not practical for some families, it is a lifestyle change that can be worth the challenges and commitment.

The information on this topic is intended as a basic introduction. Various authors have provided more complete explanations of these systems and there are a number of internet sites that provide versions of these chip and point systems. Free behavioral charts can be printed from websites and can be used along with this and other behavioral systems. Some therapists who provide behavioral management training for parents may be able to teach or assist parents with using these systems. This may be necessary for some families because these systems can be complex.

Here are the basic steps:

1. Younger children should use tokens or chips. These chips can be those used for poker or other different colored plastic one. The child can keep their chips in jars. For older children and adolescents, the point system should be used. The point system is a more involved version of the token system. Large numbers of points should be used for teens for their earnings and spending. A notebook ledger will be used and managed by the parent only, but the teen should view this. For either system, each day tokens or points are added or subtracted based on their behaviors. Additionally, they will spend tokens or points daily for their desired privileges from a menu that includes "prices" of the privileges.
2. Parents should write out all daily desired and unwanted behaviors that occur. List what behaviors are expected for the morning, after-school, evenings, and weekends. Then list the common undesired behaviors that occur. Then determine how many chips or points they will earn for each of the daily expected desired behaviors, and how many chips or points they will lose for the unwanted ones. Lastly, create a list of rewards and pleasurable activities they enjoy, and then attach their price in chips or points. Chips or points should be able to be converted to money as well, such as one chip or 25 points equals 25 cents.
3. Parents will need to spend some time calculating and writing down how many potential tokens or points a child can earn each day for performing their normal daily expected behaviors, such as brushing teeth, getting dressed, doing homework, etc. Then parents should write down how much the child will want to spend daily for pleasurable activities such as snacks, privileges, playing with others, and so forth. With these systems, all expected and unwanted behaviors will earn and lose chips and points. They can carry balances or amounts to following days. The daily amounts of earning and spending should be calculated to be somewhat in check with each other, but they should earn a little more than they can spend each day and should earn more than they lose each day or the program will not work. Initially, parents will need to adjust the amounts to get proper levels. For many, this can be the most complicated phase of this approach.
4. To use the system, parents should award tokens or points immediately when they perform the listed desired behaviors. Bonus points or chips can be given as well as for good attitudes or other positive behaviors. Tokens and points are taken away when they perform predetermined unwanted behaviors, and children and teens will need to pay tokens or points when these occur. Finally, the child or teen should be permitted throughout the day to spend or cash in chips or

points for items on a menu of rewards (favorite foods, toys, activities they desire, money, and other privileges).

Allowance Systems for Chore Compliance

One of the most effective ways to motivate children and teens to consistently complete their chores is through the use of an effective allowance system. Many parents complain that their children and teens do not help out or do their fair share around the house. Because those with ADHD have difficulties doing things they do not like, it is no surprise that chores are battlegrounds for many families. Some parents just give up on chores, and the child or teen is not expected to do these. Some may believe it is not worth the yelling and begging for the chores to be done. Yet, these parents may harbor resentments and grudges about this. Allowance systems can be antidotes, and are highly effective for most children and teens, not just those with ADHD.

Allowances systems are wonderful because they teach the important skill of money management and financial responsibility. Children learn the value of money and how to budget it only when they can earn their own money, not when it is given to them automatically. These systems teach good work ethics as well. Allowance systems also teach how the real-world works, including the concept of employment and the costs of goods and services. When children are given a vehicle to earn money, they will then have to learn how to make better choices about using their money.

Allowance systems are great for parents as well. Parents will receive chores that are completed in a consistent timeframe without much complaining. Some families report that they actually save money by using allowances instead of giving their children money when they ask.

Some parents may say, "My child doesn't get a regular allowance, but they know I buy them things they want when they are good." This approach is less effective and teaches children to beg and harass parents for what they want. It does not create a clear link between the responsibility of completing chores regularly and the money they earn. Further, when these parents are asked if the child does chores regularly with this approach, they often say no. This method teaches children that their parents are ATM cash machines, but nothing about money management.

Some parents also say, "When I was growing up, I wasn't paid for chores. I won't pay my kid to help around the house. Families should pitch in and help out." The response is parents are not their children. These are different times. In addition to teaching a good work ethic and money management skills, allowance systems significantly increase children's and teens' motivation to do chores. ADHD is a behavioral disorder that affects motivation, and money is a great reinforcer.

Parents who don't use allowance systems can be asked, "How is it working out at your home with chores? Does your child complete chores regularly? How much arguing and threatening occurs each week about chores?" If these questions generate negative responses, the question can then be asked, "How much would you pay for your children to magically start doing chores consistently without complaints?" Almost all reply, "A lot!" The answer to them is, "This is called an allowance system." Allowance is a master parent wizard tool.

There are many different ways to use allowance systems. With the version presented here, each chore that is completed earns a specific amount of money. Allowance money is earned and should not be automatically given. Parents should spend some time and list on paper or computers what chores are expected to be done on specific days, and then how much they will earn for each chore. A common guideline is that a child earns one dollar per year of age. For example, a 10-year-old could earn 10 dollars per week. However, they should perform ten dollars of work each week. Also, more chores should be added as the child ages so they may be paid more but will be required to do more. If parents cannot afford a dollar per age each week, then they can pay a lesser predetermined amount.

The length of time a chore takes and the complexity of the chore should dictate how much is earned. Brief chores should earn less than more involved chores. Also, some families may choose to leave more involved and longer chores for weekends, such as cleaning bedrooms, pet cages, or bathrooms. Chores should be written down with indicated days and times when they should be completed. This makes the expectations very specific and clear for everyone. When chores are completed, they can be tracked by marking what was done on a calendar or chore checklist. On pay day, these can be reviewed and the child should be paid for what was done that week. Children and teens can also be expected to record these after chores are completed.

The way to calculate the allowance system chore payments is to work backwards from what will be paid to the child. First determine the total amount that will be paid each week. Suppose a 10-year-old is permitted to earn a total of 10 dollars a week. The parent will then make a list of all of the desired chores the child should complete each week. Some chores may be daily, such as making their bed or doing dishes after dinner, while others will be once or twice a week, such as cleaning a bedroom. Then determine the amounts for each completed chore based on the entire amount to be paid (such as $10 for the 10-year-old).

For example, a child will be expected to wash dinner dishes on Monday, Wednesday, and Thursday evenings (perhaps a sibling does them on other days), bed-making each morning before leaving for school, cleaning a pet guinea pig's cage each Saturday at 11 a.m., and bedroom cleaning each Sunday at 10 a.m. The dinner dishes can earn one dollar per day (3 dollars total), making the bed could earn 25 cents each time (for $1.75 total), cleaning the pet cage could earn $2.25, and room cleaning could generate 2 dollars. This makes a total of ten dollars that can be potentially earned each week if all of their chores are finished. Because allowance does not have to be all or nothing, the child is paid only for the chores completed.

Allowance money is earned only if the chore is done on the expected day and to the standard that the parents sets. Parents should spend some time initially explaining how they define the chore and how the chore should be properly done. Chores done poorly should not be paid, and children should be told they are only paid when it is done properly. Also, children and teens can initially be given one reminder to start their chores. Parents should not be expected to repeatedly remind or beg them to do their chores.

Bonus chores can be utilized as well. These can include yard work, extra cleaning projects like basements or garages, washing windows, and so forth. These bonus chores can be written down with the amounts they earn. Each window cleaned could earn 50 cents. Mowing the yard could be 10 or 20 dollars for older children or teens that are permitted to do this. Bonus chores are excellent opportunities for children or teens who want to save for more expensive items. When children and teens ask for things they want, parents can have the standard responses of "Where's your allowance money? Have you been doing your chores to earn allowance? Should you start doing bonus chores to earn more money?"

Pay day for allowance should be the same day each week. Fridays are good pay days because it is the start of the weekend and children may want to make purchases or go out on the weekend. It is not recommended paying children every two weeks or monthly because this is generally too long for some children or teens to wait, and this may reduce their commitment to completing their chores consistently. Parents should also be mindful to pay when they should, and not delay payments ("I do not have the money now, but I will pay you next week when I get paid"). Additionally, parents should be accommodating sometimes to take children and teens to stores or activities to let them spend their allowance. This should help with their participation in the program, and will be fun for them. Parents can also supervise and assist with online purchases as well.

Participation with allowance systems can be optional, or not. Some parents may pay allowance only when chores are done, and no negative consequences for not doing these. Others may pay when chores are completed but also give negative consequences if not completed. While both approaches work, it is suggested initially that allowances are an optional system without negative consequences. Some parents may make allowance optional because they are working on improving other behaviors that the child is struggling with, such as homework compliance or school behavior problems, and these other targeted behaviors are more important and time consuming. However, other parents may decide that doing chores is very important, and so the hassle of consistently applying negative consequences if they do not complete their chores each week is worth it.

If parents use the allowance system along with negative consequences when the child does not complete chores, they will be improving their chances of compliance because they are "double stacking" a child's motivation. They will receive money for doing the chores, and they will receive a negative consequence for not doing the chores. If a negative consequence will be applied, then this should be standard, pre-determined, and explained to the child. They can be told "If you do all of your chores, you will be paid for these. If you choose to not do your chores, you will receive no allowance money for the things you want, and you will be grounded in your room each Saturday for 3 hours with no electronic screen time." If they refuse to do chores and do not cooperate with their negative consequences, they can lose all privileges and electronics until the negative consequences are completed. Then they can make their choices about participating the next day.

If no negative consequences are used when children or teens refuse to participate, then parents should explain that this is acceptable, but they will receive no money for anything they want. Eventually, if parents are consistent with not giving them money, then children and teens should want to participate. If they do not do the chores, or only do minimal chores, but ask their parents for things, then parent should ask, "Where is your money? If you did your chores you would be earning an allowance." As children grow older and money becomes increasingly important, they will be more motivated to do their chores.

Another interesting aspect of an allowance system can be the option of money allocated for savings and/or for charity or religious donations. Some families may require savings and/or donations as part of this system. A child who earns ten dollars a week may be required to put one dollar away in a bank savings or child investment account and one dollar a week for a chosen charity. This means the child can have 8 dollars a week for free spending. Of course, parents can decide that children must allocate more money per week for savings or charity. However, if this number is too high, some children and particularly teens will not be motivated to participate. Glass jars can be used for savings and donations, and parents can hold onto these. A child's savings account can be opened at a bank, and periodically the child can make deposits at the bank with the parent. This will expose children to banks and help them understand how they work. What are considered acceptable purchases from their savings accounts should be discussed with the child. Generally, savings money should be used for more important and infrequent purchases approved by parents.

To help the child use the allowance system consistently, parents and generous grandparents should not regularly give the child extra money, except for special occasions or bonuses. This will be particularly important for children or teens who refuse to do chores. Families should not give money outside of the system so they will be motivated to consistently do their chores. When using allowance systems, parents should pay for only the most basic things, while the child can pay for everything else that is wanted. Books bags, school clothes, and other essentials should be purchased by parents. However, extras like additional clothes, video games, more expensive sneakers, or snacks in stores should be paid by children and teens. For families that go to the movies, parents can pay for the movie ticket but the child can pay for their own popcorn or snacks. Buying their own things can help children and adolescents feel more mature as well.

Parents should not combine the allowance system with other forms of negative consequences. The allowance system should occur even if other negative behaviors occur. Parents should not remove a child's allowance for defiance at home or school suspensions. This is because parents should reinforce chore compliance so children and teens are consistent and do not stop doing these. However, they can pay fines as a negative consequence from their allowance money, and can do extra chores if they have no money to pay off fines. Lastly, there are apps for child debit cards that parents control with their smart phones that pay allowances, including savings and charity options (such as Greenlight).

BE PREPARED WHEN OUT IN PUBLIC

For younger or very hyperactive and impulsive children, parents should plan ahead for recurrent problematic situations outside of the house. This includes shopping, restaurants, family outings, and birthday parties. Parents should review the expectations and consequences with the child before entering the situation. A reward can be given at the end of the activity if the expectations were followed (snacks from home, screen time, or a small purchase). Negative consequences can include loss of privileges, immediate time-outs in or outside the store, or a delayed time-out at home (Barkley, 1997).

GO TO THE NEXT LEVEL TO MAINTAIN CONSEQUENCES

If a child or teen steals items from others in the home or does not respect assigned negative consequences (such as no video game, cell phone or computer use), parents should manage this by an extended removal of these items. They can be locked up in the parent's bedroom or car trunk. Parents should also lock up all valuables that they believe may be stolen by the child or teen, particularly those with ODD or conduct disorder. If this is a recurrent issue, parents may want to invest in a small safe in their room to secure their valuables as well.

When parents go to the next level with these responses, some children and teens may escalate further due to their poor frustration tolerance and as a way of maintaining control in the home. When enraged, some children and teens may resort to more extreme behaviors to lash out at parents. In some of these situations, parents may require assistance from experienced behavioral health therapists or other treatments to address these volatile and potentially dangerous situations. Please refer to the sections below regarding addressing aggressive and suicidal behaviors, and when more intensive treatment is needed.

RESPOND TO PROPERTY DESTRUCTION

If children or teens destroy property in a rage, tantrum, or in response to consequences they don't like, parents should not respond emotionally. Rather, caregivers should inform them that they will be forced to pay back the cost of replacing items or repairing the damage. If it is their own property they destroyed, parents can simply do nothing and do not replace it. If it is something that must be replaced (like a school book), repaired (like walls, doors, or windows), or is someone else's property, parents can create a chore list with dollar amounts for each chore item. Children and teens can be informed that they will need to do chores to work off the money they owe for what was broken or destroyed. They can be informed that they will be grounded with no or minimal privileges and/or lose their cell phones or electronics indefinitely until they finish paying off the amount with the chores.

ADDRESS AGGRESSIVE AND SUICIDAL BEHAVIORS

Parents should call 911 if a child or adolescent becomes significantly aggressive, violent or makes serious threats that they will hurt the caregiver, themselves, or others. Unfortunately, children and teens with ADHD, ODD, bipolar disorder, and conduct disorder are at greater risk for suicidal and aggressive thoughts and behaviors. Teens or older children may try to prevent parents from enforcing consequences by threatening or acting violently. This escalation can be an attempt to prevent caregivers from maintaining healthy and appropriate parental control.

If they escalate with threatening or aggressive behaviors, parents should not respond with yelling, screaming, or physically enforcing consequences. Rather, parents can call the police to show children and teens that if they escalate, more serious consequences will result. When the police arrive, they may only talk or mediate with the family about the situation, or they may call for an ambulance for the child or teen to go to a medical or psychiatric hospital for an evaluation. Parents can request they go to a hospital for an evaluation as well. Admissions to psychiatric hospitals or intensive outpatient programs (IOPs) may occur if the child's or teen's aggressive behaviors are excessive, if they have a significant suicidal risk, if they seriously threaten to harm another, or if they demonstrate other severe difficulties.

Some parents are reluctant to "call the cops" in these serious situations. However, it is critical that parents maintain appropriate control in the home. When children or teens have severe behaviors or are excessively defiant, they may have histories of antagonizing parents to get their way. This can be particularly true for older children or teens with ODD, conduct disorder, or bipolar disorder. The severe defiance can create a significant dysfunctional imbalance of power. A serious safety issue occurs when violence is threatened or happens. Calling the police can demonstrate to the child or teen that these severe behaviors are not acceptable and will result in a serious response to maintain safety. Finally, obtaining higher levels of care is humane and is a sign that the child or teen is out-of-control and needs more intensive assistance.

WHEN MORE INTENSIVE TREATMENT IS NEEDED

For children and teens with more severe ADHD, ODD, conduct disorder, bipolar disorder and/or other serious co-existing conditions, parents may have to modify their methods and apply consequences somewhat differently within their behavioral management systems. Children and teens with chronic and more extreme levels of moodiness, irritability, behavioral rigidity, instability, reactivity, aggressiveness, explosiveness, and poor frustration tolerance may require different types of treatment providers and approaches. These children and teens often benefit from a team of coordinated providers, including psychiatrists for medication to better balance their brains to increase stability and functioning.

Therapists and psychiatrists should work with the family to create more effective treatment plans and approaches to address the serious behavioral concerns. Parents may have to alter or stop their use of negative consequences because some of these children cannot tolerate these, and only use positive consequences for desired behaviors. Children and teens with diagnostically complex conditions may require additional assessments, such as yearly psychological testing, to explore their functioning and evolving conditions. Some may have undetected conditions that require specialist providers to better understand and treat their difficulties.

The more severe the conditions and behavioral problems, the more the child or teen will require psychiatric medications, more frequent family and individual psychotherapy sessions, and possible admissions to Intensive Outpatient Programs (IOPs), Partial Hospitalization Programs (PHPs), and psychiatric hospitalizations. Concerning substance use, suicidal or aggression risks, and other serious and risky behaviors should be addressed by behavioral health providers and not ignored. IOPs, PHPs, and psychiatric hospitalizations may be needed periodically or frequently, depending on the situation. Furthermore, if children or adolescents continue to experience instability and severe symptoms, additional opinions from different psychiatrists may be needed to explore other psychiatric medications options. Consultations from experienced clinical psychologists to explore other diagnostic options and treatment recommendations may be needed as well. Finally, neurofeedback treatment and the Walsh Biochemical Imbalances and Nutrient Therapy approaches may be helpful with more challenging cases (please refer to the last chapter for more information on these topics).

SUMMARY POINTS

- Effective behavioral management approaches involve parents utilizing more effective parenting principles and changing their interactional styles.
- The use of effective, consistent, and timely positive and negative consequences is one of the most essential keys to ADHD behavior management.
- Parents can create a written behavioral plan listing specific expectations with positive and negative consequences to target desired and unwanted behaviors.
- Parents can promote behavioral changes with time-outs, ignoring behaviors, token and point systems, and allowance systems.

- At times it may be necessary to call the police to maintain safety, or utilize intensive outpatient services and programs or psychiatric hospitalizations when serious threats or acts of property destruction, aggression, or suicidal behaviors occur.

REFERENCES

Barkley, R. (1997). *Defiant children* (2nd ed.). New York, NY: The Guilford Press.

Barkley, R. (2013). *Taking charge of ADHD* (3rd ed.). New York, NY: The Guilford Press.

Flick, G. (1996). *Power parenting for children with ADD/ADHD*. West Nyack, NY: The Center for Applied Research in Education.

Gershoff, E. T., Goodman, G. S., Miller-Perrin, C. L., Holden, G. W., Jackson, Y., & Kazdin, A. E. (2018). The strength of the causal evidence against physical punishment of children and its implications for parents, psychologists, and policymakers. *American Psychologist, 73*(5), 626–638. Retrieved from http://dx.doi.org/10.1037/amp0000327

Phelan, T. (2016a). *1-2-3 Magic* (6th ed.). Naperville, IL: Sourcebooks, Inc.

Phelan, T. (2016b). *1-2-3 Magic Teen* (4th ed.). Naperville, IL: Sourcebooks, Inc.

Tarver, J., Daley, D., & Sayal, K. (2014, November). Attention-deficit hyperactivity disorder (ADHD): An updated review of the essential facts. *Child: Care, Health, and Development, 40*(6), 762–774.

Chapter 6

MAXIMIZING PARENTAL EFFECTIVENESS AT HOME

STOP EXCESSIVELY TALKING!

Many parents of children with ADHD talk too much when unwanted behaviors occur. Parents should stop over-explaining the rules and expectations, consequences, and rules of the house. They should end the long unproductive discussions and lectures. Too many parents waste tremendous energy and time complaining to children about their negative behavior and providing ineffective lectures about their own childhoods, the future, or other unhelpful topics. When a child earns a negative consequence, the parent should deliver this in an emotionally neutral manner and then detach from the subject. They should not raise their voice or give rambling monologues. These bad habits do not motivate the child or change behavior. Many of these children and teens are now parent-deaf and tune out quite quickly.

Parents should also not engage in arguing with children or teens about their rules and expectations. Instead, they should give a consequence and walk away. With some children and teens, particularly those with ODD and conduct disorder, the more parents argue, the worse the situation becomes. When children attempt to argue, parents can respond causally to the child's persistent complaints and comments with "I understand" or "Could be." Some children and teens with ADHD and ODD have lots of energy and enjoy arguing. Many act like little lawyers, passionately litigating their case in an imaginary courtroom for what they want or why something is so unfair. Parents should not participate or engage in these unproductive debates. Escalations can be prevented by being brief when giving consequences and not overexplaining expectations. When caregivers argue, explain their reasoning, threaten, or discuss the importance of the rules or respecting elders, they are giving away their parental power. While it can be tempting to respond and argue when misbehavior or defiance occurs, it is usually unproductive, and particularly when all are emotional. When people are upset and reactive, their frontal lobes (the more developed and rational portions of the brain) are less in control, and more primitive responses will occur. Parents should instead teach their children through their actions that when they give a consequence, it is written in STONE. It takes time to become a master parent wizard.

Additionally, consequences should not be negotiable. Consequences for repeated unwanted behaviors should be predetermined and written down so there are no surprises when they occur once again. It is not helpful to make deals or lessen consequences after unwanted behaviors occur. If it is necessary to discuss or review the rules and consequences with the child or teen, parents should do this the next day or at a later time when everyone is calmer. Discussions about expectations and consequences should not happen in the moment when unwanted behaviors occur. Finally, it can be quite productive to have occasional discussions about expectations and consequences, particularly with older children and adolescents. These discussions can be helpful in adjusting consequences so they seem reasonably fair to all. This can motivate children and teens to have more "buy in" and compliance with the behavioral systems.

CALMLY GIVE CONSEQUENCES

Most parents work too hard by yelling, raising their voices, arguing, lecturing, and threatening to try to force their children or teens to do what they want. Instead, parents should let the consequences do the work. In a calm and neutral voice, they should tell the child or teen what is expected and what the consequences will be if they do or do not do the expected behavior. The child should be given the option of choices, without parents raising their voices and threatening. In time, if the caregiver is neutral and consistent when giving consequences, then the child can learn to make better choices in a calmer environment. In a sense, the parent is removing themselves from the situation and providing the child choices about what will happen. With behavior management, parents are focusing on what they have control over, and this includes their emotional states and the actions they can deliver.

Because behaviors are contagious, it is important for parents to be as calm, neutral and non-reactive as possible when using behavior management approaches. If a parent or teacher is even mildly dysregulated when disciplining a child, then this can negatively activate a child, and particularly if they have other conditions or have experienced psychological trauma.

The negative behavior of children or teens can easily escalate when parents are not calm or neutral when delivering consequences (B. D. Perry, personal communication, April 14, 2014).

When parents become upset, they give away their parental power and can lose control of the situation. Removing the caregiver's emotional charge can help prevent the child from escalating and may stabilize the situation. Additionally, parents who practice remaining calm during conflicts model positive behaviors for their children and teens, as well as self-discipline and personal responsibility. It is ironic how many parents will yell and become upset with children and teens while demanding respect and self-control from them. Actions speak louder than words.

Calming down when unwanted or escalating behaviors occur can be difficult to learn, particularly at first. Practicing maintaining a calm and neutral attitude when interacting with difficult children is a skill that develops over time. Master parent wizards have learned to not become emotionally reactive during stressful interactions, and have learned to manage their emotional states. Many parents of children and teens with ADHD get lots of chances to practice! The emotional management skills presented in Chapter 7 should help with this, and therapists can assist as well. Some parents will struggle more with calming down in the moment than others, particularly if they have "hot-headed" tendencies or if they have ADHD themselves.

When parents remove their own bitter and angry reactions and attitudes, they will improve their relationships with their children. Better relationships are more enjoyable for everyone, and children and teens will be more compliant and display fewer behavioral problems when they experience improved relations. Once again, parents have to change first.

If parents become angry or upset when a child or teen misbehaves, they should not give consequences at that time. Unless it is a safety issue that needs to be addressed immediately, the parent should inform the child or teen that they will address the issue later and they will receive consequences soon. Some children and teens with ADHD, and particularly ODD, are talented at provoking and antagonizing caregivers. Caregivers are at risk of hitting or verbally abusing their children when they are overwhelmed, frustrated, and believe they have no control. When individuals become upset, they are not in full control, and can say and do things they regret later. Their frontal lobe is offline, and parents should not discipline during these times. Using more self-care practices can help reducing stress and negativity as well (more on these later).

CHANGE UNPRODUCTIVE THINKING

If parents do not fully grieve and accept a child's disability, they can remain stuck in the unproductive cycle of yelling and negatively reacting to their challenging children. Parents can become lost in ineffective thinking patterns that propel the cycle, such as "Why does she keep doing this! This is so unbelievable! It's unfair! I can't handle this." These self-programming thoughts are counterproductive, maintain negative emotional reactions, and will not inspire more effective parental responses.

Thoughts and beliefs direct feelings and behaviors. Thoughts create reality, and there is a tremendous power in changing one's thinking patterns to create new outcomes. More accurate and positive thinking patterns can help shift parent's frustrations and reactions, and support acceptance and better moods. Changing negative attitudes and perspectives help break the negativity cycle. Parents can practice replacing unproductive thoughts with ones that focus on accepting the ADHD ("This is his ADHD brain operating right now, and that's why he's arguing"), not taking the behaviors personally ("This is not about me, she would do this with any parent"), self-reminders of healthy detachment ("I need to let this go and take a break now; I can handle this") and the use of consequences ("I need to give a time-out and stop debating with him").

To help accelerate this change process, caregivers can take some time to notice and write out some of their most frequent and unhelpful negative thoughts and beliefs about their children and teens, ADHD, family dynamics, and parenting experiences. Curiously, thoughts rule our lives but are often invisible until examined. After identifying the unwanted thoughts, parents can make lists of new thoughts and beliefs they wish to adopt. Some parents leave themselves reminder notes with the new thoughts they wish to use.

Parents who are stuck in negative thinking and response patterns can also take some time to reflect upon their reactions and why they become so upset. Obviously behavioral problems are frustrating, however there may be additional components. Perhaps they have specific fears about the child's future, or are unconsciously triggered by the disrespectful behaviors. Maybe these actions remind them of someone from the parents' past who mistreated them, such as an abusive parent, romantic partner, or toxic co-worker. Conflictual parent-child relational dynamics can be ongoing painful reminders, and can trigger some parents to feel like a victim without control. These and other strong emotional reactions from parents, particularly ones that happen repeatedly, can provide important information if they are examined. Once uncovered, these issues can be addressed and may contribute to improving parent-child relationships.

AVOID POWER STRUGGLES

Power struggles promote escalations during confrontations and should be avoided. A power struggle occurs when the child wants something and a parent says "No," or when a child or teen refuses to do something a parent wants them to do. Power struggles can involve escalations of their voice, behaviors, or threats. Caregivers should learn to quickly recognize the signs of power struggles and disengage as soon as possible. Parents should provide children and teen with choices, and they should be permitted to choose. If they decide to persist after a warning or counting, they will earn a negative consequence. When they refuse to accept the limits or consequences, this is a power struggle. "You can't make me!" or "I refuse!" are common themes in power struggles.

The challenge is for the parent to remain calm, resist the urge to argue and threaten, and give the child their options. Parents can imagine that they are using their master parent wizard training to practice detachment and disengagement from power struggles and escalations. This mentality can help caregivers unhook from provocative negative comments and behaviors, and not participate in the tug of war. When a consequence is given, parents can practice giving this and walking away, without yelling or becoming emotional. Finally, parents can use the parent–child/teen conflict resolutions skills presented in the next chapter when conflicts arise and to prevent or minimize escalations.

WORK ON HEALTHY DETACHMENT

While similar to avoiding power struggles, it is essential that parents learn to disengage and detach themselves from their children's and teen's antagonizing and challenging behavior. Parents should practice the emotional management skills to notice, accept, and cope when they become upset with their children (these are discussed in the next chapter). This can be very difficult at times because some children will curse, tease, or say hurtful things when they are upset with parents. Healthy detachment is a critical aspect of maintaining parental control, particularly for children with ODD. As much as possible, caregivers should not get emotional in front of the child. Becoming upset and reactive to children will only reinforce their difficult behavior and lessen parental control of the situation.

Instead of negative reactions, parents should have a plan of what they will do when difficult behaviors occur. Parents can give a consequence, walk away, and not discuss the problems with child at that moment. When upset, parents also can go into their bedroom, lock the door, and do some type of relaxation, coping, or stress-relieving behaviors to calm down, including emotional management skills. Taking a disability perspective and practicing forgiveness can also help parents detach when their children are provocative, nasty or difficult. These are part of master parenting wizard training.

Due to their own poor frustration tolerance and as a possible attempt to control their parent's reactions, some children and teens with ADHD can easily escalate with nasty language, particularly those with ODD. If parents emotionally respond, they are taking the bait. Instead, parents can state, "When you use that language with me, the conversation is over." Then walk away. They should not get emotional or react to this language because this will reinforce and encourage them to use it again. If necessary, parents can use a standard regular consequence for cursing or disrespectful language. However, it may be best to detach from this and concentrate on other behaviors because it can be difficult to control children and teen's negative language. Thus, caregivers can practice detachment and pretend not to get upset. While not easy, it is a skill that takes practice. Finally, if parents want cursing and negative language to end, they should model this themselves and end this bad habit when around them.

Sometimes when parents give a negative consequence and walk away from the child, the child may follow the parent around the house and continue to argue with them. Some parents feel abused or stalked by their children and teens when they give consequences. Others may have stopped giving negative consequences because of this escalation. Children and teens with ODD can be particularly skilled at harassing and following caregivers around the home until parents give in to what they want. One way to address this is for parents to invest in a good working key lock on their bedroom door that the child cannot break into or pick easily. If the child follows them or wildly screams, parents can then go into their locked bedroom and play music after delivering a consequence.

LEARN TO EXPECT CERTAIN BEHAVIORS

Many caregivers continually react with surprise and outrage when their children or teens exhibit difficulties. When children and teens with ADHD act in challenging ways this should not be a surprise. Many parents who react this way have not accepted the rainy climate and their child's condition. Parents should learn to expect certain problematic behaviors and have a specific plan to calmly respond to these. This will give the caregiver more control and minimize their emotional reactions. "No surprises!" should be spoken internally as a master parent wizard mantra when a child or teen with ADHD commits the same unwanted behaviors. Similarly, parents should also not take the ADHD behaviors personally. The disorder causes interpersonal and behavioral challenges with all parents. Once again, grieving and acceptance can help.

Another aspect of this perspective involves learning to identify and better prepare for situations when a child or teen is more likely to demonstrate certain unwanted behaviors, tantrums, or frustration episodes. Behaviors have specific causes, and parents and children may not be aware of these. Parents can reflect on the most common situations that provoke and precede their behavioral difficulties. These situations may include being hungry, too hot or cold environments, feeling overwhelmed by parental expectations, the pressures of homework or reading, chores, difficult social interactions, not getting their way, or rules they dislike. They may also have episodes when they are bored, want attention, have anxiety or depression symptoms, have had poor quality sleep, or experienced stressful days with peers or teachers at school. Another reason for unwanted behaviors may be related to certain situations that lack clear expectations or structure. ADHD medication factors should also be considered as well. These include not taking their medication that day, medication wearing off, annoying side effects, or other medication issues. Over time, if parents can identify their children's triggers and patterns, these situations can be anticipated and managed better. Often understanding and compassion can warm parents' reactions. Emotional management skills may be helpful for children and teens to better respond to stress and frustration as well.

DON'T EXPECT CHILDREN AND TEENS TO UNDERSTAND PARENTS' LIVES

Parents should not expect their children or teens to understand or appreciate their stresses, difficulties, time, and money that is spent on raising children. This is particularly true with those with ADHD. Caregivers can become bitter because the child is not appreciative enough of their efforts. Some parents persist in this thinking and it can increase their resentments and bitterness. Parents should not expect children or older teens to thank them or act in grateful ways for all of their hard work. Again, understanding ADHD as a neurobiological condition, taking a disability perspective, implementing self-care (see below), and practicing forgiveness are all antidotes to this unhelpful thinking.

INEFFECTIVE PARENTING STYLES

Every parent has a certain style in their interactions with their children. Unfortunately, ADHD parenting stresses can bring out the worst in parents. Caregivers respond in different ways. Some parents are highly permissive, cannot tolerate conflict, and prefer to be "buddies" with the child or teen. This permits them to be less of a "bad guy" and avoid some problems, such as children's frustration episodes when they are told "no." Other parents respond to non-compliance and difficulties by becoming a task master and attack through harsh, rigid, and punitive interactions. Some have highly reactive temperaments and may quickly raise their voices when they are frustrated. They may yell and curse when the child is forgetful or non-compliant. Other parents can become depressed, anxious and overwhelmed, acting more disengaged and distant with their children. These caregivers may emotionally avoid their children or retreat into their own interests. Still other parents are inconsistent in their responses to children's unwanted behaviors. They may be unpredictable and vacillate between harsh, permissive, or disengaged responses, which will confuse the child and reduce stability. Parents with their own ADHD are at higher risk for committing these highly reactive, inconsistent, and volatile parenting behaviors.

All of these styles can contribute to negative relationships with children. These are unhealthy for the entire family and can cause the ADHD problems to persist or magnify. Parents too often accept their unhealthy parenting behaviors as just something that happens, with an attitude of "that's just the way I am." Some parents may be unaware of how ineffective or even toxic they are. While some of these negative communications are bad habits, others may have deeper roots. Parents may be unconsciously impacted by how they were raised and may be acting out certain parenting behaviors that they themselves resented as children. Parents can also have their own mental health issues, substance use, and unhealthy aspects of their personalities, as well as significant other stressors and problems in life.

Research has shown that parents of children with ADHD experience more stress and dysfunctional interactional styles with their children than parents of neurotypical children. This can have implications for the potential maltreatment of children and teens with ADHD. One group of researchers shared that parents of children with difficult temperaments and ADHD may experience higher levels of parental stress and distress which can then lead to abusive parenting. This toxic parenting can then accelerate aggressive tendencies and behavioral problems in the children and teens with ADHD, and further aggravate their ADHD-related difficulties (Briscoe-Smith & Hinshaw, 2006). Indeed, a vicious cycle can result, and everyone loses.

Children and teens with ADHD, ODD, and behavioral problems can elicit excessive negative reactions from parents. This is a sensitive topic because children and teens should not be blamed for parents' toxic actions. Some parents may believe they have lost control of their home and become desperate to reclaim control. Other parents are incredibly overwhelmed, angry, and resentful of their disobedient and difficult children and teens. At times, some parents react to these challenging situations with emotionally and/or physically abusive behaviors. Additionally, children who have poor relationships with caregivers are less compliant with them, and so a negative spiral of dysfunctional interactions between parent and child can develop and continue, with abuse sometimes resulting.

Because parental reactions can easily escalate when they are emotional and disciplining, it is strongly recommended that they not use physical consequences. While parents are permitted to use corporeal punishments in many states as long as they do not leave bruises or marks, it is easy to cross the line and hurt the child more than was intended. Over the years, increasing research has indicated that corporeal punishments are not as effective as other forms of behavioral management. They negatively impact the child, and do not improve parent-child relationships.

A group of earlier studies have found that there are four types of parenting styles which tend to use different discipline approaches.

- *Permissive Parents* provide less structure and discipline, are more lenient, and can be more of a friend than parent. They may encourage their children to communicate and discuss their problems, but do not adequately discourage or deal with their negative behaviors (Morin, 2017). Permissive parents permit their children to make decisions whether they are ready or not. These children perform worse academically, and may have more problems with authority and accepting responsibility (Joseph & John, 2008).
- *Authoritarian Parents* demand their rules are followed without explanations or exceptions, do not engage in problem-solving, and frequently say "Because I say so." They are like lion tamers and drill sergeants, and love to be in control. Their punishments tend to generate anger in their children and do not teach effective lessons to promote improvements (Morin, 2017). Because they are overcontrolled, their children tend to have lower self-esteem, happiness, and social abilities. They can lack curiosity, self-confidence, and may take initiatives less often (Joseph & John, 2008).
- *Uninvolved Parents* are more disengaged and neglectful, may have mental health or substance abuse issues themselves, and may not meet their children's basic or emotional needs. They can lack rudimentary

knowledge about parenting and child development, and can be chronically overwhelmed by life. They have few expectations or rules. These children often lack attention, guidance, and nurturing (Morin, 2017). Research has shown these children have the worst outcomes, with low self-esteem, self-control, and social abilities (Joseph & John, 2008).
- *Authoritative Parents* are the healthiest. They have clear expectations but can have some flexibility. They explain their rules and will consider children's feelings when setting limits. They use consequences instead of punishments, and will utilize more praise and reward systems to reinforce desired behaviors (Morin, 2017). This style creates the best results, with children who are happier, more socially competent, and experience better mental health. Their teens also experience greater scholastic achievement and fewer behavioral difficulties (Joseph & John, 2008).

LeMasters presented other parenting styles, some of which have similarities to the styles already mentioned.

- *The Police Officer* ensures rules are always followed, with punishments for even little infractions (Joseph & John, 2008).
- *The Pal* is a buddy with a relaxed approach to expectations and discipline, and may provide little direction. Some with this style may temporarily try to become stricter if there are serious difficulties, but it can be hard to regain authority (Joseph & John, 2008).
- *The Martyr* does anything they can for their children, but often feels guilty and struggles to maintain this style (Joseph & John, 2008).
- The *Teacher Counselor* strives to be this role with their children, and places children's needs above parents. While this may be effective, it can generate parental stress and pressures (Joseph & John, 2008).
- *The Athletic Coach* can be the most effective style, and utilizes a benevolent interactive coach role to help children succeed (Joseph & John, 2008).

The impact of parenting styles on children will depend on a number of interactive factors, including characteristics of the child and parent, family dimensions, socioeconomic factors, and cultural aspects (Joseph & John, 2008). Additionally, parenting styles can fluctuate and exist on a continuum. Parents usually have more complex blends and variations than just these parenting styles. What can be most helpful is to identify which ineffective styles or tendencies parents exhibit. Once noticed, then parents can practice increasing their awareness of the unwanted parenting behaviors so they can be changed. Parents can strive for an authoritative and benevolent coaching parenting style, along with other master parent wizard approaches.

To accelerate this process, parents can honestly reflect upon what they should change. This can take some deeper soul searching, and are great opportunities for personal improvement. Once these less productive parenting traits are identified, then change can occur. Awareness will be the first step because people cannot change what they do not know. Journaling on these topics, discussing this with close friends or significant others (who can also remind the parents when they slip back to old behaviors), and exploring these topics in therapy sessions can be helpful. The next task is to make a commitment to change, determine what new behaviors should be practiced, and then take the specific action steps to accomplish this. Some caregivers use lists of daily parenting goals or reminder notes around the house to encourage consistent practice to form new parenting routines.

IMPROVE PARENT-CHILD/TEEN RELATIONSHIPS

A large problem many caregivers of children and teens with ADHD experience is negative parent-child relationships. This can result from years of conflicts, defiance, and behavioral difficulties. The child often learns that a powerful way to get the caregiver's attention is to act negatively. While this may seem ineffective, it does work ("the squeaky wheel gets the grease"), and the child will receive the caregiver's lectures, anger, and punishments. Yet, too often this is associated with minimal pleasant or positive interactions between the child and caregiver. The spontaneous and natural love, fun, and joy in the parent-child relationship can greatly decrease or end. Over time, caregivers may learn not to trust the child, become increasingly angry, and hold grudges. In turn, the child or teen can react to this by becoming angrier and act out with more unwanted behaviors. Another negative bitter cycle develops.

When these issues exist, stopping the negative cycle and improving the parent-child relationship is crucial. The most obvious first step is to treat the child's ADHD, and any other conditions. The ADHD*ology* treatment approach can provide this framework, and effective ADHD medication can sometimes dramatically and quickly change a negative environment. The next step is for parents to reverse the process and improve the relations. When the relationship has improved, the child should act less negatively and will not need to be seeking as much negative attention with their difficult behaviors. As stated previously, almost all children and teens, with or without ADHD, are more cooperative and compliant with adults they like.

One of the best ways to improve and rebuild the relationship is to implement the technique of together time. Barkley and Benton (1998) discuss this approach. During together time, parents should spend at least 15 to 20 minutes with the child or adolescent daily or at least four days a week, doing some activity the child enjoys. For younger children, parents can offer games or activities they can do together and avoid watching TV or screens if possible. Together time involves parents connecting with the child and spending time alone with them, without siblings. During this time parents should not teach anything, correct their actions, or be judgmental. Parents should make positive observations about the child's actions, such as "Wow, you can really throw the ball." If the child becomes difficult during together time, the parent can turn away briefly or end it for the day (Barkley & Benton, 1998).

For teens, together time can be more challenging, but parents should try to join their activity or ask if they can watch their video game or computer use. Some teens may enjoy parents' interests or questions about their activities. The key to have positive interactions while doing activities they enjoy. While they may be negative at first, parents must persevere (Barkley & Benton, 1998). Together time does not mean that parents should spend money or go out to eat together, but they can. Additionally, parents should expect that most adolescents will naturally disengage from them. Teens are often less interested in interacting or spending time with parents. While this is developmentally normal, it can make together time more difficult, particularly when there has been a poor parent-teen relationship.

Additional goals of together time are to learn to pay attention to the positives with the child (their interests, talents, and positive behaviors), and to regain the child's trust. Often this alone can dramatically improve fractured child-parent relationships. The improvements can take weeks to months, so users should not expect immediate results. If possible, both parents should do together time, but separately. With progress, it can be phased down and continued as long as necessary (Barkley & Benton, 1998). Also, even if parents do not commit to doing together time multiple times a week, they can incorporate these elements in their interactions. They can participate in their children's and teens' activities and interests more often, and do more enjoyable activities together, in and out of the home.

In simple terms, to improve the quality of their relationships, parents need to decrease their negative communications and interactions, while greatly increasing the number of positive communications and interactions. Human relationships require five times as many positive than negative interactions to be healthy. Parents who are frequently critical, nagging, and complaining should replace these communication habits with the use of consequence and allowance systems, healthy detachment, and acceptance. Parents will be challenged to transform old grudges and negative relational patterns.

When the child or teen is not having behavioral difficulties, parents should try to show genuine interest in them as a unique person. They can ask questions about what they care about, not just "How was school?" and other boring general questions. Examples can be "What was the most interesting thing about school today?" "Tell me about what's most important to you now," "What are you most looking forward to this week?" and "What's the funniest/weirdest/most exciting thing that happened today?" Committing to family dinners multiple times a week can facilitate more face time and connections together as well. Some families implement routines of playing a board game, watching a movie, or doing an activity outside of the home once a week to spend more time together. Finally, the use of parent–child/teen conflict resolution skills presented in the next chapter can enhance relationships by helping children and teens feel they are treated with fairness and respect by parents.

Phelan (2016) has presented several helpful parental approaches to improving parent-child relationships. The first is the use of effective listening skills. These include making sincere attempts to really listen, showing genuine interest without quick reactionary comments, and using reflective listening skills where parents paraphrase what children say. Also, parents can disclose appropriate things about their childhood or their current thoughts or feelings. This may make them more interesting and human to the child. Finally, providing honest compliments can enhance bonds (Phelan, 2016).

For families with ADHD, focusing on enhancing relationships can provide a healthy balance with firm behavioral management approaches. Parents of teens have a more difficult job because their relationship with the child will change more dramatically. They need to work on accepting their teen's developmentally-appropriate disengagement from parents, friends coming first, and moodiness. Staying warm in the relationship despite rejections, increasing flexibility, and increasing opportunities to connect and talk about non-conflictual things, particularly teen interests, can be important as well (Phelan, 2016). Additionally, utilizing the parent-child/teen conflict resolution skills of discussing problems that arise and using negotiation and compromise can help relationships as well. This approach will be further discussed in the next chapter.

Parents may need to work on forgiveness, including forgiving themselves for having bad days, losing their patience, and not sticking to behavioral programs at times. Family therapy can be very helpful for assistance in improving parent-child relations. A psychotherapist can teach more effective communication skills, ways to connect more, and addressing conflicts or issues that may be impacting the family.

Finally, parent-child relationships can be impacted when the child or teen is upset, angry, or struggling with a range of issues that may or may not be related to their parents. Children and teens who are depressed, anxious, have experienced significant stressors or psychological traumas, and adolescents who are developmentally disconnecting from parents can be more challenging. They may also be holding a grudge toward parents related to difficult past experiences or episodes. They may have deeper wounds regarding family issues and dynamics, such as dysfunctional adult relationships, domestic violence, parental substance misuse, parental separations or divorces, step-parent challenges, financial difficulties, harsh discipline, negative or toxic family communication styles, or various other family issues. These topics can be complex, and family and/or individual therapy may be an effective way to address them.

ADDRESS PARENTAL STRESSES AND INCREASE SELF-CARE

Parents need to work on their own stress levels, depression, anxiety, grudges, and other problems that are a result of or accompany their difficulties with their challenging children. Parents of children and teens with ADHD, ODD and other conditions are often overwhelmed and burned-out, particularly when the conditions are not effectively managed. This is especially true if multiple family members have ADHD, including spouses. Research has shown that parents of children with ADHD experience more stress, self-blame, depression, and isolation than parents of children without ADHD (Briscoe-Smith & Hinshaw, 2006). Parents of children with special needs often have imbalanced lives, and their children's struggles and conditions can dominate their worlds.

Parents may also have their own marital, work, personal, or other family issues. These additional problems can negatively impact their parenting abilities and may be contributing to the child's acting out. Parents and particularly mothers are at increased risk for depression and anxiety from raising children with ADHD and ODD. Caregiver's marriages and romantic relationships can be deeply damaged by the difficulties and parental differences that can occur when raising children with disabilities. Research has confirmed that mothers of children with ADHD hyperactivity are separated or divorced more often than mothers of children who do not have ADHD (Briscoe-Smith & Hinshaw, 2006).

Depending upon the severity of their own problems, parents should consider getting their own individual and/or family therapy with their spouse or partner. Blended families often have their own special challenges, and they can require additional assistance. Parents may procrastinate to obtain their own treatment if they are already receiving services for their children, or believe they lack the time, energy, or resources. However, waiting can increase the difficulties. When parents address their own needs, their effectiveness to help their children and the entire family can be enhanced.

At a minimum, parents should have a long-term and realistic stress-reducing plan to help them unwind and disengage from parenting stresses and difficult interactions at home. Parents should focus on activities, hobbies, and socializing that are invigorating and helps to "recharge the batteries." A commitment to self-care is essential and not a luxury. This may seem idealistic. Many parents think, "I don't have time or energy for that, I'm just trying to survive each day." However, this mentality will only worsen the situation. Emotional management skills can greatly assist in this area. Practicing basic healthy lifestyle routines can also go a long way. While not exciting, increasing sleep by going to bed earlier, regular exercise, and reducing unhealthy and increasing healthy food choices can all contribute to parents' well-being. Getting out of the house more on dates with significant others without the children and/or socializing more with friends can help inject more joy and fun and provide more balance. Finally, therapy can help with creating and using self-care practices and specific long-term stress reduction plans.

ADDRESS PARENTAL ADHD

Because ADHD is highly genetically transmitted, many children and adolescents with ADHD will have one or both parents who have ADHD as well. Since ADHD is two to three times more likely to occur in males than females, fathers tend to have ADHD more than mothers. Also, if one child has ADHD, the siblings are at increased risk of having ADHD as well. The more people in the home with ADHD and other conditions, the more challenges the entire family will have. ADHD is a family problem that affects everyone in the home. When it is better managed, the entire family will benefit.

Parents of children with ADHD who have undiagnosed or untreated ADHD themselves can often become easily overwhelmed and frustrated with their challenging children. This can sometimes contribute to unhealthy parenting behaviors and ineffective disciplining efforts. Parents who have untreated ADHD can possess more dysfunctional parenting behaviors and styles, and can suffer from increased difficulties that may negatively impact their parenting abilities. These can include decreased frustration tolerance (which makes them more overwhelmed and stressed by children's behaviors), lesser patience, higher rates of yelling and physical punishments, organizational difficulties, trouble following through on promises and commitments (including treatment appointments), less consistency in parenting approaches, more infrequent homework and school assistance, as well as other personal and family difficulties and other co-existing psychological conditions, such as depression and anxiety.

Some parents learn they may have adult ADHD when their children first begin their services for ADHD. If mothers have ADHD, it can be particularly difficult for the entire family. Parents with suspected ADHD should consider obtaining their own services, including evaluations or assessments first, then psychiatrists, ADHD therapists, neurofeedback providers, and ADHD coaches. Services are important for parents because when their ADHD is identified, treated, and managed, there is a better prognosis for the children or teens with ADHD. Clinicians who evaluate and treat ADHD in children and adolescents should expect to be interacting with parents who also have ADHD, diagnosed or not.

Finally, as discussed in Chapter 1, when one or both parents have ADHD, a number of significant marital or adult relational difficulties can occur. These home environments can be highly dysfunctional and stressful for everyone. Parents can seek appropriate services to address these difficulties, including the above-mentioned services for the parent suspected of having ADHD, as well as individual therapy for the other spouse. Couples therapy for the parents may be helpful as well, but this typically is more effective after adult ADHD is diagnosed and treated. Addressing these parental relational issues can also help stabilize and improve the entire family.

CONSIDER FAMILY MEDICAL LEAVE ACT (FMLA)

Parents who have children diagnosed with chronic psychological or medical conditions that require more frequent or intensive treatments and impact their work schedules should consider utilizing FMLA. This federal law permits qualifying employees who work for covered employers to receive job protection and unpaid leave from their work, for a period of time, to care for their children with serious health conditions, including ADHD. Parents can bring a FMLA certification form to the child's providers to complete, and then submit this to their employer for FMLA approval. This protected job leave can be helpful and necessary especially if the parent is missing work due to the child's services and treatment appointments.

For parents to be eligible for FMLA, they must have worked for at least 12 months and 1250 hours or more during this time frame. FMLA provides 12 weeks of coverage during a 12-month period, but it can be used intermittently and only when needed. While FMLA will not protect a job indefinitely, it can help and provide some relief. Parents can perform web searches for more information about FMLA and to print the form for providers to complete.

SUMMARY POINTS

- Parents can improve their parenting effectiveness by not talking excessively, calmly giving consequences, changing negative thinking and attitudes about children's behavior, avoiding power struggles, and practicing healthy detachment from negative interactions.
- Ineffective parenting styles include permissive, authoritarian, uninvolved, police officer, pal, and martyr styles. Caregivers should use authoritative and benevolent athletic coach styles.
- Parents can improve and rebuild their relationships with children and teens with together time, decreasing negative and increasing positive communication and interactions, and practicing forgiveness.
- Parents should address their own stresses and personal difficulties, increase their self-care practices, and considering obtaining Family Medical Leave Act if they require time off from their work for their child's services.
- Parents with ADHD should treat and better manage it to greatly improve their ability to manage their children's ADHD and help the family.

REFERENCES

Barkley, R., & Benton, C. (1998). *Your defiant child.* New York, NY: The Guilford Press.

Briscoe-Smith, A. M., & Hinshaw, S. P. (2006, November). Linkages between child abuse and attention-deficit/hyperactivity disorder in girls: Behavioral and social correlates. *Child Abuse & Neglect, 30*(11), 1239–1255.

Joseph, M. V., & John, J. (2008). Impact of parenting styles on child development. *Global Academic Society Journal: Social Science Insight, 1*(5), 16–25.

Morin, A. (2017, May 03). *4 types of parenting styles.* Retrieved from https://www.verywell.com/types-of-parenting-styles-1095045?

Phelan, T. (2016). *1-2-3 Magic Teen* (4th ed.). Naperville, IL: Sourcebooks, Inc.

Chapter 7

ADDITIONAL WAYS TO ADDRESS ADHD AT HOME

FAMILY AND INDIVIDUAL THERAPY

For more personalized assistance to improve results, particularly for families with more challenging ADHD, family therapy or counseling can be quite helpful. This specialized treatment should incorporate the previously-mentioned education about ADHD, behavioral management skills training for the parents, and an ADHD solution-focused and problem-solving approach for the family to address home and school difficulties. Other issues may also be addressed. The American Academy of Pediatrics has determined that parent management training is a Level One treatment option for ADHD. This means they found it has the best scientific support as an evidence-based child and adolescent treatment intervention (Practicewise, 2016).

Therapists who provide this type of family treatment should have experience working with ADHD. Effective ADHD-focused family therapy can help parents and families master the topics discussed in chapters four, five and six, as well as address school issues. Many of these competent ADHD therapists may also provide ADHD evaluations in the beginning phase of treatment. As discussed in Chapter 3, parents can interview some therapists on the phone to discuss their child's issues, as well as learn how the therapists specifically treat ADHD. This can improve the chances of families obtaining an effective therapist for their needs. Also, families may require additional rounds of therapy over a period of years to continue to address issues and polish their management skills, particularly when children grow older and encounter new developmental phases and challenges. Additionally, as mentioned previously, family therapy can help improve parent-child relationships and address significant family issues and conflicts.

Individual therapy alone without the parent-focused behavior management training is not an effective primary treatment for true ADHD. Psychotherapists and counselors cannot really teach children or adolescents with ADHD how to improve their attention or become less hyperactive. The American Academy of Pediatrics had determined that attention training, client-centered therapy, cognitive behavioral therapy, play therapy and self-control training were all Level Five primary treatment options for ADHD. This means these therapies were found to have no support as evidence-based interventions for this condition (Practicewise, 2016).

Individual psychotherapy can be a potent treatment for co-existing psychological conditions and other issues. Those with ADHD can have lower self-esteem and secondary depression and anxiety due to the failures, disappointments, and negative interactions they have experienced. Academic problems, underachievement, social problems, discord with parents and siblings, and chronic feelings of ineffectiveness can add to these difficulties. If these struggles exist, the core ADHD condition is often treated first, and then these other conditions can be addressed. Fortunately, many times these secondary issues improve with effective treatments, and particularly with ADHD medications. If not, then individual therapy and/or additional medication can be utilized. ODD often requires more extensive family therapy to address the relational issues and provide more intensive parental management training. Finally, debilitating depression, self-harm risks, severe anxiety, and other serious conditions should be evaluated by behavioral health professionals to determine the most appropriate treatment.

ADHD COACHING

During or after therapy, parents can also consider utilizing coaches to maximize results. While personal coaching has existed for a number of years, child and adolescent ADHD coaching is newer. Coaches can help to promote and create positive changes. They provide encouragement, help identify and enhance strengths, and teach skills to achieve established goals. Effective ADHD coaching can provide training to improve organizational, social, and time management skills, as well as meeting behavioral expectations at home and school. This coaching can also improve academics by enhancing homework, classwork, and study skills.

While similar in some ways, personal coaching is not therapy. ADHD coaches do not replace psychotherapists, educational therapists, tutors, or medication. Coaches do not treat psychological disorders, but teach skills to help provide improvements with the difficulties that result from the conditions. There are different types of coaches. Coaches are not required to be licensed, and the coaching field is much less regulated than for psychotherapists or physicians. However, a number of ADHD coaches are also licensed mental health therapists. Some may have various coaching certifications or credentialing, and while others may have only their personal experiences. Some licensed providers offer both personal coaching and psychotherapy, and others have specialty practices that just provide coaching. Group ADHD coaching sessions may be offered also, but these seem to be less common. Some coaches do not provide in-person sessions beyond the first session, and offer Skype or phone sessions, or email or text check-ins.

While there are benefits to coaching, there are some challenges. Their fees vary, and are typically not covered by health insurance. There are far fewer child and adolescent ADHD coaches available than those who work with adults with ADHD. Additionally, the effectiveness of coaches can obviously vary greatly. Parents should research and interview coaches to explore their approaches, what types of results they may expect, costs, and level of experience working with children or teens with ADHD.

Another challenge will be children's and teens' receptiveness to coaching. To be effective, children and teens will need to be fairly open and motivated to work with ADHD coaches. If they have ODD and/or are highly resistant to accepting feedback, improving their behavior, and setting goals, then ADHD coaching is probably not for them. This is similar to the results that can be expected from individual tennis or music lessons. When children are not invested, they will probably not practice the skills outside of sessions. Of course, rewards can be provided for positive efforts. Adolescents may desire change and participate more actively if they can acknowledge their ADHD limitations and wish to set goals to improve their lives. Younger children may require more direction and parental support in utilizing ADHD coaching. Coaching may also be more effective when medication is utilized, and after completing therapy treatment. Parents with ADHD can also obtain their own coaching. Finally, parents may wish to YouTube child or adolescent ADHD coaches for more information.

MANAGEMENT APPROACHES FOR YOUNG CHILDREN WITH ADHD

Preschool age children can have many ADHD-like symptoms. Consequently, it can be more challenging to firmly diagnose true ADHD in young children. Some may outgrow the symptoms by age six to seven. While some children can be diagnosed with ADHD at age three or four, the diagnosis can be less accurate. This can be difficult for parents of young children with behavioral problems who are unclear about the diagnoses or if the problems will continue. Some younger children with ADHD may also experience difficulties transitioning from half days of preschool, kindergarten, or daycare to full days. They may be taking shorter or less frequent naps or no naps, and their problems adjusting may persist for months. They may consequently experience even greater irritability and behavioral difficulties. As mentioned previously, young children with high levels of hyperactivity should receive occupational therapy evaluations to explore if they really have sensory processing disorders that are causing ADHD-like difficulties.

One of the most challenging aspects of younger children with behavioral problems is their difficulties at school and daycare. In these settings, aggression towards peers and staff, refusal to follow rules, poor frustration tolerance, frequent tantrums, and high levels of hyperactivity and disruptive behaviors can be quite overwhelming for the staff. Dysregulated children with high levels of ADHD-like symptoms can also have greater difficulty remaining in day cares or preschools due to their more extreme behaviors. They may be asked to repeatedly leave different settings because they are so difficult to manage. Of course, these dismissals can be quite overwhelming for working parents.

Even though it is frustrating to lack diagnostic clarity with younger children, a definitive diagnosis of ADHD is not necessary to address the behavioral difficulties. The behavioral management approaches discussed in prior chapters can be used with young children at home and school, including the use of daily structure and expectations and consistent consequences for positive and unwanted behaviors. Parents can modify some of the negative consequences previously mentioned to address younger child behaviors, and time-outs can be effective.

The rewards will need to be as immediate as possible and focused on younger child interests, including stickers, enthusiastic praise, snacks, reading or other enjoyable activities with parents, earning short amounts of screen time, and small prizes and toys. Some families combine surprise along with inexpensive prizes and toys by creating "a trip to the treasure box" as a reward. This is a decorated cardboard box that parents fill with dollar store items, and as a reward the child picks one item from the box but cannot see inside.

To best manage these behavioral difficulties at school and daycare, parents will need to work closely with the staff. Behavioral approaches in these settings can include the use of token systems of earning and losing poker chips for positive and unwanted behaviors (with a reward menu at home and school), closer proximity to teachers, more frequent breaks, the use of time-outs, and positive and negative reinforcers implemented at home for preschool and daycare behaviors on a daily "report card" (Smith, 2011). Indeed, these behavioral systems will be critical. Therapists experienced with providing behavioral management training for young children may need to be engaged as well.

For children with the most severe presentations, their very high levels of impulsivity and hyperactivity can pose safety risks, and thus can warrant medication trials. Preschool age children with severe ADHD can impulsively run out of their homes, schools, and daycares into the streets and traffic when they are frustrated, upset, or curious. They are at risk for more dangerous and lethal play activities as well, including playing with harmful objects and poisons, and climbing into unsafe areas. For more severe cases, ADHD medications can be attempted for children ages 3 to 5. However, it is generally recommended that young children first receive behavioral approaches for their ADHD-like difficulties before medication is attempted.

Studies of preschool-age children on ADHD medications have yielded mixed results. While ADHD stimulant medications have been shown to be effective and safe for school-age children, these drugs have shown fewer positive results for children under age 6. The Food and Drug Administration has not approved methylphenidate hydrochloride (Ritalin) to be used on children under six (Smith, 2011). Because a number of pediatricians and family practice physicians may be uncomfortable prescribing ADHD medications for children under age 6, parents can visit child psychiatrists for the medication.

MANAGEMENT APPROACHES FOR ADOLESCENTS WITH ADHD

A. Teens with ADHD need more parental assistance and interventions than teens without ADHD. This can be difficult because adolescence is a developmental phase when many teens wish to detach themselves from caregivers, and may resist parental help. They may resent the very structure and guidance that they require. Additionally, adolescents with ADHD can have more challenging presentations and interactions, and may be more volatile, moody, argumentative, defensive, and less likely to assume responsibilities. Creating a balance between providing the parental structure they need while their natural detachment process occurs will be a key challenge during this time.

B. As mentioned previously, children and adolescents should receive information so they accept that their ADHD is a long-term brain-functioning disability that requires management skills. Understanding this is important because teens will need to manage their conditions increasingly more without their parents as they advance to young adulthood. Internet articles or books can be shared with them, and they may even read some of these along with their parents. Conversations should include how they may have acquired the condition, and ADHD does not mean someone is crazy, dumb, a loser, or a bad person. Teens can experience their own grieving processes, and may bitterly struggle against learning about or accepting the condition. Some may believe ADHD is a phony condition. In these situations, a series of conversations about ADHD may be the best approach. Parents should be mindful not to lecture or create power struggles about acceptance. Providers can be engaged with these discussions as well. Discussing how other family members may have ADHD could help too.

C. Teens should be informed about the importance of ADHD medications. Some do not take medication consistently and may not see the positive effects, while others may resent it and the side effects. Adolescents may also believe they are admitting they are "mental" or something is wrong with them if they take medication. Teens who have not accepted their condition may refuse to cooperate with this treatment. If compliance continues to be a problem, parents should administer the medication each day, with positive and negative consequences utilized if necessary. Some parents make the mistake of assuming that their teen is old enough to handle taking medication on their own. However, some teens are simply not able to responsibly take this important treatment each day, and thus require more structure and support.

D. Teens with ADHD may need additional adjustments with their academic schedules to maximize school functioning. If possible, families can consider arranging the high school class schedule to reflect the student's best time of day for their most difficult classes. They can try to schedule these when the student has the most focus. This is typically in the morning when the medication effectiveness is highest, or perhaps after a second stimulant dose in the early afternoon (if these are given at the school). Classes right after lunch may receive increased focus for some teens as well. If students have 504s or IEPs, it may be easier to arrange schedules with the schools, but parents can still advocate for schedule adjustments even if they do not have official school plans.

E. Compared to younger children, teens will require modified negative consequences. These can include loss of cell phones, computers, electronics, internet access, driving privileges, socializing with friends after school and weekends, and the privilege of working at outside jobs. Other consequences can be essays on various topics, math problems, copying pages from the dictionary, mandated charity work (such as working several weekends at a local food pantry), paying fines, increased chores at home (yard work, dishes for the entire week, cleaning windows or garages), electronic groundings (no electronic use), and groundings in the home or bedroom. While these may not stop them from doing what they wish, these "fences" can slow many teens down. They can certainly get over the fence if they want to, but it will still be a deterrent. Part of a parent's job is to help protect them from the risky temptations and choices they will certainly encounter, and these deterrents can help.

F. Parents should have clear curfew expectations for their adolescents and older children when they are out of the home. As teens work and socialize later on weekends, coming home on time can become increasing important, as well as a safety issue. Teens with ADHD do not manage their time well, and the topic of lateness can be a battleground for families. They often have excuses for being late, and parents can lose trust in them. To address this topic, a set regular curfew time should be established. Parents can inform adolescents that there is one main clock in the house, such as the stove or oven clock, that is the official time that will be used. They can be told that they will receive standard consequences for being late one minute or more for curfews, such as loss of one or more days of going out with friends at night. Caregivers can help them work on time management and setting alarms on watches or cell phones before they leave. A reminder alarm can also be used to signal when they need to leave for home so they will not arrive late.

G. Inappropriate and/or excessive cell phone and internet activity can be a complicated topic for parents and teens. Teens, and particularly those with ADHD, can be constantly tempted and distracted by their phones. Cell phone use can also keep teens up at night and reduce their amount of much needed sleep. Teens may also abuse their access to the internet by looking at pornography and sending inappropriate images and interactions. If inappropriate use occurs, parents can remove their phones and access to the internet in the house for a period of time, and then regularly review their history of use. Adolescents may be quite clever in avoiding detection, and are often more knowledgeable about electronics than their parents.

Adolescents' love of phones can be quite helpful to parents because it can be a highly motivating consequence for them. Most teens are incredibly attached to their phones, so earning the privilege of phone use can be incorporated into their specific daily behavioral expectations. Teens can earn and lose cell phone use on a day-by-day basis. Routines can be created where the teen surrenders their phone before bed, and then earns its use the next day. Further, parents should have access to their cell phone plans so that they can review their phone and internet use if necessary, and can shut down the cell phone service if the teen refuses to give the parent the phone when they lose their privileges. Parents can also consider the option of adolescents being expected to regularly contribute to the cell phone plan costs through a portion of their allowance or if they work.

Finally, parents can consider using special apps and software that monitor teens' cell phone and computer use, including their texts, online communications, and internet activity. These can monitor inappropriate use and a range of concerning topics they may discuss in their communications. These include Net Nanny, Bark, and Circle with Disney.

H. Older children and teens may benefit from written contracts regarding behavioral expectations and consequences. These can be signed and dated, and may help them take more ownership. These written details can literally keep everyone on the same page. When there are disagreements about expectations, these contracts can be reviewed.

I. Most teens, and particularly those with ADHD (as well as ODD or conduct disorder), should be expected at times to experiment with or commit certain unsafe and risky behaviors. These include inappropriate internet activity, using cigarettes or nicotine products, alcohol and/or marijuana use (and other drugs), shoplifting, driving while intoxicated, getting in cars with impaired drivers, committing vandalism, performing non-lethal self-harming behaviors (such as cutting or burning body parts), skipping school, violating curfews, and other risky behaviors. Additionally, teens with untreated ADHD are at greater risk for earlier sexual activity with higher rates of sexually transmitted diseases and teen pregnancies when compared to their peers. These behaviors can generate significant stress and worry for parents. They can also cause significant conflicts between parents and adolescents, and may negatively impact their relationships.

Adolescents can become involved in these problematic activities for a variety of reasons. Friends and peer groups can be enormous influences. Developmentally, adolescence is a time of disconnecting from parents while desiring and striving for deeper affiliations with peers. It is a time of lesser supervision, more autonomy, and greater access and opportunities for tempting and unsafe activities. This can be a perfect storm for risky behaviors, particularly if there is existing family discord and negative relationships with parents. Those with Combined ADHD can have more thrill-seeking and impulsive tendencies, contributing further to these choices. Teens who abuse substances may be self-medicating and can have genetic influences to their use. Some behaviors, particularly substance use, can be unhealthy coping approaches. Other disorders may contribute to their actions as well. Some risky behaviors may be acting out, and can be related to underlying anger, depression, ODD, psychological trauma, painful stressors, and/or difficult family situations. Finally, teens who do not take effective ADHD medications or commit unsafe behaviors at night (when the effects of stimulants have worn off) can have greater chances of making poor choices.

When these risky behaviors occur, there will be four main issues to address. However, before addressing these, parents should first try to understand why the adolescent committed the behaviors. While a number of teens will shut down or speak minimally after parents learn about their actions, some may be surprisingly honest about the details of what they did, and why. If parents can use self-control and not react emotionally or with lectures, they may be able to dialogue with their teens to learn more about what occurred and their reasons for this. Of course, this restraint can be quite difficult and will challenge many parents. However, this will help parents most effectively respond to the situations.

The first issue will involve examining the larger context of their actions to better understand the behaviors. Did they commit multiple risky behaviors and a pattern exists, or was this an isolated incident? What was the severity of the behavior, and its frequency? Other questions include, do they plan to do it again or do they show genuine remorse; was it a cry for help; is the behavior related to being upset or angry about specific issues, including family issues; is their peer group a significant influential factor; do they require more supervision; was this thrill-seeking behavior; was this related to their ADHD and making poor and impulsive choices; did they take their ADHD medication or did their stimulant medication "wear off" by the time the poor choices occurred; do they have co-existing ODD or conduct disorder; does boredom play a significant factor; are they starting to identify as a "bad kid;" and do they have an underlying depression or anxiety disorder, unresolved psychological trauma/s, or other impacting behavioral health conditions. These considerations and others can affect how the risky behaviors will be addressed.

Due to the complexity of some situations, psychotherapists may be needed to assist families to better understand and navigate these challenges. If medication is not used, parents may need to consider using it for the first time or returning to medication use to help improve self-control. There may be other medication issues as well, including ways to use medication more consistently, and exploring with the prescribing physician if the ADHD medication is working effectively. A second opinion from a new psychiatrist may be helpful.

Second, parents can conduct internet searches on the unsafe behaviors to prepare for informational discussions with teens. These should be provided in creative ways (Phelan, 2016). Parents can also use printed web pages when discussing these topics. Parents may give writing assignments on these topics as part of their consequences, and then they can review the information together. Many teens will not like this approach and may believe they already know everything about the topic. These parent-adolescent conversations may be awkward and tense initially, particularly if they have poor relationships. The challenge will be to continue with discussions in stimulating and calm ways, and avoid lectures.

All parents should provide specific discussions and education on the topics of substance use, inappropriate internet use and electronic communications, and sexuality, including pregnancy, sexually transmitted diseases, the use of birth control, and teen romantic relationships (Phelan, 2016). These discussions should occur whether risky behaviors have occurred yet or not.

Teens should be warned that they will be exposed to these situations and to peers that participate in these activities. Peer pressure and ways to handle these situations should also be addressed. These conversations should start no later than age 10 for most children, be developmentally appropriate to the child or adolescent, and occur periodically until late adolescence. Generally, the younger the child, the more influence parents will have. While these discussions can be uncomfortable, they are obviously important to help protect the youth, particularly those with ADHD. Internet searches can provide tips for parents in approaching these topics, and what to specifically discuss at the various ages.

The third issue is to establish better monitoring routines and determine the specific consequences for risky behaviors in and out-of-the-home. This will provide structure that is critically needed and can help reduce or deter future occurrences. For more serious infractions, in-home groundings (with or without electronic groundings) of one to three weeks can be used. Some parents may include other negative consequences as well. If teens refuse to cooperate, they can lose their phone, screen devices, and all other privileges until they agree to do their time. Discussions with the teen about the expectations, along with their feedback and input, can be helpful and should be held periodically. Parents may also need to work on monitoring their teens more, and greater supervision out of the home may be needed. This could mean an increase in structured activities with adults present, required periodic check-in calls, and parents connecting and coordinating more with their friends' parents. Some behaviors may not generate consequences, such as sexual activity, but may require more education and less unsupervised time. Self-harming behaviors will require a different approach from consequences, and should involve a psychotherapist.

The fourth issue involves improving adolescent-parent relationships. Parents need to be honest if relational difficulties exist. Positive parental relationships are important when helping teens who commit risky behaviors. Negative parental relationships can cause more distance and alienation when risky behaviors occur at a time when teens need their parents the most. Conflictual relations and dysfunctional family dynamics cause stress, and can further worsen teens' behaviors. Conversely, when adolescents have a more trusting and open relationship with parents, it is easier for them to talk about their concerns and issues. They may also be somewhat more receptive to parental influence, which is particularly important when they are attempting to make better choices. Parents will be challenged not to become sour when mistakes and conflicts arise, and should strive to improve their connections despite disappointments. If the parent-adolescent relationship needs improvement, parents should make this a priority as part of the plan to address unsafe adolescent behaviors. Ways to enhance these relationships were addressed in the prior chapter.

J. While already partially addressed, adolescent substance use requires additional attention. As stated, teens with ADHD are at higher risk for experimenting with and developing substance abuse problems. Substance use during adolescence can have serious impact on brain development, and their brains can become more vulnerable to the effects of substances. The brain experiences dramatic changes during adolescence, including the reorganization of millions of neurons, pathways, and networks through synaptic pruning and myelination. Synaptic pruning helps the brains become more efficient by reducing lesser used brain cells and connections. When substance use occurs in teens, these behaviors can become neurologically "stuck" or reinforced in their brains. One reason is the substance-related brain activities do not get pruned, but can be strengthened through myelination. The process of myelination promotes the pruned neurons in adolescent brains to connect and communicate more efficiently, enhancing brain activities that occur repeatedly, whether they are healthy or not, including substance use thinking and behaviors. Finally, teens who repeatedly abuse substances will have much greater risks of developing serious substance abuse conditions later in life.

If a teen has been using drugs, alcohol, or nicotine products, parents can address these in multiple ways. First, education on substances and adolescent substance use will be important. Increased monitoring and supervision should occur also, and trust will need to be earned over time. Peer groups may play a substantial role in their use, and this may need to be addressed. If substances are misused as a way of coping with uncomfortable feelings, the use of healthy coping skills will need to be taught. The use of emotional management skills can help, and is presented later in this chapter. Obviously, any other related factors and issues should be explored and addressed, and professional assistance should be considered in these situations.

Boredom is an often overlooked factor for teen substance use, as well as in certain other risky behaviors. This can be a significant issue for some, and increased supervision may be necessary. There are additional ways to address this issue and to replace use with stimulating and healthier activities. These include cultivating new hobbies, taking new after-school classes and lessons, increasing participation in organized sports, becoming involved in clubs or other groups, and becoming active with volunteer or community service organizations. Parents can support teens in exploring and engaging these new activities through heavy encouragement, assistance in finding them, and, of course, rewards for participation.

Parents can also create a clear expectation with standard groundings for any future alcohol or drug use. For example, "Every time you come home smelling or acting like you have used alcohol or drugs or *appear* to be intoxicated, you will be grounded for 2 to 3 weeks." The groundings should be specifically defined and can include no electronics or going out of the house, except for school and essentials. If these substance-using behaviors continue, substance use treatment may be engaged along with the groundings. After the groundings are completed, earlier curfews, increased monitoring, and no to minimal driving privileges can be enforced until trust is rebuilt.

Additionally, random drug screening can be conducted periodically by parents to monitor compliance. These kits are sold online and in drug stores and can be inexpensive. There are more expensive kits that can test for a greater range of substances which may help provide more information about their use. Firm groundings and random screenings can actually help teens with peer pressure by providing an honest way to decline use because they can say that their parents give them drug tests and groundings.

Earlier and milder professional interventions when experimentation first occurs may be the safest approach, and adolescent substance use professionals can be consulted about what is needed. Teens with repeated substance use should receive treatment from adolescent substance use intensive outpatient programs (IOPs) or services from certified drug and alcohol counselors. These providers can also work with families about the use of consequences when more serious substance usage occurs. For repeated nicotine use or dependence, adolescents can start with treatment or referrals from their primary care physicians.

K. Parents need to monitor the automobile driving of teens with ADHD more than other adolescents their age. Teens with ADHD have more driving difficulties, accidents, and moving violations. Radio use and cell phones while driving should be addressed and monitored due to their increased issues with distractibility. Teens who take stimulant medications should drive cars during the day when these are actively working. Other specific expectations, including the adolescent's financial responsibilities for their automobile use (insurance and gas), should be discussed and reviewed over time.

EXPECT CHANGES OVER TIME

The ADHD condition can evolve as children grow older and the symptoms and life situations change. Some parents assume that a child's ADHD medication will correct all of their ADHD problems. Some may even forget about the ADHD altogether because things have been going fairly well for a long time. Indeed, effective treatment with medication and/or therapy can greatly improve ADHD challenges for years. However, families that have effectively managed ADHD in a child's younger years can be blindsided by

ADHD issues that emerge later. Also, when adolescents experience hormonal and bodily changes with puberty, their ADHD symptoms can increase or appear differently.

Naturally, it is expected that all older children and teens will experience new developmental challenges. These can include having more complex homework and school tasks, involvement in new sports and after-school clubs and activities, driving cars, increased chores at home, employment, later curfews, sleep schedule changes, different social interactions and patterns, romantic interests and relationships, and exposure to alcohol and substances. These new experiences can be impacted in varying degrees by their ADHD, which may make navigating these more difficult. New problems with self-esteem, moodiness, and risky behaviors can emerge as well, causing concern and confusion for parents.

It can be beneficial for parents and teens to understand how their ADHD specifically impacts them as they grow older. Obtaining new ADHD evaluations and assessments can help with this, and can track the evolution of their ADHD. Adjustments in parenting, medication and other treatment approaches may then be needed with these changes.

TREATING OPPOSITIONAL DEFIANT DISORDER (ODD)

As mentioned in the first chapter, a difficult and common co-existing condition is ODD, which is defined as having a persistent pattern of anger, irritability, argumentativeness, and defiance lasting for a minimum of six months. These behaviors often persist and intensify over time, along with deteriorating parent-child relationships. Parents can become extremely frustrated and angry with the negative and disrespectful attitudes. Children and particularly teens with ADHD and ODD are at much greater risk for more severe behavioral difficulties, aggressive behaviors, vandalism, theft, substance use, and delinquent actions. Families with children and teens with these conditions often suffer from increased conflict and discord. Parents may become more aggressive in their attempts to maintain control in the home. Conduct disorder with ADHD can be even more challenging with greater risks.

If a child has been diagnosed with or suspected of having ODD, it is vital to address the ODD as a separate but related part of their ADHD. It is important for parents to understand the condition of ODD, and learn to recognize which behaviors are resulting from this. Once again, taking a disability perspective and expecting and detaching from the negative behavior can be very important. While medication itself is not often used to treat ODD, children and teens with both conditions often experience improvements with effective ADHD medications. If the ADHD medication is not effective, families may obtain second opinions with psychiatrists. Additionally, treatment for ODD involves implementing the ADHD behavioral management approaches, including parents not reacting to their negativity, setting and maintaining clear written expectations for their daily behaviors, consistently applying clear consequences to their unwanted behaviors, and working on improving the parent-child relationship.

An important aspect of the treatment for ODD involves repairing and rebuilding the fractured parent-child relationships common in these families. The years of bitterness, mistrust and conflict need healing, but this takes time. One helpful approach can be the use of together time, which was addressed in the prior chapter. Finally, families may require assistance from experienced family therapists for their more complex behavioral and relational challenges.

ENHANCE SOCIAL SKILLS

Many children and adolescents with ADHD, and particularly the combined type, have social skill deficits, difficulties with peers, and more immaturity than other children. Social problems can result from their brash and intensive style, excessive talking, tendency to dominate conversations, struggle to listen to others, aggressive responses when upset, and lesser awareness of other's feelings and non-verbal social cues. Their impulsive and reactive interactions often get them into trouble and hurt other people's feelings. Conversely, children and teens with Inattentive ADHD may be more passive and reserved with others, and are at risk for being be easily influenced and controlled by peers.

Children and adolescents with ADHD can require specific instruction and assistance in learning basic ways to effectively interact with peers and adults. However, teaching social skills to children and teens with ADHD can itself be challenging, and is not a "one and done" task. Social skills can improve when children and teens are motivated to work on these skills, parents help them rehearse positive social skills, more social opportunities and activities for practice exist, and effective ADHD medication is used.

A list of social skills that all children should possess includes responding and listening to others, demonstrating interest by asking questions and smiling, greeting others warmly by name, playing cooperatively, learning to join a game or activity in progress, giving and receiving positive and negative feedback, solving problems in nonaggressive ways (Rief, 2003), giving good eye contact, practicing taking turns, sharing, learning how to make and maintain friendships, conflict-resolution skills, learning how to apologize and make up after conflict, dos and don'ts for getting along with friends, managing frustration with peers when things don't go their way, not cursing or name calling when upset, handling negative interactions, managing teasing and bullying experiences, and giving compliments.

There are approaches parents can utilize to improve social skills. First, obtaining more information about the specific social challenges can be important. Parents may already have a good understanding based on their observations. Other family members or adults may witness them interacting with others and may provide helpful insights into which skills may be needed. Parents can obtain specific social feedback from peers and school staff to better understand their deficits.

Parents may utilize bibliotherapy by obtaining age-appropriate books from their library or purchasing books online that teach specific social skills. Parents can repeatedly read and review this information with their children to help them. Using lists of specific skills to practice over time and viewing YouTube videos may help as well.

Next, parents should arrange numerous opportunities for them to interact with peers. This can include group activities, lessons, and play dates or "hang sessions" (Rief, 2003). After the socializing, a review of the experiences and self-ratings can beneficial during this learning process. These social experiences should occur over time, and the skill development will take practice with different friends and social settings. Rewards for reading these books and practicing these skills can be utilized to enhance motivation and compliance.

Additional services may be necessary to support these changes. School services may help, including social skills groups lead by social workers and/or school counselors who can address these deficits in individual sessions with students. These services may be added to their IEPs, but this may not be necessary. Individual psychotherapy and social skills groups can be engaged outside of school. Finally, an important aspect of addressing deficiencies of social skills is the use of ADHD medications. It cannot be overemphasized how effective medication can improve some social skill difficulties. However, when the medicine is not taken, these difficulties can return, unless there has been significant skill mastery.

PARENT-CHILD/TEEN CONFLICT RESOLUTION SKILLS

It is important for families to have effective approaches to resolve conflicts and disagreements. This is even more essential for children and teens with ADHD and other conditions who become easily frustrated, reactive, and argumentative when they do not get their way. Ross Greene (2001) has presented an approach for families to navigate conflicts though the use of negotiation and compromise. This can help minimize outbursts and teach problem-solving and frustration management skills. However, it should not be used when the topic involves a safety issue. This approach can also contribute to child/teen-parent relationships as they evolve over time. This is a good technique to periodically adjust expectations and consequences, particularly as children grow older. This should not be used to alter pre-determined expectations because it will undermine the behavioral management approach. Yet, it can be used to occasionally negotiate mutually agreeable changes to these expectations, but not during power struggles.

When a conflict arises, parents can first ask the child to discuss the problem as calmly as possible to better understand it. Second, parents should use empathic statements to convey understanding, but they do not need to agree. Reflective listening skills can be used to paraphrase their statements, such as "So what I hear you are saying is …" or "What I think you do not like is. . . ." Third, parents ask the child if they will help solve the conflict together. Fourth, parents share their views on the issue, and in time children may learn to improve their listening skills. Fifth, parents will ask for possible solutions to compromise and negotiate with the child for an acceptable resolution for all, with parents having the final decision. At first, parents can provide potential solutions if children cannot (Greene, 2001).

When children and teens with ADHD become overwhelmed, they can have difficulty thinking rationally. Therefore, this process is most effective before deep frustration occurs and at the start of escalations. Parents should explain these steps and say they want to use them. Starting with small or imaginary conflicts should help, and practice makes perfect for this important relationship skill (Greene, 2001). Parents can create the habit of using this approach when disagreements occur that are not pre-established expectations. This can help prevent arguing and other unproductive reactions.

After children and teens successfully use and trust this skill, families can request to use this approach at a later time if they are unable to use it when a conflict arises. For example, if a disagreement occurs about something a child wants to do tomorrow, parents and the child can agree to use this approach after dinner when there is more time to properly discuss the issue.

As stated previously, when used effectively and fairly, this approach can improve child/teen relationships with parents. Children and especially teens may feel more respected if parents sometimes negotiate with them. It can balance behavioral management approaches by adding child and teen inputs, and may help some parents seem less harsh. It can also help to address parent-teen conflicts that may require compromises, such as curfews, socializing activities with friends, bedtimes, larger purchases, and appearance issues. For more information on this approach, read Ross Green's book *The Explosive Child.*

SIBLING ISSUES

Siblings of those with ADHD can suffer and experience their own unique hardships. These siblings often receive less attention from parents due to the energy spent on those with ADHD. The "squeaky wheel gets the grease." Siblings without ADHD usually have greater achievements and fewer problems, and are commonly assumed to be normal. Parents may be relieved that these children do not have ADHD difficulties, yet they can expect more from them while spending less time with them. Siblings may be dragged along to multiple provider appointments, and endure their parents' burnout and bad moods. Indeed, their needs may not be met while the family experiences the ADHD struggles. Over time these children and teens can feel less important and ignored. They can also resent the siblings with ADHD. Additionally, siblings with ADHD can be quite conflictual and difficult. They may steal their things, argue, tease, aggravate, and become more aggressive with their brothers and sisters.

Siblings can react to these challenges in several ways. They can have their own grieving processes, and may even develop their own problems as a result of the family environment. They may experience anxiety and depression because of the stresses in the home. They may also become chronically resentful of the sibling with ADHD, their parents, or both. They may withdraw, avoid family members, or use unhealthy ways of coping.

Parents should be aware that their children without ADHD often need their own special attention and care. They may even need protection at times from their siblings with ADHD. Parents can address these difficulties in a variety of ways. They should talk to them about their sibling's conditions and help them understand how the inappropriate behaviors are related to their disability. They should know that the sibling would act this way with any brother or sister, and to not take this behavior personally, even though it is difficult and seems very personal.

Siblings of children with ADHD often feel like victims. They may feel overwhelmed by their siblings' chronic annoying, thieving, or aggressive behaviors. One way to reduce this is for parents to consider allowing older siblings to have a separate bedroom with a door lock, if they are old enough and if separate bedrooms are possible. Parents should ensure that these door locks are the kind that can't be picked or opened easily. Giving them their own space with a locking door can help them feel like they have more control. Also, siblings can be given safes they can keep in their room to secure small valuables, whether they share a room or not.

Additionally, siblings need their own together time with their parents. Parents should make efforts to spend more time alone with the other child or children, as challenging as this may be. They may also receive extra privileges or rewards at times for their patience. Siblings should be taught how to practice healthy detachment from negative interactions and the use of emotional management skills to deal with their stressors and frustrations. Siblings may also benefit from their own psychotherapy or counseling sessions to help them better understand, adjust, and cope. Finally, family therapy that includes all the siblings together could address their relational difficulties in deeper ways.

EMOTIONAL MANAGEMENT SKILLS

Overview

Children and teens with ADHD unfortunately can become more easily overwhelmed and frustrated. They simply struggle more with the stressors of daily life. To help them, parents and clinicians can teach effective emotional management skills. This involves using a three steps process to Notice, Accept, and Cope (NAC) (Jongsma & Peterson, 1995). These skills teach children and adolescents to practice noticing, accepting, and coping with their challenging and unwanted emotions and thoughts. The sooner they do this when they experience these feelings or thoughts, the easier it is to do. Parents can help by reminding them to recognize their feelings in the moment, and start using these skills immediately. For children who struggle with parental warnings for impending time-outs or have temper tantrums, emotional management skills can also help. Rewards from parents can be important to reinforce its use. Finally, the NAC method is not just for children, and can be effective for stressed, frustrated, and overwhelmed parents as well.

The 3 Steps of Emotional Management: The NAC

1. **NOTICE**. During this first step, the child or teen should recognize the uncomfortable feeling or thoughts they have. Parents can ask the child to share how they know they are feeling sad, nervous, worried, scared, angry, or aggressive in the moment. Do they recognize the feelings in their body? Do they notice the thoughts in their mind? Are they crying or screaming? Is their body tense or jaw clenched? Encourage them to recognize the signs that indicate they are having feelings or thoughts in the moment. It's vital

that children learn to catch their feelings or thoughts as they occur so that they can then do something about them. If they cannot notice them, then they cannot do anything about it. This is really a mindfulness activity. To assist, parents can print from the internet examples of faces depicting feelings, or children and teens can draw faces that display uncomfortable feelings. These can then be posted in their rooms to help with this step. Parents can also encourage them to practice identifying and labeling these feelings and thoughts as independently as possible.

2. **ACCEPT**. During the second step, parents should encourage children to accept their uncomfortable feelings and thoughts when they occur. The more they learn that it is OK to have these feelings, even though they do not feel good, the more tolerant they will become of their emotions and thoughts, and the less distressing they can become. Children can write down that "It's OK to feel or think or worry about _____." While this can be a difficult concept for some children, it is a powerful skill. Most people are afraid or hate their unwanted feelings and thoughts, and so they desperately avoid or distract themselves from them. However, feelings can change when they are noticed and accepted in a non-judgmental way. They offer feedback of important information about how we perceive things. As with the Notice step, accepting without judging is a mindfulness practice. If this step is too difficult, particularly for younger children, they can skip it and go to the last step.

3. **COPE**. During this last step, the child or teen should perform a specific activity to manage the uncomfortable feelings or thoughts. Coping can be almost anything the child likes to do that will shift their focus and disengage from the upsetting experience. Coping activities should not cost money and should be able to be done easily by the child alone. Initially, parents can do coping activities along with the child to support them. Ideally, over time and with practice, the use of coping will be regular, automatic, and a habit. A good goal is to create a written and posted list of three to 10 coping activities that can be regularly used. Coping activities that can be used quietly may be helpful when the child is at school or out of the home and doesn't want anyone to know they are using them. These may be different from the ones used at home, and families can create a separate list for school as well.

One of the most powerful coping skills is deep breathing, also called belly breathing. It can provide relaxation immediately, and can be done almost anywhere. This is not just breathing quickly, but involves long and slow breaths through the nose, filling and expanding the abdomen area with air, and then exhaling slowly through the open mouth, making a whooshing noise. To add more impact, the person can also silently repeat a single calming word like "relax" during each in and out breath. This should be done at least 5 times, but can be done more for a greater effect. Also, deep breathing can be combined with other coping approaches, with the deep breathing first and then others.

Other coping activities include relaxation exercises, such as progressive muscle relaxation, where a person tenses and relaxes all the muscles groups, starting with their feet and moving up to the head; doing physical exercises, like jumping jacks or push-ups (exercise can be quite effective because it changes the body's biochemistry quickly); playing with pets; drawing; writing down thoughts and feelings in a journal; imagining a special place that makes them feel good, such as the beach, park or field with horses; thinking about their favorite activity; thinking about their favorite character, superhero, real-life person or a family member; thinking about a favorite part of a movie or book; listening to music; recalling a cherished memory; silently or out-loud singing the lyrics of a favorite song; watching an upbeat TV or internet show or movie, or playing a video game, if screen time is permitted; playing with a favorite toy; reading; and counting from 1 to 50, or counting backwards by 5s or 3s.

The caregiver can also help the child to create a special "power phrase" or "magic words" to use to repeat to themselves several times to improve their emotional state. The phrase can be something simple, such as "I'm OK the way I am," "Mommy loves me," "I'm doing the best I can," "It's OK to make mistakes." These phrases may have spiritual components as well. Mindfulness can also be used as coping; however, children will require instruction and practice with this before it will be effective (see Chapter 13 for more information on this).

While using coping skills, the child should focus only on that activity as much as possible. Some coping activities such as reading or watching TV may not be engaging enough, so more active coping may be needed. If the uncomfortable thoughts and feelings continue or return after coping, they can cope again or may want to try different activities. The more they practice, the faster and better coping tends to work. Repeated coping activities help create new neural pathways and grooves in the brain to help improve emotional regulation skills, and with practice can become increasingly effective. Various coping approaches should be tried to find what works best. Combining a series of coping activities can help as well.

While the NAC system will not "fix" underlying issues or conditions, it can assist in reducing the emotional discomfort associated with these. The emotional management process should be practiced regularly and as often as needed throughout the day. The child may even need to use the three steps several times in one hour. Just like riding a bike, the steps become easier as they are used more. If a child or teen has aggression difficulties, they can be encouraged to do something physical for coping that can be a release of energy, such as exercise or a physical activity. Punching pillows or kicking things for coping is not suggested. If the struggles are more chronic or serious, emotional management skills can be utilized, but a mental health practitioner should be consulted in these situations.

Parents and children together should create an individualized list of the three NAC steps as a reminder sheet. Parents can then post this one-page reminder sheet on the back of their bedroom door, on the refrigerator door, or in any highly visible place in the home. Some children may be embarrassed by this sheet and want it posted somewhere more private, while others will be happy to have it anywhere. Parents can review this sheet with the child daily, encouraging them to practice these often, and praising and rewarding their efforts liberally (and especially when they do these on their own). Finally, parents and adults should not forget to use and "get the NAC" themselves to better manage their own difficult or challenging feelings and thoughts. When parents model the use of this system, it can help children and teens use it more consistently as well.

When families first start using the NAC, it is suggested that parents frequently use reinforcers. Practice helps almost any skill, and repeated use creates new habits. Rewards should be specific and pre-determined for each time they use it, and a special NAC rewards menu can be offered. This way the child will know what they will receive and parents do not have to think of rewards on the spot. Examples include receiving 15 additional minutes of electronic screen time or one dollar. Rewards can be phased down once the skills are used more often.

Also, parents can reward children's use of the NAC even when children report that they used it, but the parent did not see it, such as at school. The only requirement is the child must describe in detail how it was used. Children and teens should share what was the stressful or upsetting initial event, how did they notice and accept their difficult feelings, what coping did they use, and what happened after the coping. Parents may think, "What if they are just lying to get the rewards?" The response is that even if they are lying, at least they are thinking about the skills and are rehearsing and practicing them verbally by describing a fictional experience.

The ultimate goal is for children and teens to create the habit of using the emotional management skills on their own. With time and practice, the child or teen should be encouraged to do these activities as independently as possible with less and less assistance from caregivers. Some may struggle to do this on their own. Each child and teen's ability to do this will differ, and can require varying amounts of encouragement, reminders, and rewards. Important other adults, such as teachers or family members, can be enrolled to be supportive and encourage use of the NAC outside of the home.

SUMMARY POINTS

- Families can utilize family and individual psychotherapy and ADHD coaching to better address and treat ADHD.
- Specific ways to address a younger child's ADHD difficulties include younger child rewards and preschool and daycare management approaches.
- Adolescents with ADHD often require different approaches, including providing more ADHD information, school schedule adjustments, updating consequences, and specific ways to address technology use, driving, risky, and unsafe behaviors.
- ODD and social skills deficits should be addressed and treated.
- Families should practice the parent-child/teen conflict resolution skills of negotiation and compromise to navigate clashes and arguments.
- Siblings often have their own unique challenges and require specific parental support.
- The emotional management skills of notice, accept, and cope (NAC) should be taught to address difficult feelings and thoughts. Parents can use these as well.

REFERENCES

Greene, R. W. (2001). *The explosive child* (2nd ed.). New York, New York: HarperCollins Publishers.

Jongsma, A., & Peterson, M. (1995). *The complete psychotherapy treatment planner.* New York: John Willy & Sons, Inc.

Phelan, T. (2016). *1-2-3 Magic Teen* (4th ed.). Naperville, IL: Sourcebooks, Inc.

Practicewise. (2016). *Blue menu of evidence-based psychosocial interventions for youth.* Retrieved from https://www.practicewise.com/Community/BlueMenu.

Rief, S. F. (2003). *The ADHD book of lists.* San Francisco, CA: Jossey-Bass.

Smith, B. L. (2011, July-August). ADHD among preschoolers. *Monitor on Psychology, 42*(7), 50–52.

Chapter 8

ADDRESSING SLEEP PROBLEMS

The importance of addressing sleep difficulties when treating ADHD cannot be overstated and was briefly discussed in Chapter three. To improve sleep, including insomnia, inadequate sleep duration, and a variety of sleep issues related to resistance and behavioral difficulties, sleep hygiene and behavioral interventions should be utilized as a first approach, whether ADHD medications are used or not. These approaches can be used along with other sleep treatments. Providing education to parents and children about sleep issues and more effective sleep practices will be important as well (Brown & Malow, 2016). Sleep-disordered breathing, periodic limb movement disorder, restless legs syndrome, and other sleep disorders will require sleep studies, sleep specialist providers at sleep centers, and other experienced health care providers. Neurofeedback treatment may be helpful for some sleep difficulties as well. This will be discussed further in Chapter 14.

OBTAINING THE OPTIMAL AMOUNT OF SLEEP

It is recommended that children ages 3 to 5 consistently obtain 10 to 13 hours of sleep per 24 hours (including naps), and most do not require a nap after age 5. Children ages 6 to 12 consistently require 9 to 12 hours of sleep per night. Adolescents ages 13 to 18 consistently require 8 to 10 hours of sleep per night (American Academic of Pediatrics, 2016). These are guidelines for the age ranges, but needs may vary. Even if a child is obtaining the lower end of the range amount, they still may need more than this minimum number due to individual differences.

Parents should calculate the number of typical hours of sleep per night a child or teen obtains. To do this, determine when the child/teen typically goes to bed with lights out, how long it usually takes them to actually fall asleep, and when they wake. These can be averages or ranges. Parents should calculate two sets of sleep hours, one for their number on school nights, and the other for non-school nights, such as during weekends, summers, and holidays. They can then compare these numbers to the suggested guidelines.

SLEEP HYGIENE APPROACHES

The process of implementing healthy sleep hygiene practices will be a lifestyle change for the family. These new routines will be difficult at first, but parents need to be advocates and remain firm. Explaining the new sleep expectations and using daily reinforcers for compliance and increased motivation may be critical. Parents should not give up on these processes prematurely, and should expect fluctuations in success until steady progress is achieved. Master parent wizards will be firmly committed to these sleep enhancement goals because achieving healthy sleep can significantly improve children's and teens' lives, as well as the lives of the rest of the family.

Older children and especially teens should be more involved with these sleep management behavioral approaches so they understand these approaches and have adequate "buy-in" and agreements. One simple reward can be earning a predetermined amount of electronic screen time for each prior night that they cooperate and no screen time the next day for lack of cooperation. Other rewards as well as negative consequences can be used daily.

Consistent Sleep Schedules

A regular and consistent sleep schedule is vital. The time of going to bed with lights out and the waking up time should be the same each day, whether it is a school night or not. Consistent wake times permit sleep pressure to increase by the evening so the child is sleepy enough by bedtime. Naps can be avoided after age 5 or 6 because these can increase sleep onset difficulties ("Healthy Sleep Habits for Children," 2017). These schedules can assist children and teens to fall asleep more easily and help them consistently obtain adequate amounts of sleep.

Their time to go to sleep should be calculated by determining the number of hours a child or teen needs, and then counting backwards from the time they will wake up. This will be their sleep time with lights out, not the time they start winding down for bed. For school days, the time to wake up should be clear for most families. Parents should start with the middle time within the range of sleep times that are required for each child age group. They can adjust this number over time to see if the child needs more or less sleep (Kurcinka, 2006).

If children and teens are obtaining less than what is optimal for them, parents should work on getting them to bed earlier and/or addressing any existing sleep onset or insomnia difficulties. Shifting towards earlier bedtimes may need to occur slowly, with a slightly earlier time every few days or week. Over time parents can increase sleep time to determine their optimal number. Chapter 13 will further address the importance of obtaining sufficient sleep.

Parents should be aware that putting some children and teens to sleep earlier can cause increased frustrations and delayed sleep onset if they are not ready for sleep. To address this, the time they go to sleep should be gradually decreased over time (Brown & Malow, 2016). The wind down bedtime can help the child or teen transition to sleep as well. The goal is for children and teens to awake refreshed, without difficulties and sleep deprivation indicators (see Chapter 13 for more on this topic).

For adolescents, the sleep schedule should not deviate more than two hours on any night, including weekends or non-school days. Younger children should have less than two hours of deviation. Sleeping in on weekends should not occur, and the need to sleep in should decrease if set sleep times are made a priority and maintained. An important goal will be to achieve the required number of hours of sleep, and all efforts should be made to achieve this nightly (Schwartz & Thomas, 2016). Teens may argue they are older and should be able to sleep when they choose, and some resistance should be expected. Compromises with this may help. Parents may need to repeatedly discuss the importance of improving their sleep, along with web articles on the topic. Motivating rewards and negative consequences should be used to increase compliance as well.

Bedtime and Sleep Time

Another important sleep hygiene approach is utilizing bedtime to help transition to sleep. Sleep time is when the child or teen is in bed with the lights off, while bedtime is a wind down period that is the preparation and shift towards sleep time (Kurcinka, 2006). Before sleep time there should be about 30 to 60 minutes of this nightly quiet bedtime. While this amount may vary depending on the child, it should not be too brief. Activities before the lights go off can include putting on pajamas, bathroom hygiene, baths or showers, reading calming books without stimulating or scary themes, quiet music, prayers, and relaxation exercises. Watching TV, movies, computer/laptop use, video gaming and vigorous play should not be part of this winding down. These quiet time activities do not need to occur exclusively in the child's bedroom, but they should end there for the last 10 to 15 minutes. Parents should not drag out saying goodnights, with interactions being consistent, warm, and brief. To maintain positive associations, bedrooms should not be used for time outs or where punishments occur ("Healthy Sleep Habits for Children," 2017). A dim nightlight is acceptable if children fear the dark, however shifting towards eliminating this with encouragement and rewards is best.

Some families and teens are so busy that they do not use adequate bedtime periods to help the child transition to sleep. They may be on the go with activities in or outside of the home, and then just expect the child to suddenly shift gears and fall asleep quickly. Each child will differ in their time and specific activities they need to calm down before bed, so exploration and adjustments should be made to fine-tune this. These wind down practices should be considered pre-sleep rituals that help the child associate these behaviors with becoming sleepy and going to sleep. Younger children and teens will benefit from this process.

Screen Time and Sleep

Children with electronic screens devices and TVs in their rooms tend to go to bed later and get less sleep. Children getting less sleep are more likely to spend two or more hours per day watching screens (Breus, 2005). TVs, mobile screen devices, phones, and video games should all be removed from bedrooms permanently. Screens can emit blue light that can lower the hormone melatonin that naturally promotes sleep. Screen use should not be used at least one hour before bed. Additionally, nothing should be watched that is stimulating, violent, or potentially upsetting at least two hours before bedtime. This includes news, talk shows, arousing video games, or shows with more anxiety and intense drama. Additionally, there should be no bright light exposure during the bedtime period, but bright light exposure in the morning can be helpful ("Sleep Tips for Your Family's Mental Health," 2016). Social media use before bed may be too arousing as well.

Routines can be created where there are firm times that all electronics are off at night, such as 60 minutes before bed to minimize any overstimulation. Cell phones should be surrendered to parents before the lights go out as well, particularly if children or teens are using this when they should be sleeping. Phone can be returned to the child or teen each morning, and lack of cooperation can generate a loss of the phone for a time. Some may protest, and say they need the cell phone for a morning alarm and it "calms me down." Alarm clocks should be purchased, and discussions can occur about other soothing bedtime activities. If parents do not remove phone nightly, turning off the home's Wi-Fi at night may be necessary for those who sneak internet use.

Additional Sleep Hygiene Approaches

Other ways to enhance sleep include having a light snack before bedtime if hungry. Sleep enhancing foods include milk, turkey or a half turkey sandwich, low sugar cereal, or a banana. Heavy meals within two hours prior to bed should be avoided. Caffeinated drinks and foods including chocolate should be avoided. Regular exercise can help too; however, this should be finished at least three hours before bedtime because it can be stimulating. The bedroom should have a comfortable bed and temperature (not too hot and slightly cooler is better). It should be adequately dark (room darkening shades may help), and quiet. Fans, white noise or soothing sound machines can be used. Additionally, beds should be for sleeping only to create a positive and strong association with sleep. There should be no phone or screen use, eating, or homework while in bed, day or night (Smith, Robinson, & Segal, 2018). Potentially upsetting discussions or arguments should be avoided before bed or in bedrooms as well.

DIFFICULTIES FALLING ASLEEP

Some children and adolescents may experience difficulties falling asleep or insomnia, and this can decrease their amount of optimal sleep. These may be short or long-term struggles, and can occur for a variety of reasons including poor sleep hygiene, perfectionistic personalities that are prone to excessive planning and thinking, various stressors, depression, anxiety, excessive worrying, medical conditions that cause discomfort, and unresolved psychological traumatic experiences. Sleep onset difficulties may also result from delayed sleep-phase disorder, restless legs syndrome, as well other conditions.

Children and teens who experience difficulties falling asleep should receive specific education about this. For those who lay in bed worrying and overthinking, a nighttime or "unloading" journal can be helpful. This can be used to write down their worries, concerns, frustrations, events of the day, or anything they wish to expel from their minds so they can be dealt with the next day. Creating a list of things they are grateful for can be helpful as well, including recognizing any small acts of kindness or things they were proud of ("Sleep Tips for Your Family's Mental Health," 2016). Children should be taught that the purpose of the journal is to write down things on their mind so they do not need to think about them in bed, and once written should not ruminate or return to thinking about them. They can return to thinking about these the following day. Also, if this journal is used, the writing should be finished about one hour before the lights go off and it would be best to do this outside of the bedroom.

Watching the clock for hours and forcing oneself to fall asleep usually makes falling asleep worse. Getting out of bed to do boring and relaxing tasks can help break these frustrating episodes. The child or teen can also use emotional management skills during bedtime, including calming coping and relaxation skills. Parents can assist and support this, including the use of rewards to increase compliance with this bedtime practice.

To address insomnia that is related to depression, psychological trauma, anxiety and excessive worrying, a competent child or adolescent psychotherapist should be consulted. Assessments, more extensive therapy, and/or medications may be necessary for more severe cases.

Some children and teens who take stimulant medications may experience insomnia as a side effect. This should be discussed with their prescribing physician. They may also benefit from a second opinion from a psychiatrist experienced with ADHD treatment. Additional medications or supplements for sleep, such as clonidine and melatonin, may be suggested for some children or teens who take stimulants and struggle with difficulties falling asleep. Please refer to Chapter 12 for more information on this topic.

SLEEP STUDIES MAY BE NECESSARY

Finally, for sleep problems and sleep disorders that are more complicated or persistent, a sleep study at a sleep center may be necessary. Sleep centers diagnose and treat sleep conditions and difficulties. They can have clinical psychologist behavioral sleep specialists and board-certified sleep medicine physicians on staff.

SUMMARY POINTS

- Children ages 3 to 5 should consistently obtain 10 to 13 hours of sleep per 24 hours (including naps); ages 6 to 12 consistently require 9 to 12 hours; and ages 13 to 18 consistently require 8 to 10 hours (American Academic of Pediatrics, 2016).
- Sleep hygiene practices can improve sleep quality and duration with consistent sleep schedules, effective bedtime and sleep times, understanding and limiting the effects of screen time on sleep, and other approaches.
- Several approaches to address difficulties falling asleep can be utilized.
- For more significant sleep problems, a sleep study may be necessary.

REFERENCES

American Academic of Pediatrics (2016, June 13). *American Academy of Pediatrics supports childhood sleep guidelines.* Retrieved from https://www.aap.org/en-us/about-the-aap/aap-press-room/pages/American-Academy-of-Pediatrics-Supports-Childhood-Sleep-Guidelines.aspx

Breus, M. J. (2005). *Back to school, back to sleep.* Retrieved from www.webmd.comM/sleep-disorders/features/fixing-sleep-problems-may-improve-child-grades-and-behavior?print=true

Brown, K. M., & Malow, B. A. (2016, May). Pediatric insomnia. Contemporary Reviews in Sleep Medicine. *CHEST, 149*(5), 1332–1339.

Healthy Sleep Habits for Children. (2017, June 1). Retrieved from https://my.clevelandclinic.org/health/articles/pediatric-healthy-sleep-habits?view=print

Kurcinka, M. S. (2006). *Sleepless in America.* New York, NY: HarperCollins Publishers.

Schwartz, B. S., & Thomas, J. H. (2016, August 24). *Adolescent sleep issues: Why are they so tired?* Retrieved from http://www.chop.edu/news/adolescent-sleep-issues-why-are-they-so-tired

Sleep Tips for Your Family's Mental Health. (2016, November 4). Retrieved from https://www.healthchildren.org/English/healthy-living/sleep/Pages/Sleep-and-Mental-Health.aspx

Smith, M., Robinson, L., & Segal, R. (2018, July). *How to sleep better.* Retrieved from https://www.helpguide.org/articles/sleep/getting-better-sleep.htm

Chapter 9

THE HOMEWORK AND SCHOOL BEHAVIORAL NOTEBOOK SYSTEMS

ACADEMIC PROBLEMS AT SCHOOL

Due to their brain-functioning problems, children and teens with ADHD typically have a multitude of academic difficulties. Often, they are chronic school underachievers. While they may do adequately or even well in the lower grades, as they age their grades typically drop because of the increasing requirements of middle and high school. Their scholastic performance can suffer as a result of their disorganization, inconsistency and motivation problems with completing their classwork and homework, tendency to be easily bored with academics, poor study skills, reading and comprehension difficulties, lesser mastery of subjects, and inattention during class lectures. To further complicate their school functioning, various studies have found that from about 19 percent to 45 percent of children and adolescents with ADHD also have additional formal learning disorders, such as reading learning disorders, math learning disorders, and handwriting disorders (Weyandt & Gudmundsdottir, 2015).

ADHD impacts learning and academic performance in numerous ways. Inattention, poor concentration, and daydreaming can cause reduced comprehension of lectures, missed assignments, careless mistakes in academic work, errors in spelling and grammar, sloppy writing, and misunderstandings of assignments and test questions. These students can struggle to persist with tasks, and are easily distracted during classwork, lectures, and tests. They may also become easily overwhelmed and frustrated with the time and effort academic work requires. Additionally, those with hyperactivity and impulsivity may rush through or not complete their work, take short cuts, and talk excessively (Dendy, 1995). Additionally, those with ADHD often do not enjoy or practice leisure reading and may have weaker reading skills. This can make reading more difficult and unpleasant. This lack of reading can further weaken their academic abilities, particularly at the higher grades. Ultimately, these challenges can cause academic procrastination, avoidance, incomplete schoolwork and tests, poor grades, and a chronic dislike for school and learning.

Due to slower cognitive processing, many students with ADHD process information, read, write, and recall information more slowly. They have greater listening comprehension difficulties and can become lost in teachers' instructions and lectures, losing the main point. Due to their poor organizational skills, they can have difficulty organizing their thoughts when writing, struggle with knowing the proper steps to complete their work, and have inadequate time management with tests and writing assignments. Decreased memory can impact their ability to learn facts, the proper spelling of words, and reading comprehension (Dendy, 1995). These difficulties can contribute to lower test scores and ineffective studying strategies for tests as well. Collectively, all of these problems can cause academic underachievement and lower and failing grades.

Because of these challenges, students with ADHD also frequently struggle with homework. Their decreased reading comprehension, tendency to become easily bored and distracted, slower cognitive processing, difficulty maintaining focus and staying on task, and poor organizational skills all contribute to their homework challenges. They may forget to bring home their books or assignments, may not write down the homework assignments, and may forget what and when it is due. They can have great difficulties becoming motivated to actually complete homework after school, so they procrastinate, and avoid finishing the work. Some students lie and say they had no homework or did it at school. Others may wait until the last minute and then do it late at night, after much arguing with parents and losing precious sleep time.

There is a growing trend in the United States of teachers assigning less homework, and particularly within elementary schools. Some research exists that suggests that homework does not significantly contribute to learning and educational achievements for students in elementary school. However, homework still exists for many children and teens, and typically is a portion of their grades. For students with ADHD, homework can be a significant struggle. It may take much longer than their peers, sometimes hours each day. When completed, it may even be forgotten at home. Students can fail to submit the completed homework while in class because they are not paying attention when the teacher asks for it. Or, they may not be able to find the homework because it is lost in their messy book bag. The arguments over the many homework difficulties can be exhausting for everyone in the house. Alas, it starts all over again the next school day.

BEHAVIORAL PROBLEMS AT SCHOOL

In addition to their scholastic struggles, children and teens with Combined ADHD frequently have greater school behavioral and disciplinary problems as well. For these students, school can feel like a prison, with their desks becoming strange torture devices. Because of their hyperactivity and impulsivity, staying seated and quiet can be extremely difficult. Their natural desire is to move, but because they must remain seated, they will wiggle, endlessly shift in their seat, fidget, and fiddle with pencils or anything else. These students can struggle terribly to stay focused on what the teacher is saying, and anything else will become more interesting. Their boredom and difficulty to stay in their seats and remain quiet can generate considerable frustration and can influence some to act out and become the class clown. Because of their brain-functioning challenges and higher levels of activity, they can talk excessively, annoy neighbors, and experience a range of behavioral problems, much to the exasperation of a teacher with 25 other students and a lesson plan.

Their in-school behavioral problems can also distract them from effective learning and academic success. Due to their immaturity, poor frustration tolerance, behavioral problems, and social skill deficits, students with Combined ADHD can have more problems in their relationships with teachers, school staff, and peers. These can also cause them to be less liked by others at school, making school a more negative experience. They may bully other children at recess or lunch, become bullied themselves, or both. They can struggle with getting along with peers and teachers, and experience fluctuations in their school relationships, but never understand how annoying they are to others. They may be more verbally or physically aggressive than their peers as well. Unstructured times during hallways, recess, or lunch time can be opportunities for mischief and behavioral difficulties. School discipline problems can ensue, including more detentions, suspensions, and calls of complaints to parents. These ongoing problems and lack of positive relationships with teachers and others can further compound their challenging school environments.

WAYS TO MANAGE SCHOOL DIFFICULTIES

To better manage these numerous learning, homework, and behavioral difficulties at school, parents can use a number of approaches. First, parents should firmly engage the school staff to address the academic and behavioral difficulties. Parents will play a critical role in their children's educational experiences and should be assertive and direct about their requests and needs with teachers and the school administration. At the start of the year, parents can inform the teacher/s about the student's ADHD condition, and discuss their strengths and weaknesses. Parents should not wait for recurrent problems to emerge again. Parents should also not expect the school to understand or effectively handle the child's school problems without their involvement and oversight. Parents should not assume teachers understand ADHD, and may choose to give them reading materials about this condition.

Obtaining official school plans of 504s and Individual Education Programs (IEPs) can be one of the most important steps in addressing ADHD and other conditions at school. These plans may be challenging to obtain at first, but once secured can create helpful accommodations and services. When a student's special school and learning needs are known and formally acknowledged by the school, parents should continue to be their advocates. Caregivers can continue to work with the school staff to ensure that the child's difficulties are being addressed properly, and that the school services and accommodations are actually being provided. Chapter 10 will explain what 504 plans and IEPs are, and how to obtain them. Chapter 11 will address additional ways to address school issues as well.

This chapter will present two powerful behavioral approaches parents can use to address homework and behavioral problems at school. These are the homework and school behavioral notebook systems. These will work whether a student has official school plans or not and with only minor assistance from teachers.

THE HOMEWORK NOTEBOOK SYSTEM

If the child refuses to do homework, forgets to bring it home, doesn't turn it in to the teacher, is inconsistent, or sabotages their homework in any number of ways, then parents can utilize the homework notebook system. Variations of this homework notebook and the school behavioral notebook program have been discussed by a number of authors and it has been used successfully by thousands of families for decades (Barkley & Murphy, 2006; Flick, 1998; Garber, Garber, & Spizman, 1996). Parents should probably not use these systems to target homework and/or school behavioral problems until they have mastered at least some of the behavioral management principles and approaches at home. For many families, it will be more important to first address the home problems before working on the school difficulties. Some parents can be eager to address all the ADHD issues right away, but this can lead to ineffective results if the behavioral management skills are not adequately mastered. However, if the family does not have home behavioral issues, then they can start using these homework or school behavioral notebook systems.

Often a parent will initially say "We have already tried that homework notebook. It doesn't work. My child only got the teacher signatures for a few days and then stopped." The clinician can then ask, "Did you give the child daily negative consequences at home for not obtaining the teacher signatures?" Parents rarely answer in the affirmative. When told that this approach is different and effective, most are skeptical but want something that works.

To utilize this homework notebook approach, parents should explain to students that they will be expected each school day to write down the date and their assigned homework for each subject in a designed homework notebook. They should also write down when the teacher says there will be a quiz or test. These can be recorded in regular spiral notebooks, with the date, list of classes, and an area for the teacher to initial. A new page should be used for each new day. Many schools require students to use planners, and these can be used as well, as long as it has enough room and separate spaces each day for listing the homework, upcoming announced quizzes or tests, and the teacher initials for each class. At the end of the class or school day for those with only one teacher, the student must go to their teacher/s to ask them to initial next to what they wrote for the assigned homework that was given that day, as well as any announced upcoming quizzes or tests. It is not the teacher's job to chase them to sign this. If there is no homework they must write "No Homework," and have this signed as well. If there were no announced upcoming quizzes or tests, they should write "No Quizzes or Tests."

The teachers are expected to initial only if the student has written the correct homework assignment and quizzes or tests. If inaccurate, teachers can inform them of the correct homework assignment and/or upcoming quizzes or tests, and they can re-write this. Also, teachers can also comment on any in-school behavioral problems or if they were missing homework, or anything else they wish to share with parents about that school day. This notebook system creates a direct daily communication line between parents and teachers. For students in middle school and high school with multiple teachers, they will be expected to get signatures from each of their subjects' teachers at the end of every class. If the child forgot to turn in the homework that day, the teacher can ask the student to submit it if they have it. This initialing process should be quick and requires very little time or effort for teachers, particularly after the routine is established.

As soon as they come home from school, the student will be expected to immediately show the parent the homework notebook, or as soon as the parent can check it. Additionally, the child will be expected to bring home all homework due the next day that may have been done in school already so the parent can check this also. When the child or teen comes home, they can have a brief break, but it is best for most students to begin their homework and studying for quizzes and tests soon after school, particularly if they are on stimulants that will be wearing off shortly.

After the homework is done, parents should check the homework and compare this to what was written in the homework notebook, including if there were quizzes or tests. The student should then receive a daily positive consequence if the notebook is properly initialed by the teacher/s and after the homework is completed and checked. If the child does not have all the teachers' initials or if the notebook is missing ("I forgot it at school" or "Aliens stole it from me"), then a predetermined and standard daily negative consequence should be given.

The simplest version of this system is that students can earn cell phone use, screen time, or going out to play with friends each day after they show the initialed notebook and completed homework to the parent. If they lack the properly signed notebook or they did not complete the day's homework, then there should be no use of electronics or phones, and they should not be allowed to go outside or have friends over the house for the remainder of day and evening. Other consequences can be used as well, such as requiring the child to do special "homework" of copying one or more pages from a dictionary, writing an essay on a topic, or doing math problems from books at home.

Initially when this program begins, bonus rewards should be added for successful compliance of one full week to help them develop the homework system habits, such as extra privileges on the weekend. For older children and teens, they can lose their cell phone privileges on longer-term bases if they continue to refuse to comply with the program. Parents can discuss with their children and teens which daily consequences and motivators will be effective. Parents should also "high five," energetically thank them with big smiles, and praise liberally on successful days. Additionally, after each positive test outcome, or weekly to monthly for older students who have online posted grades, students can receive monetary or other rewards to increase their efforts.

Before the program starts, it is important for parents to first speak with all of the student's teachers to make sure they will cooperate with the program. Parents should not give negative consequences if teachers will not participate. Teachers should be told that this is a daily commitment to initial the notebook, and the student will receive groundings daily if it is not signed by them. Teachers should know that it is not their job to chase students for signatures, which they will appreciate. Most students will be motivated to obtain signatures if the parents are consistent with daily consequences at home. Many teachers actually like this program because it addresses the homework problems, with little effort on their part. Additionally, teachers can be asked to comply with signing the notebook each day if this system is part of the child's 504 Plan or IEP.

This is a powerful daily system, with each new day being a fresh opportunity for the student to make good choices by writing down the homework, getting teacher signatures, and completing the homework soon after coming home from school. Parents must stay firm with enforcing consequences, and not make deals, give students extra chances, and feel sorry for them when they forget. Because ADHD is a disability, this system may be a challenge for them initially. However, with persistence, this system should motivate the child to remember to do the tasks necessary to create homework success.

Reminders can help initially. Parents can briefly review each morning the notebook expectations and the consequences that will occur if they do not comply. The child can write themselves reminder notes, and teachers can help with reminders as well. Also, parents or therapists can create pre-written templates and sheets that can be copied that have the student's subjects listed, lines for the date, space for the assigned homework for each class, space for announced upcoming quizzes and tests, and the area for teachers to sign or initial. Other information can be listed on these copied forms as well. The daily forms can be placed in a three-ring binder at the start of each week.

This notebook system can be used with students in elementary, middle, and high school up through their senior year. As with most behavioral approaches, this notebook system works whether the children like it or not because they will be motivated to avoid the negative consequences at home. Sometimes students, particularly those in high school, will complain that they are embarrassed to go to the teacher with a notebook at the end of class. In these situations, teens can tell their friends or classmates that they are doing a special system to help them improve their grades, and their parents give them extra privileges or stuff they want from this. Also, after this system is implemented, many students get used to this quickly after the first several weeks.

As with most behavioral systems, adjustments may be necessary over time if bumps arise. However, parents should be patient and do not give up too soon. This is a highly effective system as long as the expectations are clear and the parents are consistent in enforcing effective consequences. Therapists who are familiar with this approach can be consulted while using this system, especially if there are challenges or problems.

ADDITIONAL HOMEWORK SUGGESTIONS

1. Create a homework routine. Find the right location for doing homework. This place should have the fewest distractions, with minimal exposure to TVs, siblings or other distractions.

2. Children and teens with ADHD may need parents to be accessible during homework. Due to their disability, they can require help to supervise, structure, organize and assist with their homework, but may not ask for this. If their homework is a struggle or determined to be problematic by teachers, parents can commit to a culture of accessibility and encouragement for homework. Perhaps there are only certain subjects they require help. Parents may need to work on their own unwelcoming reactions for assitance requests, particularly if they get frustrated or believe they do not have time. If two adults are in the house, perhaps one should be the designated homework helper, or they could alternate.
3. Homework should be done as soon as possible after school. Some children may need a brief break. Students on stimulant medications are "on the clock" because these medications will wear off at about dinner time or earlier. Additionally, studying for quizzes and tests is also homework, and should require time and attention. See Chapter 11 for information on how to study effectively for quizzes and tests.
4. Background music or white noise machines may help some students with ADHD to better focus while doing homework, and parents can ask if this helps them. TV or electronic screen use should not be an option because these are too distracting.
5. Students may need a series of brief focus or motor breaks while doing homework and this may help decrease overwhelmed feelings. Timers can be used to take breaks, such as every 15 to 20 minutes.
6. Parents, tutors, or educational therapists should teach homework organization, including breaking down homework into smaller parts. Before beginning homework, parents can help to organize and divide each subject work into smaller manageable parts. Timers can be used for math problems and reading assignments, gradually extending the time as the student sustains attention. Students can use folders clearly labeled for all subjects. At the end of the session, the homework should be put in these subject folders and in the book bag. Book bags should be in one specific place at home, and after homework these should be in this designated place ready for the morning.
7. Homework should be checked by parents to see if it is completed and matches the assigned homework every day. Parents and students need a daily checking routine. Some students have accuracy problems or are not consistent or honest with completing homework. Homework checking by parents is also a commitment. Students and parents should accept this and not become defensive about this important final step of the homework process. This checking process can be implemented whether the family uses the homework notebook system or not.

8. The process of checking homework assignments and grades can be easier with technology. For middle and high school students, many teachers use special apps and websites so parents and students can have direct access to daily assigned school and homework assignments, as well as when upcoming projects are due. The grade for the class, as well as dates and grades for quizzes and tests are also often included. This online checking can help parents slice through the mystery and uncertainties about if their students are being honest about their school performance. Apps like PowerSchool permit access to this information, and help families monitor academic functioning and progress. While this technology can be extremely helpful to get immediate information on assignments and grades, it can also be used as a back-up for the homework notebook system. However, it should not be used to replace the notebook system. Students need the organizational habit of writing down assignments, as well as teachers verifying these. Additionally, this technology is not perfect, and errors, delays of assignments, and confusion can occur.
9. Some students with ADHD can have serious handwriting problems, such as dysgraphia, or written expression learning disorder. For these difficulties, parents should consider evaluations and treatments, as well as using laptops for schoolwork and homework as an accommodation.
10. If possible, students should receive from the school an extra set of books to be kept at home for homework and studying. This can be part of the 504 or IEP, and can help to minimize forgetting books at school.
11. Parents can encourage and reward the use of various educational websites to help students enhance their learning in weaker subject areas, such as Khan Academy. Parents should specifically ask teachers which websites they suggest.
12. Students with ADHD require book bag management assistance due to their problems with disorganization. Messy book bags can contribute to lost important school papers and homework. Parents should routinely help them clean and organize their book bags, and one day a week can be designated to this task. Similarly, parents should work with teachers on regularly organizing their desks. If the student has a messy book bag regularly, assume their desk is the same.

THE SCHOOL BEHAVIORAL NOTEBOOK SYSTEM

Consequences given by school staff are typically less effective in changing behavioral problems at school. For most, suspensions, detentions, classroom scolding, and visits to the principal are insufficient reinforcers to end behavioral problems. The Combined ADHD brain functioning difficulties make it more difficult for these children and teens to control themselves. Thus, they need greater motivation to follow class rules and expectations. Students with ADHD know the rules but struggle to follow them consistently. When parents can link unwanted school behaviors with effective reinforcers at home, children's behaviors at school can improve. Children typically care much more about electronic and media screen use, cell phones, going outside and seeing friends, and therefore they will be much more impacted by these home consequences than those from school.

The school behavioral notebook system is very similar to the homework notebook system, except this will focus on behavioral issues at school. These will be any behavioral problems or complaints observed by teachers or other school staff in the classroom, cafeteria, and recess. It can also be used for unwanted behaviors on buses. This system can be effective for preschoolers to high school seniors. The behavioral notebook system provides verbal or written performance ratings for the student each school day to help them become more accountable for their behaviors. Most students will work harder to modify their behavior, practice increased self-control, and make better choices when they know they will receive consequences at home.

Similar to the homework notebook, each day students will ask teachers to rate or list their behaviors, and then initial or sign next to their class in the notebook. Each day on a blank sheet of notebook paper the student (or parent in the morning or night before) can write the date, list the classes, and leave an area for teachers to give that day's behavior rating or list the unwanted behaviors. There should also be a place for the teacher to sign or initial for each class. The school behavior notebook can be a planner already used, but it needs enough room and separate spaces each day for listing unwanted behaviors, ratings, and the teachers' initials. If there are behavioral concerns on the school bus, the bus driver can be asked to sign the notebook each morning and after school before they leave the bus, along with teachers.

For younger children with more frequent class behavioral problems who use the school notebook system, their teacher can provide three ratings a day (late morning, after lunch, and near the end of school day) or even hourly ratings. This should give students more frequent feedback and check-ins for their behavior. For elementary school students with one teacher, they can have one rating at the end of the day, but can also have three or more per day. For middle school and high school students with persistent in-class behavioral problems, they should obtain signatures and behavioral ratings from all their teachers at the end of each class, or just the ones in which they have behavioral problems.

It may be helpful for teachers to use Phelan's counting techniques to give students warnings to change their behavior before they receive a lower rating. By holding up 1, 2, or 3 fingers to students, teachers can give warnings to change their behavior. By signaling a "3" with their fingers, the teacher can indicate to the student that they will now receive a lower behavioral rating. Younger children will need more frequent counting and feedback during the school day.

Next, a rating system should be utilized by teachers. Before implementing this notebook system, parents should discuss with teachers what behavior rating system the teacher/s will use each day. Many teachers will be open to the proposed systems discussed below, while some teachers may wish to use or design their own. Different systems will work, they just need to be specific and clear to teachers, students, and parents. Teachers will rate younger students for the entire day, or multiple teachers will offer ratings for their class for older students.

For a simple version, elementary to high school students can receive a behavior rating system of 1 to 3, where a "3" rating is a positive day with no unwanted behavioral problems, "2" is a day with a fewer or mild behavioral issues, and "1" was a day with unacceptable behavioral problems. Then these numbers need to be translated into specific consequences at home. A "3" or positive day would earn full privileges at home after homework is done. A "2" could earn the less privileges, or a parent could add on a mild negative consequence. A "1" rating would be no privileges, and another option is no privileges plus a negative consequence. The numerical system can also be changed to be 1 to 5, or 1 to 10 for more specificity. This system can also be converted to colors, with a "3" becoming a green rating, "2" a yellow, and "1" a red.

For kindergarten to elementary school children, some schools may already use various classroom behavioral systems. Parents can incorporate the behavioral rating systems that are already being used by teachers into this school behavioral notebook system. A popular one is the color behavior system, with a range of colors indicating the daily rating. This can include behaviors exhibited at recess, in hallways, at lunch as well as the classrooms. Some schools may use red to indicate that a number of unwanted and negative behaviors occurred, yellow for some negative behaviors but at a milder level or intensity, green for positive and expected behaviors, and other colors for above average behaviors such as pink, purple and blue. Pink may be a better than average day, blue is a superior day, and purple indicates the child showed exemplary and outstanding behaviors. For older students and teens, more colors can also be translated to numbers, such as red is 1, orange is 2, green is 3, pink is 4, blue is 5, and purple is 6.

Some schools have systems that allow children to move the colors up or down (or "clip up" or clip down") based on their classroom behaviors on a large chart for the entire class. Teachers may give warnings to students (such as two strikes) before they will move down to a lower color or number on the chart.

One advantage of the school behavior notebook approach is that it is private and not publicly posted, such as with in-class color charts or other behavior systems commonly used in elementary schools or preschools. In these systems, all the students in the class know who is on a negative rating such as a "red" ranking. While these classroom systems can work effectively, critics argue that these are shaming for some children and may cause them distress and anxiety.

Parents can also use other existing behavior systems currently used by teachers by attaching specific consequences to the teachers' ratings. The student can indicate in their notebook the rating they achieved, and then have this signed by the teacher at the end of the day for verification. Then parents will review their rating when they come home, and they will earn pre-determined positive or negative consequence based on this. If a rating system is not used, teachers can list any unwanted or previously determined unacceptable behaviors and then initial the notebook. A combination of a daily rating (colors or numbers) and listing the unwanted behaviors would probably be the most specific and provide the most feedback for the student and parents.

When the student comes home, the behavior notebook should immediately be shown to the parent. If the student received one or more negative behavior ratings and does not have all the teacher's initials, then they should receive a pre-determined and standard negative consequence after school for that day. Also, if the notebook is missing ("I forgot it at school" or "A dog ate it"), then the standard maximum negative consequences should be given. The negative consequence can vary, as previously mentioned, and they can also be combined and changed as needed, as long as they are pre-determined and clear.

The severity of the consequences should be appropriate for the child's age and behaviors. Preschool or kindergarten students should have briefer reinforcers. For younger students that cannot be trusted to bring home the notebook each day, the teacher may email or call parents with the daily ratings, or parents can get the notebook from the teacher if they pick up the child after school. In these cases, the goal would be to motivate the child to bring home the notebook, and stronger consequences may need to be used.

Parents should spend time writing out this system and posting this on the refrigerator, in the student's room, or both. Parents can design this on their computers so they can adjust the modifications that will occur over time. It also helps to have this on a computer to be able to print out extra copies if the child rips these up or lose them. The list should have what positive or negative consequences the numbers, colors, or unwanted school behaviors will earn after school at home. This list should be reviewed each morning before school with the student, at least initially.

Just like the apps and websites used by teachers to share current information on homework assignments and grades, similar technology exists regarding school behaviors. For example, the app ClassDoJo captures and creates data on school behaviors that teachers can share with parents and other school staff. This type of technology can be used on a daily basis as a "behavioral report card" for the student. However, parents should not rely only on this technology to manage behavior, but they can be creative in utilizing the technology feedback into their behavioral systems or as back-ups.

Also, parents should ask students for their ideas and feedback on the program periodically. They may have interesting and surprisingly fair ideas on what their consequences should be. Like all daily behavioral systems, each day presents new opportunities for better choices. For families with more severe school behavioral problems, they should use this system with an experienced therapist's direction.

ADDITIONAL SUGGESTIONS FOR THE SCHOOL BEHAVIORAL NOTEBOOK SYSTEM

1. Parents can provide daily morning reminders before school about the system and give pep talks to motivate the student each day. Parents should be positive and encouraging ("You can do this!").
2. If the student continues to experience school behavioral problems and is on ADHD medication, explore with the prescriber various medication issues, including is the medication effective, is the student taking it daily, is an additional stimulant dose needed at school, and is the medication wearing off too soon.
3. Parents should try to determine why the behavior problems are occurring at school. They can partner with teachers and school staff about detecting triggers to the school difficulties and finding ways to help the student improve. Parents can make a list of the most problematic recurrent unwanted behaviors that occur at school to understand the patterns and help the student do their best to improve these. Different teachers can have different requirements from students, and have their own criteria about what they expect behaviorally. Parents should explore these factors, and assist the student to target these. Questions to discover include when does the behavior occur typically, why does

this happen, what reinforces this, and what are the situations or signs of this occurring so they can avoid or stop it if possible? Rewards for these efforts can be utilized as well.
4. Parents should permit and encourage the child with bonus rewards for excellent efforts at school, such as when they have several days or the entire week of reduced or no unwanted school behaviors.
5. There should be extra standard negative consequences at home for suspensions or detentions if these are recurrent. Suspensions should earn more serious, pre-determined, and motivating consequences, such as weekend groundings.

COMBINING THE HOMEWORK AND SCHOOL BEHAVIORAL NOTEBOOK SYSTEMS

If the child is having homework and school behavioral problems, then these two notebook systems can be integrated. However, it is recommended that at first, only one issue is targeted at a time. With experience, parents can graduate to using a combined notebook system. When first learning to use these behavioral approaches, families should initially decide which types of problems they wish to improve more, the homework or behavior. If the behavior problems are more severe, disruptive, and concerning, then these should probably be the first target.

When parents are ready to use a combined notebook system, the one notebook will have areas for teachers to initial next to the assigned homework and another separate area for the daily behavior rating and/or a place to list unwanted behaviors. The student will then receive daily consequences at home for homework signatures and a separate rating/s for school behaviors by the teacher/s. The challenge with a combined homework and behavior notebook system is to separate the homework compliance and daily behaviors ratings so they are distinct from each other.

Parents will need to determine which school behaviors or school behavioral ratings, such as a "3" or "negative" colors, will earn what daily consequences. Then the second focus on homework expectations should earn a separate standard daily consequence. Remember that parents should have clear pre-established consequences that are easy to administer, something the parent has control over, and something that motivates the child. With a combined system, the child could earn a negative consequence for not submitting or writing down a homework assignment, and a positive consequence for no school behavioral problems (or vice versa).

While these systems are not perfect, if created and used effectively they can create a clear and logical routine to help students and families address homework and/or school behavioral challenges. If either notebook system is not working, parents can spend some time to review this with the teachers and student to figure out why it is ineffective. Of course, parents must be diligent and consistent with the consequences. Also, perhaps the consequences are too mild or too severe. Finally, parents should not give up too soon with this system. There will be some bumps that can take weeks to work out. Engage a therapist familiar with these behavioral approaches for help if necessary.

EXAMPLE OF A COMBINED HOMEWORK AND SCHOOL BEHAVIORAL NOTEBOOK SYSTEM PLAN

This is a behavioral plan that is written for Franco, age 10, to address his ADHD-related difficulties with completing and submitting his homework, and his self-control difficulties in class. It uses the same color behavioral system that his teacher already utilizes in her class. It was written by his mother on their computer and posted on the family refrigerator.

Franco's Notebook System Expectations

1. *Homework Notebook:* All homework assignments should be written down and the homework notebook should be signed by all five teachers at the end of each class every school day. If any teacher indicates that homework was missing and/or if any teacher signatures are missing in the homework notebook, then Franco will go to his room immediately after school. He will remain there until he completes a two-page writing assignment of copying the dictionary or math problems, or a two-page essay on how he plans to improve his homework and homework notebook compliance. If the writing assignment is not completed that day, then the consequence will continue the next day until the writing assignment is completed, with no privileges until it is done.

2. *School Behavioral Notebook:* At the end of each class, all teachers should rate Franco's behavior with a color from red to blue and sign the school behavioral notebook. If any signatures are missing, this will be an automatic red color day. The positive consequences for green days and higher colors will be earned only after homework and chores are done for the day. Screen time that is earned will occur after any writing assignments are completed for missing teacher signatures for homework as noted in the homework notebook.

    a. Purple day—a visit to Dairy Queen or blue day privileges, and one extra hour of screen time on Saturday and Sunday.

b. Blue day—one hour of screen time earned for the day and one dollar
c. Pink day—forty minutes of screen time earned for the day
d. Green day—twenty minutes of screen time earned for the day
e. Yellow day—no screen time privileges for entire day
f. Orange day—in bedroom without screen time or any electronics for 90 minutes, and no screen time privileges for the day
g. Red day—in bedroom without screen time or any electronics for entire day

SUMMARY POINTS

- The homework notebook system can be utilized to increase homework organization, help students take more responsibility, and better motivate homework completion from using daily consequences at home.
- The school behavioral notebook system can be used to target daily school behavioral problems.
- These two systems can be combined for homework and school behavioral difficulties.

REFERENCES

Barkley, R. A., & Murphy, K. R. (2006). *Attention deficit hyperactivity disorder: A clinical workbook* (3rd ed.). New York, NY: The Guilford Press.

Dendy, C. (1995). *Teenagers with ADD: A parent's guide.* Bethesda, MD: Woodbine House.

Flick, G. (1998). *ADD/ADHD behavior-change resource kit.* San Francisco, CA: Jossey-Bass.

Garber, S. W., Garber, M. D., & Spizman, R. F. (1996). *Beyond ritalin.* New York, NY: Harper Perennial.

Weyandt, L. L., & Gudmundsdottir, B. G. (2015). Developmental and neuropsychological deficits in children with ADHD. In R. Barkley (Ed.), *Attention deficit hyperactivity disorder: A handbook for diagnosis and treatment* (4th ed., pp. 116–139). New York, NY: Guilford Press.

Chapter 10

OFFICIAL SCHOOL PLANS: 504s AND INDIVIDUALIZED EDUCATION PROGRAMS (IEPs)

THE IMPORTANCE OF PROVIDERS OUTSIDE OF THE SCHOOL

The information presented here is intended to help parents understand official school plans, how schools may address learning, neurodevelopmental and psychological difficulties, and to empower parents to navigate educational systems more effectively. While many school staff and districts do the best they can and have good intentions, there can be limitations to what they can provide. Parents should be aware of these certain challenges that can occur in school districts.

As a general rule, any child or adolescent who has an Individualized Education Program (IEP) or 504 Plan (both of which will be discussed shortly) related to learning, neurodevelopmental, or behavioral health difficulties should have an independent psychological testing assessment by clinical psychologists or neuropsychologists outside of the school to determine their specific diagnoses and treatment needs. Similarly, children with sensory processing and motor disorders should receive occupational therapy evaluations outside of the school. It is important for parents to understand that, if possible, they should not rely on the school to be the only evaluator and provider of services for their children with ADHD or any type of special needs. In the United States, some public schools can have tendencies of minimizing a child's problems to parents, and may avoid being more direct or honest about what additional outside services the child may need. In some cases, they may not know what else is needed as well.

Similarly, a number of parents who have children in public schools who receive special education services are unaware of the need for additional providers outside of the school system. Outside providers are often needed to objectively evaluate and treat children with behavioral issues, learning problems and neurodevelopmental conditions. Sadly, some are unaware of what diagnoses their children have and lack a specific understanding of what their children's conditions are, even though they continue to struggle. Many times, the child will have experienced academic or behavioral difficulties for years. Sometimes, if the learning or behavioral problems at school are severe enough, the school may have initiated the school services themselves.

When asked what their child's conditions or diagnoses are, some parents will say something vague like "They said he has developmental delays," "Emotional difficulties," "Learning problems," or "I don't know." When asked what the child's specific school services or plans are, parents may say, "The school did testing" or "She gets services at school," but they may be unable to articulate anything specific. This can result from schools who are not always clear about the child's problems. Schools do not use clinical diagnostic testing and diagnoses as providers do, and typically use educational terms about the child's problems that are often different and less precise than clinical diagnoses.

Parents may not know that many schools do not provide specific clinical diagnoses, such as reading learning disorder or ADHD. Public schools typically provide educational testing, while clinical psychologists and other evaluators provide psychological testing. They are different, but may have some degree of overlap. School psychologists are not clinical psychologists, and have different training, credentials, and professional roles.

Most schools do not comprehensively assess what emotional, behavioral, or psychological problems or diagnoses a child may have, and may only loosely refer to these. School systems typically address more of the learning problems that children have, but may not specifically call these "learning disorders" or "learning disabilities." This is unfortunate because parents can lack a full understanding of the magnitude of the child's conditions and limitations, and the critical need for outside providers.

Indeed, the purpose of school evaluations is to identify learning deficits or impairments that children experience so that they can receive adequate services, accommodations and remediations in their educational environment. Parents should not expect clinical diagnoses or detailed explanations of school testing results from schools because this is not what they are designed to provide (Braaten & Willoughby, 2014). School evaluations are limited and often brief. Sadly, when children receive only school services without outside providers complementing their services, parents can have a false sense that their children's problems are being adequately addressed. Many times, parents are unaware that their child has neurodevelopmental conditions that require more services and treatment that schools cannot and do not provide. Some schools are simply reluctant to complain to parents about the child's problems until they cannot be avoided any longer. Parents may be motivated to approach outside behavioral health providers only after the child continues to have severe and frequent school complaints or problems.

When students with ADHD or other disabilities receive IEPs and special education services, they can be very costly to school districts. Students with ADHD cost school systems in the United States more than three billion dollars each year (Schab & Trinh, 2004), and this is higher now. While many school districts assist students the best they can, some schools have serious financial and funding problems. To protect their school budgets, school administrations may deny, delay, or may offer inadequate or minimal school special education services. School staff may try to delay starting any school evaluations or services with parents by saying "Let's give it some time," "Let's wait" or "Let's see how it goes next year." Also, some schools may offer insufficient or unofficial assistance to delay services, such as "The teacher can work with him more." One way to protect their budgets is to minimize the number of children who receive special education services. The easiest way to do this is to delay or deter students from receiving initial education evaluations to see if they qualify for costly special education and IEPs.

When schools have dual agendas of minimizing or limiting the services they provide and providing school special needs services, they can be biased in their evaluations and lack objectivity. In addition, depending on the school district and its culture, some public school teachers and staff may not recommend outside clinical evaluations or treatments because the school might be responsible for that funding if this is suggested to parents. A number of public school teachers and school psychologists have shared that they are not permitted to discuss necessary outside services, such as an evaluation for suspected ADHD, by their school administrations. Some administrations may even have specific internal expectations that teachers handle challenging students on their own.

Consequently, some teachers may not be straight forward and minimize student problems when they have in-person meetings with parents regarding their child's academic and/or behavioral difficulties. Curiously however, they may be more honest in their comments on report cards. The discrepancy can be puzzling for parents who receive mixed messages. Perhaps some teachers are trying to avoid conflict or giving bad news, or perhaps are doing what they can without parental involvement. This lack of open dialogue is regrettable because parents may not receive all the information they need, and can miss or delay the opportunity to evaluate and treat problems sooner.

However, despite these barriers, sometimes teachers or school staff may find a way to convey their concern about suspected ADHD or other conditions and the need for additional external services. Parochial schools tend to be much more open about this because they typically do not provide special education services or resources, and do not have the potential liability of being responsible for them.

To be fair to schools, they cannot address all the child's needs, and their purpose is not to provide comprehensive medical or behavioral health services. Part of the confusion seems to arise when schools provide some services, such as individualized tutoring for learning difficulties, speech or occupational therapy, or school social work services to address social skills deficits. This can contribute to the parent's perception that the student is having their needs fully met.

It is important to acknowledge that every school district is unique and differs in their approaches. Some schools provide many excellent services. Some may actually pay for outside clinical assessments and specialized providers for students due to various specific situations. Also, many school districts have assisted students who would have never had special services or assistance otherwise. For children who are in rural settings, have Medicaid with no available providers, or no health insurance, school services can be the only assistance they ever receive.

AN OVERVIEW OF IEPs AND 504 PLANS

Individual Education Programs (IEPs) and 504 plans are official school plans designed to specifically acknowledge a child's learning or behavioral challenges at school, provide a range of special education services and/or school accommodations, and ensure the student is in the least restrictive learning environment. These school plans formally provide school services and accommodations that should address and manage their educational difficulties. Children with ADHD often require and deserve various levels of school accommodations and additional services based on their school-functioning limitations. However, these plans are not automatically given, and students are required to officially qualify for them. If the school does not initiate these plans, parents must navigate the system to obtain these services.

According to federal laws, children and adolescents with ADHD and other qualifying neuropsychological and psychological disorders, learning deficits, and medical conditions are entitled to receive a free and appropriate education (FAPE) which includes special accommodations, modifications, and school services. The two main federal laws that permit this are the Individuals with Disabilities Education Act (IDEA) and Section 504 of the Rehabilitation Act of 1973 (Section 504). Students who qualify for services under the IDEA law will receive IEPs, and students who qualify for services under Section 504 will receive 504 plans. Students with ADHD who receive an IEP will most likely qualify under the disability eligibility category of

"Other Health Impairment" (OHI) within IDEA. Special education does not necessarily mean that a child will be in a separate classroom or will be separated from a mainstream classroom. This is a misunderstanding that some parents may have. By law, students must be placed as much as possible in mainstream classes unless they are determined to require separate special education classrooms. Many services listed on IEPs occur in mainstream classrooms, and typically only students with higher level impairments and conditions will be placed in separate special education classes full time. Additionally, it is expensive for schools to maintain these classrooms, so economically it is to the school's advantage to try to mainstream students as much as possible.

It is usually in the best interest of students and families to obtain these official school plans for their children with conditions. Some parents wish to avoid official school plans because do not want the school to "label" the child, "treat them differently," or know about their histories or disorders. Often schools already suspect a child has ADHD or some other conditions. When students with ADHD do not have the proper school services and accommodations, it can make an already difficult life harder. Also, when official school plans are established, it forces the school to acknowledge that the child has a disability and conditions, and to treat the child more fairly. Of course, obtaining school plans is a personal decision. Every situation is different, and there are pros and cons for obtaining school plans and for not obtaining school services. Generally, most children and teens benefit from these versus not having this extra school support. School staff will ultimately decide which plan a student is eligible for and which services they will receive based on their school educational evaluation. However, they may accept parental requests and be influenced by these requests to some degree as to which plan students receive.

While 504s and IEPs both provide support and accommodations, they are different. A major difference is the way in which students qualify for services under each plan. It is more difficult to qualify for special education services and obtain an IEP than a 504 plan. For IEPs, a student must meet the criteria listed for one of the required categories of special education. Generally, students with more severe conditions or disorders that require more support and services will require IEPs over 504s.

Fortunately, having a mental health or medical diagnosis from an outside provider can greatly assist students to qualify for a 504 or IEP. These are required for a 504 plan in most cases. Clinicians can assist families with the process of requesting school services by writing a letter to the child's school that states their diagnoses and recommends that they receive an IEP or 504 plan. Every school district is different, and some are more flexible and open to parent's wishes than others. However, if the parents have letters or psychological testing reports from outside providers, this typically helps to substantiate the need for an IEP or 504. Indeed, it is harder for schools to minimize a parent's request for school services when an outside provider is involved.

504 PLANS

Section 504 of the Rehabilitation Act is a federal civil rights law that permits 504 plans. Section 504 protects students with disabilities from discrimination in public schools. All students who qualify for IDEA are protected by Section 504, but not the converse. A 504 would be appropriate if a student needs class accommodations or modifications, but their condition/s do not require specialized teaching or services. Often schools prefer 504s over IEPs because these are easier, cheaper, and offer fewer student protections and rights (Disability Rights Center - NH, 2015). For 504 plans, the student's disorder or disability must impair the child's ability to learn in a regular classroom. Section 504 has a less restrictive definition of a disability than those considered under IEPs.

However, a student can have a disability but not qualify for a 504 or an IEP. To qualify for a 504, a student must have a diagnosed condition that affects a major life or school functioning. Educational impact is broader for 504s than IEPs. A student with ADHD can obtain good grades but may still need accommodations for their organizational deficits. For each plan, a specific connection is required to demonstrate the disability causes school impairment (King, n.d.).

504 plans are part of general education. 504s are typically for students with milder diagnoses and conditions that don't require more extensive school services. Once a parent formally requests a 504, then the school will conduct an evaluation for eligibility. Outside provider's diagnoses and documentation are often first required. These school evaluations are usually a less intensive process than for IEPs and can vary in their depth. Schools often make decisions on a case by case basis.

There can be a number of sources schools use to determine 504 eligibility, including documentation from pediatricians, behavioral health provider reports, psychological testing assessments, behavior rating scales completed by parents and teachers, parental input, teacher or school psychologist in-school observations, school educational testing or measures, school discipline and attendance records, and student progress reports. In addition to documented evidence of a diagnosed condition, a major life activity must be substantially limited.

A 504 plan is a better option for students functioning reasonably well with accommodations within regular education. A 504 plan is less restrictive and stigmatizing, and students can still receive some accommodations and services. However, schools may be inconsistent with the accommodations or services, and reminders may be needed for school staff. Additionally, accommodations and services may be minimally documented, are less detailed, and have fewer services available than IEPs (King, n.d.). Similarly, it may be more challenging to obtain special services from schools with 504s versus IEPs.

504s do not require that schools pay for independent assessments but parents can use these for eligibility. There are no set or written 504 formats, and these are often brief and basic. They typically include accommodations, services, supports, and involved school staff. While rules vary by state, typically a 504 plan is reviewed yearly and a re-evaluation may occur when needed or every three years (The Understood Team, 2014).

Some 504 plan examples of in-school accommodations, services, and/or other supports can include teachers repeating and simplifying instructions (pre-teaching behavioral expectations and/or reteaching expectations), providing a highly structured learning environment (teacher provides verbal prompts and reminders of appropriate behaviors), pairing verbal with visual directions (visual schedule for multi-step tasks along with tasks being broken down by steps), and preferential seating where the student sits in front of the class near the teacher to minimize distractions. Additionally, other services can be added to 504 plans, such as speech therapy, occupational therapy (to address sensory processing, motor, and handwriting challenges), time with social workers in individual or groups, individual tutoring, and additional teaching instructions outside the classroom for reading or math assistance.

IEPs UNDER IDEA

The Individuals with Disability Education Act (IDEA) is a federal special education law that mandates public schools provide all educationally disabled students with a free, appropriate public education (FAPE). To meet eligibility for special education services from an IEP under IDEA, students must have a diagnosis or disability and need special education services because their conditions impair their ability to learn in general educational classrooms without services and assistances. The IEP must be created and provided by the school to meet the student's specific needs (Disability Rights Center—NH, 2015).

As part of the IDEA eligibility considerations, a student's conditions must meet the criteria under one or more disability categories. Students with

ADHD most often fit the IDEA disability category of "Other Health Impairment" (OHI). To meet OHI criteria, a student should have a health condition (like ADHD) which causes limited strength or alertness in the educational environment that adversely effects scholastic performance. Also, the adverse effects are not limited to academics and can include behavioral impairments (Rief, 2012). There are 13 disability eligibility categories within IDEA for students ages 3 to 21, including specific learning disability, intellectual disability, OHI, traumatic brain injury, autism spectrum disorder, emotional disturbance, speech or language impairment, visual impairment, hearing impairment, deaf-blindness, orthopedic impairment, and multiple disabilities.

An IEP is often better for students with disabilities that impact their education more significantly and who need greater special services. However, an IEP can be more stigmatizing, and the eligibility process for an IEP can take longer (King, n.d.). A stigma may occur because some students may have to leave their main class for pull-out services or they may receive extra attention or accommodations (such as sitting at the back of the class for extra time on tests), and their peers can know they are receiving special assistance. Those receiving this may feel different, and peers may tease them. If this occurs, parents, school social workers, and therapists can help children grieve, accept, and manage these issues and their peers' reactions. However, parents should not automatically assume that a stigma will occur, and for many students there are no negative social consequences with IEPs or 504s.

Additionally, IDEA has more explicit protections for students than 504s. IDEA is more specific about their requirements for evaluations, parental participation, education plans, criteria and time frames for reviews and reevaluations. IDEA has detailed due process requirements, while 504s permit schools to determine this. IDEA mandates written notices before evaluations, meetings, and IEP changes, while 504s permit vaguer adequate notice. Also, students with 504s or IEPs have certain protections regarding school discipline. Students with an IEP and diagnosis that causes behavioral problems cannot be disciplined by a suspension or expulsion for more than 10 days (Disability Rights Center - NH, 2015).

IEPs can permit students to receive a wider variety of services, accommodations, and special considerations in and out of the classroom. For students with ADHD, their accommodation plans should specify appropriate and specific teacher approaches and expectations to address their challenges. Some of the most common ADHD accommodations include extended time for tests, pull-out services where students receive one-on-one instructions in math or other subjects, seating changes, and taking tests in quieter areas. Children and teens with ADHD and/or sensory processing conditions who have higher levels of wiggling, hyperactivity, and difficulties remaining seated can benefit from individual time with occupational therapists. They can help the student take motor breaks during class, and to learn better ways to manage fidgeting at their desks. Another school service is time with social workers to address school organization issues, coping difficulties, social problems and skills deficits, and self-esteem issues.

School districts are not required to pay for independent assessments but parents can request this. Parents can use external assessments, but it's the school's decision what they accept. However, schools tend to incorporate these findings (The Understood Team, 2014).

There is a specific process to request an IEP. Parents or school staff can request that the school conducts a case study or educational evaluation to determine if a child is eligible for an IEP. After this received request, the school should create an assessment plan from the school's multidisciplinary evaluation team. Parents must be notified and consent to this free assessment that explores the child's academic, functional, and developmental skills. After this evaluation, an IEP meeting is held at the school, typically with the entire team and parents (Rief, 2012). This team can include school psychologists, regular and special education teachers, social workers, occupational or speech therapists, and school nurses.

Three criteria must be met before an IEP and services will be implemented. First, the school testing process must be completed. Second, this process should determine that a student meets the eligibility criteria for a disability. Third, the student's learning is determined to be impacted by the disability. Once criteria are met, an IEP will be created and implemented (Dalgliesh, 2013). The IEP should be agreed to by parents, have specific goals, and be individualized to meet the student's unique school needs. These can include specialized school services, programs, supplemental aids, modifications, and accommodations. After implemented, IEP progress should be monitored and shared with parents, and re-evaluations should minimally occur every three years (Rief, 2012).

PRIVATE SCHOOLS AND 504s AND IEPs

Students can receive 504s and IEPs at private, parochial, and non-public schools, but the process can be more difficult. Most private or parochial schools (except the more elite and expensive schools) typically do not have the special education staff, resources or budgets to provide costly services. Private schools may have no or limited access to school psychologists or school social workers. 504s by their nature will be easier for private schools to implement than IEPs. However, private and parochial schools may have their own modified versions of school accommodation plans and services.

Usually they will be less intensive and comprehensive than most public school districts.

While private school students are entitled to receive IEPs services from their home district public school, the logistics of this can be challenging. Private school students may need to leave their school during the day and go to the public school for certain special education services. However, parents may need to arrange their travel. Private schools can have a lot of "heart" and may be motivated to keep the student with special needs at their school. Although they can provide extra time, instruction, or assistance, specialized services are often beyond what they can provide. Private schools also tend to be more honest than public school staff about recommending outside assessments or services for students with possible disorders and greater special needs. Parents of private school students can explore their options with their public district school staff regarding 504s or IEP services.

Some children with more severe ADHD and other special needs may need to leave their private schools due to a greater need for structure and IEPs. Initially, many parents of children with ADHD or other conditions who attend private schools may be reluctant to enroll in a public school. Yet if the student does not improve with medication and treatment, many of these parents can become more open to public schools. Generally, the more severe the disorders or conditions and the more assistance and services they require, the more likely that the student will need to attend a public school for their increased accessibility to IEP services. Finally, students with ADHD, ODD, learning disorders or other conditions that can cause higher level behavioral problems may be expelled by private schools. Private schools, particularly in the higher grades, may have less tolerance for persistent behavioral problems.

THE PROCESS OF REQUESTING A 504 PLAN OR IEP

To request a 504 plan or IEP, parents must write a letter to the school to ask that they conduct testing to determine if the student will qualify for these plans. This school testing, often called a "case study evaluation" or "educational evaluation," is the first step. Parents should submit this letter to the principal or school social worker. Parents may want to document to whom and when they submitted this letter, keep a copy of it, and call the principal or school social worker to confirm that they received this letter (if it was not submitted to them personally). See below for an example of this letter.

Along with the letter, it will be necessary for parents to also include diagnostic testing reports or documentation from providers who have diagnosed the child with ADHD or other qualifying disorders. Prior diagnoses are not required for IEPs but they are for 504s, and supporting documentation can certainly help. Clinical psychologists, behavioral health therapists, pediatricians, psychiatrists, and other health professionals can write letters to support the parent's request. Additionally, these reports or letters can make it much harder for schools to deny the first crucial step of approving a case study evaluation or school testing.

Depending on the state, the school will typically have a set number of school days by law to respond to these requests for school testing. Parents can internet search what are the maximum time frames permitted for their state, and can contact the school to inquire how long they typically require to respond. After this, they can periodically call for updates. For parochial or private school students, the parent would submit this letter to their public school district. Families can also attempt to obtain any available but typically more limited services in private schools.

After the school receives the parent's request letter and other documentation, they will determine if the student qualifies for consideration for a 504 plan or IEP. Once the school determines the child is eligible for further consideration, they will approve and proceed with a school evaluation. This educational testing for 504s or IEPs should be at no cost for families. If the student is declined for an evaluation or approval for a 504 plan, then the parents should receive an explanation why. If school testing does occur, parents should expect to receive a copy of the report. If these are not received, parents can request the school to furnish them. The school's testing results will indicate whether they qualify for school services or not.

When parents request case study evaluations, they should ask that these also include objective and standardized measures, and not just observational approaches. Objective and standardized measures and tests can help to make the case study evaluation process less subjective and forces the school to compare the child to other children using statistical norms. Ultimately, this should make the process harder for the school to deny services. Some schools may say they did not "observe" problems during their brief testing window and may use this as grounds to deny school services. Finally, parents should be assertive with their requests for services from schools. Parents are encouraged to be firm with their requests because schools may try to delay testing or ask that they give the student "more time" to improve. Again, schools may be motivated to protect their budgets by delaying or not providing school educational testing.

Once a student is approved for a school evaluation, parents can be expected to participate in the process to various degrees. Parents may be required to sign forms for permission for the school testing process. Also, parents should be invited to a meeting about the outcome of the case study findings, as well as subsequent IEP meetings. The 504 plans tend to be less strict about parental involvement, and various states will differ on this.

SAMPLE LETTER FROM PARENTS REQUESTING A SCHOOL EVALUATION TO INITIATE A 504 OR IEP

Parent's name
Home address
Phone number

School Principal's name
School name
Address of school

Re: Request for school evaluation for 504 plan or IEP for student (name of student), date of birth (add)

School Principal's name (add name),

Greetings. I am the parent of (student's name), who is in ____ grade and in (teacher's name)'s class at ____ (school name). My child has been experiencing significant academic and behavioral difficulties that are concerning. The following are the specific challenges my child has been experiencing at your school, including *(add some of the most recent and concerning school problems, such as failing or D grades, repeated homework problems, classroom behavioral complaints from his teacher, repeated detentions or suspensions, concerns about deficient reading or math skills, etc.).*

(If the child has been diagnosed or treated by other providers, include the following:) My child has been diagnosed with (list condition/s here, such as ADHD-Combined Presentation and any other psychological or medical disorders or conditions) by provider (name and credentials of provider). We believe that this condition/s has been negatively impacting her/his academic performance and school behavior. I have included (a letter or report) from the provider about their findings along with this letter of request.

As a result of the above stated difficulties, I am now requesting that my child be considered for a school case study evaluation or educational assessment to determine if s/he qualifies for school accommodations or special education services according to Section 504 or an Individual Education Program (IEP) as a part of the Individuals with Disabilities Education Act (IDEA).

I understand that the school has a limited amount of time to respond to this request. I expect to receive information from you soon regarding the next steps in this process. Thank you for your time and consideration.

Sincerely,
(sign name)
Print name

While this letter can be handwritten, it should be typed if possible to appear more official. The above letter is only a template and can be modified to meet the needs of the family. If parents believe their child should have an IEP, the parents can remove the reference to requesting a Section 504 and just keep the IEP and IDEA references. Conversely, if parents only want a 504 Plan, then they can remove the IEP and IDEA references. Parents should make sure to make a copy of the letter and record when and to whom it was given.

ACCOMMODATIONS AND RECOMMENDATIONS FOR SCHOOL PLANS

A Section 504 accommodation plan or IEP from the child's school should include specific school accommodations, modifications, and services to support and optimize the educational environment. Clinicians and parents can review the following list of possible accommodations, recommendations, and approaches, and decide which ones they believe would benefit their student. Parents can then request that these are included in the official school plans. Clinicians may present these in a letter to the school as well. Of course, it will be the school's discretion what is utilized in the school plan.

1. Teachers should be knowledgeable about ADHD and understand how this can impact school and academic functioning. Teachers should understand that students with ADHD will have strengths and weaknesses, and can experience fluctuations in their abilities and daily performance.
2. Effective school behavioral management and modification approaches should be utilized to address the student's behavioral difficulties. These should include approaches for desired behaviors that utilize reinforcement, specific pre-determined standard consequences for de-

sired behaviors, and frequent prompting and feedback to student. Rewards should be specific and motivating, such as earned minutes doing favorite activity or using a tablet or computer. Teachers should also offer liberal encouragement and praise. Negative consequences for unwanted specific behaviors should be clear and utilized as well.

3. The student should receive pull-out services for individual tutoring in subject areas that are identified as challenging, as needed.
4. If behavioral problems occur outside of the classroom at school (such as in hallways, recess, and lunch room), the student should receive additional monitoring, supervision, and behavioral management approaches to address these situations.
5. A positive working relationship and partnership between the student's teachers and parents is critical to best address and manage the student's educational and behavioral challenges. This should include the teachers' daily checking and signing of student's homework and/or school behavior notebook with consequences delivered at home.
6. A specific school staff member can function as an ADHD school coach or positive check-in person at school. This person could be a social worker, guidance counselor, or understanding teacher. This school coach can assist the student daily or several times a week with academic goals, organizational issues, and consistent use of study skills. Additionally, this person could provide brief interactions at the start and end of day to help student prepare for the day, focus on assignments or tests, and check backpack at end of day for homework.
7. An additional set of school books should be provided for use at home for the school year to minimize problems related to forgetting books at school.
8. If possible, the student could receive homework support time during or after school that provides a structured setting for staff to assist with homework.
9. The class schedule should be adjusted so that the most challenging subjects are earlier in the day or at times that are best for the student.
10. For students with learning disorders and/or other neurodevelopmental conditions, provide appropriate services and accommodations for student's condition, including individual tutoring once or more per week, extended time for tests and assignments, modified assignments, and other accommodations as needed.
11. Permit use of laptop computer for written work if handwriting is impaired.
12. For students with hyperactivity and sensory problems that impact their learning, they should receive occupational therapy services and sensory processing deficits accommodations to help child manage fid-

geting, hyperactivity, and excessive movements in class. These accommodations could incorporate using "motor breaks" at school and sensory tools students can use at desk or in designated sensory break areas of the classroom. The use of ergonomic classroom furniture that incorporates movement into student chairs and desks may be helpful as well.
13. Any of the ADHD-friendly teaching approaches presented in the next chapter could be requested to be utilized in school plans.

EDUCATIONAL ADVOCATES AND CONSULTANTS

If families believe that they are being treated unfairly due to delays in case study evaluations or IEP implementations, obtaining an educational advocate can be a powerful resource to ensure that schools follow their procedures more appropriately. Educational advocates are consultants who can assist families to navigate the educational process, as well as protect a child's educational rights. School administrations tend to be on better behavior when other professionals become involved with disability proceedings, including educational advocates.

Some advocates are attorneys and others are not. Both types should know disability law, special education rights and needs, and relevant school policies and procedures for their state. They can review school records and plans and may interact with school staff to obtain more information to promote fairness and advocacy. Advocates guide and coach parents towards obtaining the best educational services, plans, and accommodations possible for their child. They can accompany parents to school meetings to support and assist proceedings as well.

Educational advocate attorneys may charge hundreds per hour and may require a large retainer. Non-lawyer advocates tend to cost less and may charge $50 to $200 per hour or a flat fee for a set amount of time, such as $750 for three months. Some counties or districts may have government funding for educational advocates. Additionally, some areas may also have no cost lawyers or non-attorney educational advocates paid by non-profit organizations to help families with lower incomes. To find advocates, local disability advocacy and support groups may be helpful sources for these referrals. There are various websites that can provide referrals for educational advocates as well, such as www.yellowpagesforkids.com.

AFTER THE SCHOOL IMPLEMENTS A 504 OR IEP

Once the student receives a 504 or IEP, it is important that parents monitor the school to ensure they are adequately and consistently implementing what is written in the official plan. Unfortunately, some teachers and schools may not be properly maintaining these school plans. This non-compliance can occur with all of the school staff, or it may be related to only one teacher or staff member. If necessary, parents can obtain support and information about their children's rights at schools from child disability advocacy centers, websites, or various knowledgeable individuals in their child's school district. With 504 plans, schools have lesser requirements and oversight, and may need greater parental monitoring and reminders. Parents should not wait until the yearly official 504 or IEP school meetings to address plan problems, issues, or concerns. If a student continues to have academic and/or behavioral problems at school after plans are implemented, parents should continue to request meetings to address these issues to explore options and needs to potentially modify plans. These can be amended during the school year, so parents can work with the school staff to make enhancements when necessary.

If the school continues to inadequately maintain or implement established 504 plans or IEPs, then parents can escalate their complaints to the school principal, district superintendent, and finally the district school board, which is the highest regional educational authority. Escalations to school boards will get the school's attention. There are formal policies and procedures for making complaints to school boards, and school board websites and school staff that can guide parents with these protocols. In the most difficult situations, parents can obtain private educational attorneys for greater assistance.

ALTERNATIVE OR THERAPEUTIC SCHOOLS

If students experience severe and persistent behavioral problems that are highly overwhelming and disruptive to teachers, and other staff students, school districts may eventually transfer these students to alternative or therapeutic schools. These specialized education settings are also utilized for children who have multiple and higher level special needs and educational challenges. School districts can be reluctant to utilize these placements unless absolutely necessary because they are quite costly, and often upsetting initially for parents. The special placements will be part of the child's IEP as well. These sites can be positive experiences and a relief for parents, but not always. The students' scholastic experience and learning may be secondary to the main focus of the management of their disabilities and behavioral problems within an educational setting. However, every alternative or therapeutic school is different, and some may be visited by families before the transfer occurs.

SUMMARY POINTS

- Conditions that impact learning and behavioral functioning at school often require evaluations and assessments outside of the school.
- Individual Education Programs (IEPs) and 504 plans are official school plans designed to specifically acknowledge a child's learning or behavioral challenges at school, provide a range of special education services and/or accommodations, and ensure the student is in the least restrictive learning environment.
- Students with diagnosed conditions who qualify for services under Section 504 of the Rehabilitation Act of 1973 should receive 504 plans. These are more limited services and are generally for those with less severe conditions and educational needs.
- Students with conditions that cause greater educational impairments and needs and who qualify for services under the Individuals with Disabilities Education Act (IDEA) should receive IEPs. These involve a more extensive plan, with greater services, accommodations, and school staff involvement.
- Parents must formally request that the school conduct a case study or educational evaluation to obtain a 504 or IEP.
- Families can utilize the assistance of educational advocates and consultants if they encounter difficulties with schools.
- Alternative or therapeutic schools may be necessary for students with severe conditions who cannot succeed in traditional schools.

REFERENCES

Braaten, E., & Willoughby, B. (2014). *Bright kids who can't keep up.* New York, NY: The Guilford Press.

Dalgliesh, C. (2013). *The Sensory child gets organized.* New York, NY: Touchstone.

Disability Rights Center–NH. (2015, March 15). *Individual education programs (IEPs) and 504 plans: What's the difference?* Retrieved from www.drchn.org/IDEA504.pdf

King, E. N. (n.d.). *504 plan vs. the IEP.* Retrieved on 10/27/09 from http://newideas.net/book/export/html/324.

Rief, S. (2012). *Do you know my rights?* Retrieved from www.sandrarief.com/tips/tips-ed-rights/

Schab, D., & N. Trinh (2004, December). Do artificial food colors promote hyperactivity in children with hyperactive syndromes? A meta-analysis of double-blind placebo-controlled trials. *Journal of Developmental and Behavioral Pediatrics, 25*(6), 423–34. Retrieved from https://www.ncbi.nlm.nih.gov/pubmed/15613992

The Understood Team. (2014, June). *The difference between IEPs and 504 plans.* Retrieved from https://www.understood.org/en/school-learning/special-services/504-plan/the-difference-be…

Chapter 11

ADDITIONAL WAYS TO ADDRESS ADHD SCHOOL ISSUES

PARENT AND SCHOOL STAFF COLLABORATION

Parents should maintain ongoing contact and positive relationships with teachers and other school staff as much as necessary and possible. Parents should inform teachers they wish to support their child's learning and want teacher feedback on how to maintain an effective partnership with them. At the start of each new school year parents can inform teachers about the child's diagnoses, strengths, weaknesses and needs. After this, parental collaboration should be ongoing and continue as the school year progresses. Caregivers should work not only with teachers, but also school speech or occupational therapists, principals, and school social workers to develop, maintain, and polish specific management plans to address the child's school difficulties. This may include addressing learning homework, in-school behavior, and test performance challenges.

Sometimes parents do not engage teachers because they believe they are bothering them, or they are nervous about these contacts. They may also believe that contact should wait until parent-teacher conferences. Similarly, teachers often do not reach out to parents when there are academic or behavioral difficulties because many schools expect teachers to handle difficulties on their own, particularly if there is an IEP. Other teachers are hesitant to reach out because some parents dislike or ignore their contact attempts. However, if parents wait, they are missing opportunities to address issues before they worsen, the child gets further behind, and the teacher-student relationship suffers. Many teachers may truly appreciate a partnership with parents to better address the problems. If the parents make the first efforts to show teachers they want to be more involved, this can open the door to a better partnership.

Parents can use special apps, emails, or phone calls for contacts with teachers for regular updates or to address incidents or other concerns. Parents should ask teachers how they can best maintain contact with them. Parents can say, "Due to our challenges, I would really like to have regular contacts with you for the entire year. Do you prefer emails, the use of apps, or phone calls for contacts, and how often?" Apps can be helpful as long as the teachers are already using these, and typically they will inform parents and students about the apps they use at the start of the year. Emails and apps can be particularly useful because communications do not need to be in real time, and parents and teachers can use these when they are convenient for them.

BECOME A DETECTIVE WHEN GRADES DECREASE

When grades decline, parents should spend some time to figure out why. This can be challenging at first, particularly for busy and working parents. It will take time and persistence, and multiple attempts may be necessary. Students may be of little help initially. When asked why they are getting lower grades, parents should assume their first response is "I don't know." Fortunately, how grades are determined is not complex. Grades are typically composed of homework compliance, quiz and test grades, and sometimes projects and extra credit opportunities. The challenge will be in determining why quizzes and test grades are lower, and what are the homework problems. If teachers use apps and websites to post current grades and performance on homework, quizzes, tests, and projects, these can be used by parents in this process. Sometimes children and teens are not submitting, understanding or completing homework. Their performance may be poor because they may not understand the materials and have ineffective study skills. In these situations, teachers need to be engaged to explore these factors further and to create an action plan to correct the deficits. Parents should not hesitate to reach out and request phone or in-person meetings to explore and discuss these topics. Of course, emails and app contacts may be adequate as well, but real-time conversations can be more effective.

Students who have difficulty mastering the materials may need extra time and assistance with teachers before or after school, if teachers provide this. Often, teachers appreciate the extra efforts student make, and this can help their grades. Teachers may permit extra credit assignments or allow students to re-take certain tests. In addition to parents' outreach efforts, students should also be encouraged to ask for help and try to connect more with teachers to improve their relations and material mastery. Some teachers can be intimidating, and some students may dislike certain teachers. However, it is an important life skill to learn to interact with those in authority who they may not like. Students can be coached to advocate for themselves, and to try to connect more with their teachers by asking questions during and after class.

TEACH STUDY SKILLS

Children and teens should be taught study skills to improve their test and quiz grades. Many are expected to study for tests but are never taught how to study effectively. Too often children and teens believe that studying means simply reading the materials once or twice. If the student has not learned specific study strategies, parents can teach these and request that teachers do so as well.

The following are study skills that can be taught to students. Studying for tests is a process that should be done over two to three days before the test, while quizzes may only require one to two days. When tests and quizzes are assigned they should be recorded on a calendar to plan ahead for the studying steps. Study skills involve reading the material, then creating notes or study sheets on the material, and finally memorizing the material. Reading the material twice is the first step. Next, students need to do something active with the material, such as make their own notes about the material, create lists, write out words or concepts, practice math problems, or draw pictures or diagrams. Then the last one or two days of studying should involve memorizing the material. Parents can support students by helping them create study preparation materials and then quiz them during the memorization portion. Rewards can be utilized for good efforts for practicing these studying steps.

Preparing for quizzes and tests should be done soon after coming home from school, just like homework. Sometimes children or teens will want to study later in the evening, but this can be problematic. For children and teens on stimulants, their medications have probably worn off by then, so after dinner is not the best brain-functioning window. Also, later in the evening children and teens may be sleepy and less focused. Parents can also help with a quick study review in the morning on the quiz or test day, if possible. Finally, it will take time to help the student build the habit of preparing for and memorizing quiz and test materials several days ahead. However, if parents are firm, encouraging, and rewarding, this can be a new routine that is developed over time. Obviously, the earlier this is done the faster it will become ingrained.

ENCOURAGE READING AT HOME

For children and teens and even adults with ADHD, reading can be unpleasant and frustrating. ADHD, as well as learning disorders, visual processing disorders, and other conditions, can cause significant reading difficulties. Many of these children and teens avoid reading and do not develop the habit of reading for fun. The more severe the ADHD, and particularly if these other disorders are present, the more challenging reading can be. However, reading is a critical academic and life skill, and improves with practice. Children and teens should specifically understand how their disability affects their reading abilities. Fortunately, when these conditions are effectively treated, reading skills can improve. Additionally, most with ADHD will read more successfully when they take effective medication and before their stimulant effects diminish, usually before dinner.

Parents can take action steps to encourage reading at home to improve their skills. In addition to providing treatments, there are two main tasks for encouraging reading for those who do not like to read. The first is to get them reading almost anything. The second is to guide and motivate them to read materials at or just above their reading level, after they experience some success and improvements with reading. Students with ADHD who do like reading may be more comfortable reading materials for younger ages.

To facilitate reading, parents can give large rewards for leisure reading at home. Reading sessions may need to be broken down into smaller parts, and they can receive rewards for a certain number of pages or chapters completed, as well as when the book is finished. Sessions may need to be briefer initially, and slowly extended over time. Parents should provide lots of praise, attention, enthusiasm, and appealing rewards for reading increasingly more advanced magazines and books. Routines can be created where the child reads aloud to the parent before bed. Rewards and reading together routines can help create positive associations with reading as well. Parents can even read the same materials as the child to create their own book club, and this may open the door to discussions and better rapport. Additionally, parents should remember to practice reading before stimulants wear off, when reading is easier. Reading strategies and comprehension may improve as well from effective tutoring services (see the next section on tutoring).

When encouraging reading, parents should be cautious not to turn reading sessions into negative experiences for the child or teen, with excessive corrections or critical comments. Parents should also find reading materials that appeal to the child's interests. Going to the library and selecting books together can help with this, as well as providing a treat or reward after the library visit. Finally, the earlier the better when encouraging reading. Parents should begin these approaches as soon as possible and when reading reluctance first is noticed. It is never too late to start this encouragement, even if the adolescent is in high school.

TUTORING SERVICES

Some children and teens with ADHD may need extra learning assistance due to their academic struggles. Additionally, as stated previously, ADHD and learning disorders often co-exist. Some studies have found the prevalence to be 19 percent to 45 percent (Weyandt & Gudmundsdottir, 2015). In addition to ADHD, the sooner learning disorders, visual processing disorders, and other conditions that impact learning are detected and receive interventions, the better their progress. Reading problems are best addressed when detected at a young age, and this includes preschool, kindergarten and first grade. Early math and writing deficits should be addressed as well. For learning disorders, while there are no cures, neurofeedback can provide from minimal to significant improvements. The main treatments for learning disorders are longer-term individual remedial tutoring services from specialty tutors, use of compensatory strategies, and accommodations within an Individual Education Program (IEP).

Ideally, when there are greater learning needs, tutoring should occur during school and outside of the school. Tutors should have specific training and experience working with children who have ADHD or learning disorders. Tutors outside of schools could be a special education teacher in the local public-school system, professional tutors, or those within tutoring businesses. Depending on the severity of the learning deficits and conditions, external tutoring can require a commitment of two to three or more sessions per week for adequate progress to be made, and this may be for one or more years. Tutoring fees can be expensive (about $45 to $65 per one-hour session, or more), and experienced tutors may be difficult to find. However, they can accelerate the child's learning and may be especially critical if the in-school tutors are less effective or are infrequent. Also, some schools may have free tutoring before and after school, and some libraries or churches may also offer free tutoring. While non-specialist tutors may be acceptable for some children or teens with milder learning difficulties, these well-meaning tutors may not promote improvements for those with more serious learning conditions. Additionally, parents can monitor tutoring situations for safety, perform background checks, and stay nearby.

For some, tutoring can be challenging over time. Children who receive tutoring may resent or resist this, particularly if it is several times a week and for an extended period of time. Also, outside the school specialty tutors may give additional homework to help improve the remedial deficits and enhance learning and skills. This may add to the challenges and dislike of tutoring. However, despite the struggles, tutoring can be essential. Some larger tutoring businesses try to make it more fun and engaging. Rewards for cooperation and good efforts can help as well.

As previously discussed, school plans, services, and accommodations can be essential for the educational management of learning disorders and ADHD. When significant learning problems exist, parents should demand that the child's IEP include one-on-one tutoring services during school hours. Additionally, even if a child has an IEP and receives tutoring services, families should not assume that their child is receiving quality remedial instruction. Parents should monitor these services to ensure their child is receiving the actual time stated in the IEP, as well as the overall quality and progress of the school tutoring.

EDUCATIONAL THERAPISTS

For some children and teens with greater learning struggles, outside tutoring and IEPs will not be enough. While less common, educational therapists can address learning and scholastic difficulties further. Educational therapy is a more general term that refers to an educator who provides individual services usually outside of school. They often provide more intensive services than tutors or ADHD coaches to address a wider range of attention, learning, and school-related difficulties. They typically have more experience working with these challenges, and can address various school and learning difficulties that psychotherapists and neuropsychologists do not often address. These are professionals from a variety of backgrounds who work with children and teens who have learning disorders, ADHD, and other neurodevelopmental conditions that impact their academic and behavioral functioning at school. They can provide tutoring, skills development and training, and scholastic case management services. Educational therapists tend to utilize broader perspectives with learning challenges, and may coordinate and integrate information from providers and school staff to create more effective learning plans and results (Clark, 2014-2018).

Educational therapists usually work in private practices or learning centers outside of schools, and most health insurance plans do not cover their services. Their qualifications can vary, and they may or may not have a master's degree, certifications, or training in the field. Parents can obtain referrals for a therapist from the child's providers, or The Association of Educational Therapists (Clark, 2014-2018). This field does not have state licensing requirements, so finding an effective educational therapist may be challenging. When interviewing providers, parents can inquire about their credentials and experience, ask for client references they can speak with, and meet them in person to explore if they and their child like their personal style (Patino, 2014–2018).

WEEKLY ORGANIZATIONAL REVIEW

Each week, perhaps on Sundays, parents can do a brief organizational review with their child or teen for the upcoming week. This can include reviewing if there are quizzes, tests or projects due for the new week, as well as other non-school provider appointments, classes, or other activities. This could also be a time to clean and organize the book bag. Additionally, if getting ready in the morning is a challenge, parents and children can assemble their school outfits for the week to make mornings faster. Parents can purchase labels or write the days of the week on hangers in their closet.

ADHD CLASSROOM APPROACHES

The following are some classroom and teaching approaches for students with ADHD. If 504s or IEPs exist and these are incorporated into the official plans, then teachers may modify their styles and implement these enhancements. Some teachers may be open to or already use some of these approaches. However, when stated in official school plans, some teachers may struggle to make changes in their classroom, and may even refuse these practices. Teaching is a series of professional skills, and sometimes these can be difficult to alter over time, even with the best of intentions. If these are not listed in their school plans, parents can request that teachers utilize the approaches below.

1. Having a "best fit" teacher for students with ADHD will be important, although this may not always be possible. Teachers who work with students with ADHD and other conditions need a firm understanding of the disability. Also, certain teacher personalities and teaching styles will work better. Teachers who are highly engaging, interactive, warm, patient and understanding of disabilities will be the best matches. Stricter, disengaged, demanding and "my way only" teachers will be less effective.
2. Students with ADHD will have their own unique strengths and weaknesses, and may struggle with certain tasks more than others. Teachers should identify which tasks and abilities are more difficult for them,

and then accept and expect these as part of their disability. While teachers will be challenged to be more patient when these problems occur, they should not be surprised when they arise.

3. Teachers should maintain a highly structured classroom that utilizes clear and specific behavioral management systems and routines. They should frequently review the posted classroom expectations, including expected and unwanted behavior. Positive and negative classroom reinforcers should be delivered often and immediately to maximize their effectiveness (Flick, 1998).

4. Teachers can utilize a number of attractive rewards for positive classroom discipline, including praise, reduced or no homework coupons, playing games on a computer, additional recess time, free time in class, small prizes or toys, stickers for younger students, lunch with the teacher, free reading time, time using art or clay, leading a game, free pass from an in-class assignment, permission to bring an item for show and tell, being first in line, extra credit problems to raise grade, make up a question for an upcoming test, listening to music on headphones, and leaving for lunch early (Flick, 1998).

5. In addition to positive reinforcers, negative consequences are also important in effecttive classroom management. Research has shown that rewards-only programs are typically not impactful enough for students with ADHD. Teachers should use a hierarchy of negative consequences for unwanted behaviors that are known to students, parents and administrators (Rief, 2003).

6. Corrective consequences in class can start with quiet and mild approaches, such as the teacher standing close to the student, whispering a gentle warning or reminder, or the use of private in-class signals determined earlier with the student (Rief, 2003). Teachers can also use quiet reprimands to provide feedback for milder unwanted or off-task behaviors (Flick, 1998).

7. After warnings, stronger consequences can be used, including practicing do-overs (hand raising and waiting to be called upon after speaking out), owing time (paying with a loss of minutes from recess or after school), loss of a favorite activity, a time-out at a designated in-class area, completing a misbehavior form describing what they did and should do next time, and correcting a misbehavior (cleaning up a mess or apologizing to a peer) (Rief, 2003). A certain amount of annoying in-class behaviors may need to be ignored if possible, such as fidgeting, tapping, or humming (Flick, 1998).

8. Teachers can assist student with use of the homework notebook system, including recording homework assignments and upcoming tests. If this system is not utilized, teachers can support homework efforts

with reminders to record assignments and additional requests for homework that is not submitted.

9. Teachers can encourage students to approach the teachers' desks frequently when they have questions, are confused, or need assistance. This expectation should be discussed at the start of the year, and praise should be provided to remove any stigma about this.
10. Teachers should assign only one task or give one direction at a time. Instructions should also be clear and brief (Hallowell & Ratey, 2011).
11. To reduce being overwhelmed, teachers can instruct students to divide complex or large assignments into small tasks and encourage doing one step at a time. This can make the task more manageable (Flick, 1998). For example, if two pages of math problems are assigned, they can give one page at a time. The assignments can be varied as well, giving more breaks with certain subjects or mixing more difficult assignments with easier ones. Before the student begins homework at home, parents can help them divide each subject into smaller parts as well.
12. Students can also be taught other academic and homework organizational skills, such as effective use of a daily school planner.
13. Teachers should strive for quality rather than quantity in workloads. Students with ADHD often need reduced homework and schoolwork (Hallowell & Ratey, 2011).
14. The student should be seated near the teacher, aide, or students who provide good examples. They should not be near windows or other distractions, such as noisy air conditions or high traffic areas. Research has found that four wall classrooms and seating arrangements of the traditional rows of desks are better for students with ADHD than sharing a table or more open and noisier classrooms (Flick, 1998).
15. Teachers should give students more frequent feedback and repeat directions to help them stay on track (Hallowell & Ratey, 2011). Praise should be given when the student is on-task. They can provide students with frequent prompts, previews, redirections, and reminders. The use of visual and auditory reminders (whichever is better for the student) can also be helpful, including the use of written lists.
16. Teachers can improve attention to lectures and directions by making more frequent eye contact (Hallowell & Ratey, 2011). Additionally, when students are given instructions and directions, they can be taught to review and repeat these before beginning. This can help reduce their impulse to start without fully understanding the task (Flick, 1998). The student can also be asked to repeat the directions to the teacher quietly at their desk to insure comprehension.

17. Students should be taught study skills to improve quiz and test scores.
18. School staff can remind the student of upcoming transitions during the school day, including lunch, change of classes, and recess.
19. Teachers should watch for rising stimulation and frustration levels, and intervene quickly. Students with ADHD should be encouraged to take bathroom or in-classroom breaks when they experience stress (Hallowell & Ratey, 2011). The use of emotional management skills at school can assist with this.
20. Parents and teachers can ask students how they best learn new material because they can often articulate their learning preferences (Hallowell & Ratey, 2011). Additionally, teachers should use multimodal and activity-based learning as much as possible because students with ADHD often learn best this way.
21. Teachers and parents can instruct students to actively use outlines and underlining of keywords to help maintain attention and a sense of mastery (Hallowell & Ratey, 2011). Additionally, to improve their focus while working on math problems, students can circle each problem they are working on and put a check next to each one and then the page when finished.
22. Teachers can reduce the amount of copying from the board or written work if these are difficult for the student.
23. Besides written forms, teachers can allow students to use oral demonstrations of their knowledge when possible.
24. Teachers can routinely assist and support students in cleaning and organizing their school desk and locker, with a designated day once a week or month.
25. Teachers should provide students with additional time to complete assignments and tests, including extra time for checking for errors.
26. Student can be permitted regular access to a quiet place in class to take tests, complete classwork, or take breaks. Similarly, teachers can permit and encourage more frequent breaks during class, including regular motor breaks for hyperactivity (such as every 20 to 30 minutes, or when prompted).

COLLABORATION WITH OTHERS

Finally, in addition to school staff, it can be helpful to inform important others in the child's life about their ADHD and other conditions. Aside from pediatricians and health care providers, this can include day care staff, sports coaches, after-school clubs or activity leaders, providers of music or other lessons, scout leaders, and other adults who regularly interact with the child.

Informing others can assist parents to be the best advocates for their children with disabilities.

Some parents can be hesitant or concerned about disclosing this information. There are pros and cons to disclosing, and to not disclosing diagnoses. They may not want their child labeled or treated differently, which is understandable. Others may not respond appropriately or optimally to these disclosures. While it is helpful to use discretion about who is told, the benefits of informing others can outweigh the detriments. There is a balance between parents assisting others to best support a child with special needs, and letting the child lead as normal a life as possible. Disclosures to others may depend on how severe the ADHD is, how important it is to explain their quirks and social difficulties, and if their behavior worsens later in the day due to dwindling stimulant effects. These disclosures can assist other adults to better interpret the child's difficulties as related to a disorder. These other adults may appreciate this honesty as well.

SUMMARY POINTS

- Parents should partner effectively with school staff and important others to address and manage student's challenges.
- Specific study skills should be taught to students by parents, teachers, and tutors.
- Parents can utilize specific approaches to encourage reading at home.
- Tutoring services and educational therapists outside of the school can be utilized to address and enhance academic difficulties.
- There are specific ADHD classroom and instructional approaches that teachers can use.

REFERENCES

Clark, A. (2014–1018). *Educational therapy: What you need to know.* Retrieved from https://www.understood.org/en/learning-attentioin-issues/treatments-approaches/therapies/what-you-need-to-know-about-educational-therapy

Flick, G. (1998). *ADD/ADHD behavior-change resource kit.* San Francisco, CA: Jossey-Bass.

Hallowell, E., & Ratey, J. (2011). *Driven to distraction* (revised). New York: Anchor Books.

Patino, E. (2014–2018). *10 things to look for in an educational therapist.* Retrieved from https://www.understood.org/en/learning-attention-issues/treatments-approaches/therapies/checklist-10-things-to-look-for-in-an-educational-therapist

Rief, S. F. (2003). *The ADHD book of lists.* San Francisco, CA: Jossey-Bass.

Weyandt, L. L., & Gudmundsdottir, B. G. (2015). Developmental and neuropsychological deficits in children with ADHD (116-139). In R. Barkley (Ed.), *Attention deficit hyperactivity disorder: A handbook for diagnosis and treatment* (4th ed., pp. 116–139). New York, NY: Guilford Press.

Chapter 12

MEDICATION TREATMENT FOR ADHD

Medication is often the most critical element in effective ADHD treatment. Because ADHD is a neurobiological brain-functioning disorder, proper ADHD medication can temporarily but significantly correct and improve the condition. While many parents are initially skeptical and resistant to using medications, the right medication and dose can dramatically change lives. Many studies and decades of use have significantly demonstrated that ADHD medications can improve attention and focus, impulsivity, distractibility, academic abilities, homework productivity and accuracy, memory, moods, handwriting deficits, aggression, frustration tolerance, social problems, non-compliance, disruptive behavior, and oppositional traits.

The following psychiatric medication information is intended to provide basic information about the ADHD medication treatment process. Specific questions or issues about medication use should be directed towards prescribing physicians.

THE DIFFERENCES BETWEEN PSYCHIATRISTS AND PSYCHOLOGISTS

Some parents may not understand the difference between these providers. The treatments they offer are different, and sometimes parents are unclear why they are referred to both types of providers. Psychiatrists are medical doctors who prescribe psychiatric medication for psychological and some neurodevelopmental conditions, including ADHD. Most psychiatrists do not provide therapy. Only some are board certified to work with children or adolescents, and there are fewer psychiatrists who work with children and teens than adults.

Additionally, psychiatrist sessions tend to be much shorter than behavioral health therapists and clinical psychologists, and their focus is mostly on medication issues. The sessions usually last 10 to 20 minutes and most are not designed to be therapy sessions. In a typical psychiatrist session, they may ask how the medication is working, are there changes with the ADHD symptoms, and are there any recent side effects. They can also address sleep issues, mood difficulties, and other co-existing psychiatric and behavioral conditions with other medications. Psychiatrists typically do not address in detail how families can improve academic issues, behavioral difficulties at home, behavior management approaches, and other ADHD-related difficulties. Generally, psychiatrists tend to refer families to therapists to address these non-medication topics. However, some psychiatrists will spend longer than 15 minutes and may provide sessions with greater focus on ADHD-related issues.

Licensed advanced practice psychiatric nurses or psychiatric mental health advanced practice registered nurses typically have masters or doctorate degrees, and can also prescribe psychiatric medications. Some may work in offices along with psychiatrists.

Clinical psychologists are doctors of psychology and not medical doctors. Clinical psychologists have their doctorates in clinical or counseling psychology, and a smaller percentage have their doctorate degrees in educational psychology as well. While they can be knowledgeable about psychiatric medications, unless they are specially trained, most are not permitted to prescribe medications. Generally, clinical psychologists provide evaluations, psychological assessments, and individual and/or family therapy sessions. Most of their therapy sessions last between 30 to 60 minutes, with 45 minutes as an average. Another difference is psychiatrists tend to work with children and teens with ADHD on a longer-term basis, sometimes for years, because those with ADHD often require medications on a long-term basis. However, psychologists and mental health therapists may provide services that are shorter and last a few months to one or two years. Individuals with more complex presentations and severe disorders may receive therapy services for longer periods.

Because clinical psychologists are trained to provide psychological testing and typically have longer sessions than psychiatrists, they may have more of a diagnostic focus in their work, particularly initially. Psychiatrists, clinical psychologists, licensed mental health therapists and primary care physicians can all diagnose individuals with mental health conditions. However, clinical psychologists can be particularly effective with complex presentations and are the only clinicians who provide full psychological testing. Clinical psychologists can help to accurately determine if a child has true ADHD, other psychological conditions, or a combination of these.

While clinical psychologists are one of a number of providers called psychotherapists, all licensed mental health therapists and counselors are not the same regarding their backgrounds, degrees, and training. Clinical psychologists graduate from four to five-year graduate programs after college. Additionally, in many states, another year of supervised work is required after the doctorate before they are eligible for licensure. Besides clinical psychologists, there are a number of types of mental health therapists that have master's degrees, including counselors in psychology, social workers, and marriage and family therapists, and certain clinical nurse specialists. These providers are typically from two-year graduate programs after college, and in some states an additional year of supervised work is required, before they are eligible for licensure. School psychologists typically graduate from two or four-year graduate programs and will have a master's degree or doctorate in school psychology. Their ability to provide services outside school settings is limited and different from mental health therapists.

Often, children and teens with ADHD and/or other conditions can benefit from the services of both psychiatrists and psychologists. The most effective treatment approach is medication and therapy services. For more complex diagnostic presentations, higher level ADHD, or other psychological difficulties, children and adolescents often require services from both providers since medication and therapy services work in different ways. Lastly, effective medications and doses can deliver critical biochemical balancing so that therapy and school services can work most effectively.

ADHD MEDICATION MAY BE NECESSARY

Many families are initially against medication for ADHD treatment. Some do not want their children taking chemicals that may cause concerning side effects. Others do not want children to become "dependent" on medication to function, while others do not want the stigma of medication. The process can be expensive and time consuming as well. Yet, particularly for moderate to severe ADHD, these conditions may require medication for healthy functioning. Therapy for those with ADHD cannot teach individuals how to pay attention, focus more or to become less hyperactive. School accommodations can help reduce the work load and academic demands, but cannot improve the source of the concentration and behavioral problems. Because ADHD is a brain functioning condition, effective ADHD medications can go to the source of the neurobiological imbalance and temporarily correct the brain-functioning issues. Besides neurofeedback and certain supplement approaches (such as the Walsh Biochemical approach), there are no treatments besides medication that can go to the source of the brain difficulties and correct them. With effective medication, those with ADHD can enjoy their abilities, talents, and intelligence that are often lost in the fog.

Many families who have children and teens with higher-level ADHD who are not using medications often experience continuing problems. As they become increasingly more desperate, they may start to believe there is little to lose in trying medications. Also, some families with children and teens with ADHD who were initially against medication may eventually try it after less successful use of behavioral management training as well. Many children and teens who have milder ADHD could benefit from medication, yet parents may be less motivated to try this unless they have serious academic problems. If families are willing to spend the time, money and effort to try these treatments, they may see positive results. There are no contracts with using ADHD medications. If they do not work, families can discontinue this approach under the prescribing physician's care.

PROS AND CONS OF USING AND NOT USING MEDICATION

The best practices treatment for moderate to severe ADHD is to obtain both parent behavioral management therapy and medication. However, it was reported that 32 percent of children and teens diagnosed with ADHD received both of these, while 30 percent received only medication and 15 percent received behavioral treatment alone (Center for Disease Control and Prevention, 2018).

Families should know that there are pros and cons to using medication, and there also are pros and cons to *not* using medication. When medication is first mentioned, many parents initially will say "We are against medication." While this is a choice, not medicating is also a choice, and this can have ramifications. A decision not to use medication can have serious consequences regarding academic performance, social functioning with family members and peers, and overall quality of life. Despite its flaws, medication can be a humane approach to correcting a life disability. For people who have moderate to severe ADHD, it can dramatically change their lives for the better. Many success stories exist, particularly when the right medication at the right dose have been used.

There is increasing evidence that suggests that the ADHD stimulant medication methylphenidate (the generic name for Ritalin and Concerta), can even create longer-term brain enhancements. These improvements impact the brain's neuroplasticity and can be seen in neuroimaging. Neuroplasticity is the brain's ability to reorganize nerve cell connections to adjust and respond to learning, illnesses, and injuries, including ADHD. Methylphenidate medication seems to improve these neuroplastic processes, and its long-term use seems to improve aspects of brain functioning over time (Kasparek, Theiner, & Filova, 2015).

PEDIATRICIANS VS PSYCHIATRISTS FOR ADHD MEDICATION TREATMENTS

Receiving services from a child or adolescent psychiatrist who has experience in treating ADHD can be the best way to receive medication treatment. While pediatricians and family practice physicians are permitted to prescribe psychiatric medications, working with a psychiatrist can be more effective since they are specialists in psychiatric medication treatment. Also, there seems to be an increasing trend for pediatricians or non-psychiatrist physicians to refer patients to psychiatrists because they may not want the liability of prescribing these medications. However, pediatricians who have particular interests in treating ADHD or have been successful in treating patients with ADHD may also be effective psychiatric medication prescribers. Also, in more rural areas with limited access to psychiatrists, pediatricians and family practice physicians may be the only options.

One of the limitations with some pediatricians prescribing ADHD medications is that they may be too cautious in their prescribing. They tend to under-medicate with doses that do not have enough therapeutic effectiveness. Unfortunately, this can result in mild or no improvements. Sadly, families may falsely believe that medication doesn't work for their child and is not an option. Psychiatrists are more familiar with these medications and tend to utilize more effective doses over time. If children and teens are experiencing difficulties in obtaining positive results from ADHD medications with non-psychiatrists, and particularly if they have multiple medical and/or psychological conditions, then parents should consider visiting a child or adolescent psychiatrist.

UNDERSTANDING HOW THE ADHD MEDICATION PRESCRIBING PROCESS WORKS

When receiving ADHD medication treatment, families should understand how the process works. Typically, the child or teen is usually first prescribed a low dose. Different ADHD medications can come in a variety of forms, including tablet, capsule, patch, or liquid. Over time the dose is raised progressively until the best effect is achieved. Because every person is biochemically unique, no one exactly knows how a person will respond to psychiatric medications until they are tried. If the first medication does not work or the side effects are too intense, another medication will be attempted. This process can take months of trying medications and slowly raising the doses for each until a therapeutic level is reached. Combinations of medications may be attempted as well. In the future it will probably be routine to first obtain special testing to determine which medications and doses will be most effective, but currently this is not the case. Fortunately, often the first or second medication will show results immediately. Positive stimulant medications effects should be observed the day the medication is taken. At present, there are more than twelve medications for ADHD. Sadly, some parents are not aware of this trial and error process, and can become frustrated and stop the medication treatment process too soon before finding one that worked.

The parent's job is to work with the prescribing physician to report information about the medication, including side effects and if ADHD symptoms are decreasing. The physicians are not at home and school with the child, so feedback is necessary. Sometimes families feel rushed with brief visits with prescribing physicians, and may not be assertive with their doctors to discuss their concerns. To improve this situation, families should make lists of medication topics they wish to discuss, and should not feel pressured to rush through sessions. Also, using a medication diary may be helpful in tracking when the medication was given, when it wore off, any unwanted side effects, and how behaviors were impacted before the stimulant medication effects wear off. Teachers, daycare workers, and other adults can be approached for feedback on the medication as well. A medication diary can be particularly useful during the first few months when new medications are being used.

Due to biochemical individuality, each medication is experienced differently, and so there can be a range of results and side effects. Side effects may or may not occur. Fortunately, for many number people, these often decrease over two to four weeks as the body adjusts to the medication. However, some side effects can be immediate, severe, and intolerable. In these cases, that particular medication will not be a good match, and parents can contact the prescribing physician to discuss ceasing the medication and trying another.

THE TYPES OF ADHD MEDICATIONS

There are various types of ADHD medications. While there are a number of stimulant medications, most can be classified as either a methylphenidate-based stimulant (brand names Ritalin, Concerta, Daytrana, Focalin, Metadate), or a methamphetamine-based stimulant (brand names Adderall and Dexedrine). Please refer to Tables 1 and 2 at the end of the chapter for more information on these medications.

Within each class, the various stimulants differ based on slightly different chemical compositions, how rapidly they work, and how long their effects last. About 75 percent of children with ADHD will receive good results from a methylphenidate stimulant. For those children that do not, about 75 percent of these children will have a positive response to a methamphetamine stimulant (Lougy, DeRuvo, & Rosenthal, 2007). This means that a high percentage of children with ADHD will respond to these medications. Additionally, stimulants are a day-by-day medication. They only work the day they are taken, and many stop working by the later afternoon or evening.

Stimulants differ in how long they are effective. They can be short-acting (or immediate release) with effects that can last from four to six hours, intermediate-acting (or sustained release), and long-acting (or extended release) which can last from 8 to 14 hours. The long-acting medications are the most popular because they are only one dose, but some children and teens may experience better results from the shorter cycle stimulants that require multiple doses per day. Some children and teens are prescribed a second lower dose in addition to their main morning medication. This is sometimes called the "homework dose" and is typically taken in the mid-afternoon to extend the stimulant effects through the later afternoon to help the student after school.

Another type of ADHD medication that is not a stimulant is atomoxetine (brand name Strattera). After an effective daily dose is prescribed, it can take four to eight weeks for results to be observed, but some symptoms may improve before this time. Once it begins working, it is effective all-day long. The downside of this medication is that while it can be effective for some, it tends to work less frequently than stimulants. Also, doses cannot be skipped or missed. This medication takes time to build up in a person's system before it becomes effective. If doses are missed, or worse if it is taken inconsistently, it will be less effective or not at all.

There are other medications used to treat ADHD. Bupropion (brand name Wellbutrin) is an antidepressant that can also have ADHD reducing and stimulant-like properties. It has been used with adolescents and adults, but not often with children. Its effectiveness with ADHD is also lower than stimulants. The alpha-agonist medications of guanfacine (brand name Tenex or Intuniv) and clonidine (brand name Catapress) are blood pressure medications. These can be sedating and helpful for some with ADHD, and have been used in combination with stimulants. They have been shown to lower impulsivity, hyperactivity, insomnia, aggression, tics, and ODD behaviors (Lougy, DeRuvo, & Rosenthal, 2007), while guanfacine but not clonidine has been shown to also improve inattention. Clonidine may also increase the stimulant effectiveness. Please refer to Table 3 at the end of the chapter for more information on non-stimulant medications.

THE RIGHT MEDICATION AT THE RIGHT DOSE

Finding the right medication and dose for each person is one of the most essential aspects for this treatment to work effectively. While this may seem obvious, many families do not persist in trying all the available ADHD medications because the first or second did not work. There are more than twelve ADHD medications available. Sometimes parents will say "we tried ADHD meds but they did not work." When questioned about this, most will say they only tried one or two medications. Persistence and patience are the keys when exploring these treatments. Once again, because everyone is unique, medications working differently for each person. If the available medication options are not tried, then is will remain unclear what could help.

In addition to the proper medication, finding the correct dose that is not too high and not too low is critical. If the dose is too low, then the symptoms may show only mild or no improvement. However, if there is mild improvement, this is a positive sign that the medication may be a good match for the person, and often is an indication that the dose should be raised. If the stimulant dose is too high, then the child or teen may appear highly irritable, overly sensitive, excessively emotional, robotic or mechanical, withdrawn, and/or experience increased ADHD symptoms. Also, the most effective dose may change over time, and the dose may need to be adjusted periodically. Typically, by middle adolescence doses tend to stabilize and do not need further changes. It has also been shown that those with Inattentive ADHD do not respond to medication as well as those with Combined ADHD.

ADHD MEDICATION SIDE EFFECTS

Unpleasant side effects can result from ADHD medications. The most common stimulant side effects include insomnia, lowered appetite (particularly at lunch), mild stomach distress, mild headaches, and a rebound effect. The rebound effect occurs when stimulants rapidly wear off, and irritability and worsening of ADHD symptoms results. Typically, this rebound effect lasts from 30 to 60 minutes, and tends to occur during evenings (Lougy, DeRuvo, & Rosenthal, 2007). The most common side effects of the non-stimulant medication atomoxetine can be upset stomach, insomnia, sleepiness, decreased appetite, and irritability. Guanfacine and clonidine can cause dry mouth, dizziness, drowsiness, headaches, and sedation. Guanfacine may produce less of these than clonidine.

One of the most concerning side effects from stimulant medications has been possible stunted growth. Initial studies in the 1970s reported reductions in the height of children who took stimulants. Since then additional studies have reported mixed results, with no significant growth changes to lower growth findings. Growth deficits may differ based on the child's age of starting the medication, the type, and duration of use. Stimulant use greater than three years in the pre-teen years may be associated with decreased height throughout adolescence. One longitudinal, population-based study examined adults who used ADHD stimulants as children who were born between 1976 to 1982. This research found that ADHD stimulant medication use was not associated with significant changes in growth or height later in adulthood (Harstad et al., 2014).

Some clinicians and parents may expect that ADHD stimulant medications will cause sleep difficulties for children and teens. Indeed, some studies have reported that stimulants have caused trouble falling asleep, shorter sleep duration, and night awakenings. However, other studies investigating this topic have produced mixed results, some with no sleep impairment findings. Additionally, sleep problems and insomnia may be the result of the restlessness from the rebound effect. There have been studies showing that a second or third stimulant dose taken in the later afternoon or early evening to avoid the rebound effect produced significant delays falling asleep. Some children can sleep easily after a few hours or less of taking a stimulant, while others may require 6 to 8 or more hours after the last dose was taken to fall asleep (Khoury & Doghramji, 2015).

DO NOT TAKE STIMULANTS WITH ORANGE AND CITRUS JUICES OR CAFFEINATED DRINKS

Families should be aware that stimulant medications should not be taken with orange juice, citrus juices or fruits, or vitamin C supplements (including multivitamins). These can prevent the absorption and hasten the urination of the medication, and therefore lessen their effectiveness. Children and teens taking stimulants should not take these juices or fruits one hour before and after the medication is taken. Also, caffeinated beverages can impair the effectiveness and stability of stimulants, as well as negatively impact sleep at night. Therefore, caffeinated drinks are not recommended for children and teens with ADHD.

BE AWARE OF THE CLOCK WHEN USING STIMULANTS

Stimulant medications typically show their effects after about 15 to 60 minutes of taking the medication. Stimulants only work on the days they are taken, and only during certain time periods before they wear off. This means that the medication will not reduce the ADHD symptoms early in the morning before it becomes active, or in the evening after the medication has stopped working. Sometimes parents will say they are unaware of how or when the ADHD medication is working because they do not have exposure to their children during school days. Usually, the most effective window for the medications during the week will be during the school day, and most stimulant effects wear off by dinner time, unless it is atomoxetine. Thus, parents should monitor the child or teen on weekends to see how effective the medication is. If the child does not take medication on weekends, parents will miss this opportunity.

Caregivers should pay attention to when the medicine stops working for the day. Since stimulants generally work soon after they are taken in the morning until later afternoon or by dinner time, children and teens on ADHD medications should not do homework or study after dinner because the medication has probably worn off by then. Similarly, parents should be aware that when they are not taking medication or when the medication has worn off, reading, chores and other projects may be more difficult for them. Parents can easily forget this and become annoyed when the challenges emerge. If children and teens are not taking ADHD medications during summers, weekends or holidays, then parents should be mindful that various activities as well as attending religious, social and family events, may be more difficult for them. As part of a long-term management and acceptance strategy, parents should know the approximate time when stimulants wear off so they can anticipate the returning ADHD symptoms. Keeping a medication journal can help track how long stimulants tend to work.

Too often parents only think about medication in terms of the school day and improving their school functioning. When they are off medications, many children and teens can have increased behavioral and social difficulties and oppositional behaviors. Sometimes prescribing physicians will tell parents that the medications are optional when the child or teen is not in school (weekends, holidays, and summers). These are sometimes called "medication holidays." However, for children and teens who have moderate to severe ADHD, as well as ODD, parents should observe their child's performance, social functioning, and behavior when they are off medication. If there are persistent difficulties, parents may consider giving the stimulants daily and discuss this with the prescribing physician.

MEDICATIONS FOR TREATING SLEEP PROBLEMS

Curiously, some clinicians have reported that on occasion a small dose of methylphenidate taken before bed can help facilitate sleep. While this would not help all children, it seems to be a robust clinical finding for some (Konofal, Lecendreux, & Cortese, 2010). Melatonin, an over-the-counter dietary supplement in the United States that is a regulated drug in Europe, has been found to be effective in reducing falling asleep difficulties in children with ADHD (Hvolby, 2015). For those taking stimulants, melatonin administered at bedtime has been found to lessen the time it takes to fall asleep and sleep duration, but not daytime behavioral problems. The medications clonidine, guanfacine, trazodone, diphenhydramine, cyproheptadine, mirtazapine, and trycyclic antidepressants have all been used to treat insomnia, but with mixed results (Spruyt & Gozal, 2011). While trazodone, antihistamines, mirtazapine, and hypnotic agents have been used to treat children and adolescents with ADHD and insomnia, these have not been approved usage and are not part of current clinical practice guidelines. Clonidine has also been suggested to address stimulant-associated falling asleep delays (Hvolby, 2015).

MEDICATIONS THAT STOP WORKING

Unfortunately, ADHD medications that were working well can suddenly or gradually stop working. This phenomenon can occur with other psychiatric medications as well. This can be quite frustrating and confusing for families. The prescribing physician will need to address this, and other medications may be attempted. If the stimulants work sometimes but not consistently, and fluctuate in their effectiveness, then an underlying mood disorder may exist and should be investigated (Lougy, DeRuvo, & Rosenthal, 2007). Additionally, parents should explore if the medication has been taken erratically or not at all. Sometimes it may seem like medications are not working, but this can result from parents who are inconsistent in their medication administration, or when children or teens stop taking them.

CREATE MEDICATION ROUTINES AND MONITOR MEDICATION ADMINISTRATION

Parents can create special routines to manage how children and teens take their daily medications. Consistently taking medication is a routine, and families should find ways to remember this each morning. This can be particularly difficult for parents who are out of the house in the early morning and are not at home to supervise the medication administration. Families may place the medication by the parent's coffeemaker so they will remember, and others put it in an obvious place in the bathroom where it will be easily seen.

Some parents expect that older children and teens should be responsible for taking their own ADHD medication. This however can be a set-up for not consistently taking medications because ADHD causes memory problems and forgetfulness, particularly during hectic or drowsy mornings, and when the medication hasn't been taken yet. Also, some children and teens may resent their ADHD medications. They may feel that the medication is a reminder that they are "crazy," or something is wrong with them. They may be tired of taking the meds, dislike doctor visits, or might hate the side effects. As a result, they may fake taking these and throw them out, or just say they took them when they didn't. Some teens even give or sell stimulants to peers. Therefore, parents should know the limits of what their children and teens can handle regarding taking medications consistently, and if it is realistic to expect them to take these on their own. If there are concerns with this, it is recommended that one parent commits to the managing and monitoring these each day, regardless of the teen's age.

YOUNG CHILDREN AND ADHD MEDICATION

The number of preschool age children in the United States diagnosed with ADHD between 2007–08 and 2011–12 increased 56 percent. Additionally, the number of children ages 2 to 5 who took ADHD medication doubled. The American Academy of Pediatrics stated that the best practices first line treatment for preschoolers with ADHD should be behavioral therapy. Yet since 2001, nearly half of these preschoolers have not received therapy services. One concern is that preschool children are receiving medications for ADHD, while many of these drugs have not been approved for younger children. Further, preschool children who use these medications may demonstrate greater side effects, including sleep problems, irritability, and lethargy (Novotney, 2015).

Indeed, the Centers for Disease Control and Prevention (CDC) has urged health care providers to refer parents of young children ages 2 to 5 with ADHD to receive behavior therapy before they are prescribed medications. In one of their studies, after reviewing healthcare claims of at least five million children ages 2 to 5 with Medicaid and about one million young children with employer-sponsored health insurance, about 75 percent of young children treated for ADHD received medication, while only about half of these children received non-medication psychological treatment services. Further, the percentage of children with ADHD receiving non-medication psychological services has not increased over time. The CDC has asked that physicians, nurses, and allied health professionals who work with young children with ADHD to explain the benefits of behavior therapy and refer parents for this training (APA Practice Central, 2016).

One research study indicated that the effectiveness of medication for children ages 3 to 5 with ADHD showed mixed results. Children with severe symptoms who received low doses of methylphenidate showed a marked decrease in symptoms when compared to the placebo group. However, almost one third of parents shared that their children experienced moderate to severe side effects, including loss of appetite, insomnia, emotional outbursts, weight loss, and anxiety. Also, the medicated children weighed about three pounds less and grew about one-half inch less in height than would be expected. Eleven percent of the participants left the study because the side effects were intolerable (Smith, 2011).

Generally, it is recommended that psychiatric medications are not used for children under age six. Therefore, pediatricians and child psychiatrists may suggest behavioral therapy before medication is attempted. While medications can be effective and even necessary for young children with higher levels of ADHD, this should occur after a comprehensive assessment (Novotney, 2015). Younger children who are aggressive or have more severe forms of hyperactivity and impulsivity may require medications because they can be a danger to themselves or others. Young children with higher levels of impulsivity and hyperactivity can suddenly leave their homes, run into traffic, and make sudden dangerous choices such as playing with knives, fire, or other hazardous objects.

The American Academy of Pediatrics' Clinical Practice Guidelines for the Diagnosis, Evaluation, and Treatment of children and adolescents with ADHD stated that for children ages 4 to 5 with ADHD, the primary care clinician or pediatrician should recommend evidence-based parent and/or teacher administered behavior therapy as the first treatment. Medications should be prescribed if the behavior interventions do not provide significant improvements and if there are continued moderate to severe disturbances in the child's functioning. For children ages 6 to 11 with ADHD, medication and evidence-based parent and/or teacher administered behavior therapy are the preferred recommendations. Finally, for adolescents ages 12 to 18 with ADHD, the preferred treatments are medication and behavior therapy (American Academy of Pediatrics, 2011).

A large challenge in more rural areas is access to mental health therapists who can provide effective behavioral treatment. Prescribing physicians in rural areas can feel pressure to aid families struggling with younger children who have behavioral problems, and this often translates to prescribing medications. While research has increasingly suggested that behavioral treatments for ADHD are very effective for preschool age children, it can be difficult to find qualified child behavioral health therapists, particularly in non-urban areas. Further, pediatricians and child psychiatrists may not be trained or do not have practices designed to provide behavioral interventions for children.

SUMMARY POINTS

- Psychiatrists are physicians who provide psychiatric medication treatment services.
- Clinical psychologists provide evaluations, psychological testing assessments, and psychotherapy. Most do not prescribe medications.
- There are pros and cons to using and not using psychiatric medications. Moderate to severe ADHD often requires medication treatment because it is a neurobiological condition.
- Parents, children, and teens should understand the medication process may require trying different medications, adjusting doses, and experiencing some side effects.
- There are different types of ADHD medications. Many are stimulant based, but not all.
- Families should understand that everyone will differ in their responses to medications. The goal is to find the right one at the right dose.
- Stimulants only work the day they are taken, are active for a certain number of hours, and typically stop working by dinner.
- Families need to create effective medication routines and parents should monitor this daily process.
- ADHD medications may be less effective for children under age 6. Behavioral therapies should be attempted first in many cases before medication.

TABLE 1: METHYLPHENIDATE-BASED MEDICATIONS FOR ADHD

Medication	Form	Dose/Schedule	Dose Range	Onset/duration	Most Common Side Effects	Pro	Precautions
Methylphenidate (MPH)	tablets 5, 10, 20 mg IR chewable 2.5, 5, 10 mg IR liquid	Usually given two or three times a day. Begin 5 mg early AM & noon.	Child: 5-45 mg Adoles: 10-60mg Adults: 20-80mg	onset: 15-20 min duration: 4 hrs max	Decreased appetite, decreased sleep, less common: headaches, stomach aches, irritability, weight loss, tics, "rebound." Can overstimulate or make too calm if dose is too strong. These are true for all stimulants in Tables 1 and 2.	EVERY MEDICINE IN THIS TABLE IS (MPH) METHYLPHENIDATE BASED Methylphenidate is the generic name of all these. Works quickly, effective often. The most studied. Little to no lab testing needed. Good safety history.	Caution if history of tics or Tourette's or high blood pressure or heart problems. Controlled substance. Must hand write all scripts, no refills, no call ins. True for all stimulants in Tables 1 and 2.
Ritalin Methylin	5 mg/5ml 10 mg/5ml IR					Methylin has no dye, is very small, and comes in grape chewable and liquid.	
Focalin (dexmethylphenidate)	tablets 2.5, 5, 10mg IR			Focalin: 4-5 hrs. Focalin XR: 8 hrs.	Same as above.	Focalin is a refined isomer form which may be better tolerated and smoother.	Some kids get "meaner" with stimulants, especially amphetamines in Table 2.
Focalin XR	Focalin XR comes in 5, 10, 15, 20, 25, 30, 35, 40mg						

continued

TABLE 1—Continued

Medication	Form	Dose/Schedule	Dose Range	Onset / duration	Most Common Side Effects	Pro	Precautions
methylphenidate-SR Ritalin-SR Methylin ER Metadate ER	tablet 10mg SR 20mg SR 10mg ER 20mg ER	Begin 10 or 20mg SR in AM, may need increase or noon dose. May need regular Ritalin to start in AM or extend duration to PM All 4 of these are time release tablets.	Child: 10-40 mg Adoles: 20-40 mg Adults: 20-80 mg	onset: 30-60 min duration: 5-8hrs	Decreased appetite, decreased sleep, less common: headaches, stomach aches, irritability, weight loss, tics, "rebound." Can overstimulate or make too calm if dose is too strong.	These are longer lasting versions of methylphenidate. Avoids noon dose, usually. Concerta is methylphenidate in a clever osmotic pressure release mechanism pill. Metadate CD uses a third mechanism to extend the duration and smooth the effect of methylphenidate. Metadate CD, Ritalin LA, Aptensio XR, and Focalin XR capsules can be pulled apart and sprinkled on food. Quillivant is a time release liquid while Quillichew is a chewable time release pill. Daytrana is a skin patch.	Caution if history of tics or Tourette's or high blood pressure or heart problems. Controlled substance. Must hand write all scripts, no refills, no call ins. True for all stimulants in Tables 1 and 2.
Concerta ER	18, 27, 36, 54mg	Once a day in AM	Child: 18-27 mg Adoles: 27-54 mg Adult: 36-72 mg	onset: 15-30 min duration: 8-10 hrs	Same as above.		
Metadate CD	10, 20, 30, 40, 50, 60mg CD capsule	These 2 are time release capsules	Child: 10-40 mg Adoles: 20-40 mg Adult: 20-60 mg	onset: 30 min duration: 6-8 hrs			Some kids get "meaner" with stimulants, especially amphetamines in Table 2.
Ritalin LA	10, 20, 30, 40mg capsules	Start 10-20mg AM Give once a day in AM Max is 60mg/d				Metadate CD is 30% IR + 70% ER Ritalin LA is 50% IR + 50% ER	

continued

TABLE 1—Continued

Medication	Form	Dose/Schedule	Dose Range	Onset / duration	Most Common Side Effects	Pro	Precautions
Quillivant XR	Liquid suspension 25mg/5ml (5mg/1ml)	Once a day in AM 10-20 mg start	10mg/d = 2 ml 20mg/d = 4 ml 30mg/d = 6 ml 40mg/d = 8 ml 50mg/d = 10 ml	onset: 30 min duration: 8-12 hours		The only time release liquid stimulant.	Comes as powder in bottle, add water, shake vigorously before each use. Refrigerate. Use dropper to measure. Brand only–2014
Quillichew ER	Chewable tablets 10, 20 mg scored 40 mg is not scored		Child: 10-40 mg Adoles: 10-60 Adult: 10-60	onset: 30-60 min. duration: 8-12 hours	Same as above	The only chewable extended release ADHD med Releases biphasic 30% IR + 70% ER	New formulation 2016 Brand only
Aptensio XR	Capsule 10, 15, 20, 30, 40, 50, 60 mg	Once a day in AM Start 10 mg	Child: 10-40 mg Adoles: 10-60 Adult: 10-60	onset: 30-45 min. duration: 8-12 hours	Same as above	Another capsule option. Can be sprinkled on food. 40% immediate (IR) and 60% delayed release.	New 2016 Brand only

continued

TABLE 1—Continued

Medication	Form	Dose/Schedule	Dose Range	Onset / duration	Most Common Side Effects	Pro	Precautions
Daytrana (methylphenidate transdermal system)	patch 10, 15, 20, or 30 mg/9 hours	One patch per day to hip in early a.m. Remove after 6 to 12 hours–9 hours is advised.	Child: 10-20 mg patch Adoles: 15-30 mg patch Adult: 15-30 mg	onset: 2 hours duration: 1-2 hours after patch removed	Same as above plus patch may irritate skin.	Although not designed to be cut, patch can be cut to lessen dosage. Avoids oral dosing. Should cover school day and longer. Duration can be adjusted by time patch is put on and removed. May be smoother. Patch can be removed early to shorten duration.	Slow onset. Patch may come off accidentally. Patch may rarely lastingly discolor skin. Even low dose patch may be too strong for a child. Brand only

Note: This table is intended to be a summary guide, not a full and complete list.
Source: Created by Kevin Leehey, M.D., August 2016 • www.leeheymd.com. Retrieved from www.leeheymd.com/charts/adhd_1.html

TABLE 2: AMPHETAMINE-BASED MEDICATIONS FOR ADHD

Medication	Form	Dose/Schedule	Dose Range	Onset / duration	Most Common Side Effects	Pro	Precautions
Dexedrine (dextroamphetamine)	tablet (scored) IR 5mg 10mg	Same as Ritalin	Child: 2.5-30 mg Adoles: 10-45 mg Adults: 10-60 mg	onset: 30 min duration: 4-5 hrs	Similar to Ritalin (MPH) See pg. 1	Stronger and longer effect than Ritalin (MPH). Some people do better with amphetamines. Generic available.	Precautions same as Ritalin (MPH) but more so regarding growth, heart, blood pressure, tics, speedy, agitation, anger and abuse.
Dexedrine-SR	Spansules SR 5mg 10mg 15mg	Begin 5mg in early AM. May only need once a day. May need regular Dexedrine in AM to start effect early, or afternoon dose to extend effect in afternoon.	Child: 5-15 mg Adoles: 10-30 mg Adult: 10-40 mg	onset: 30-60 min duration: 6-8 hrs	Similar to MPH-Pg. 1 Less rebound in longer lasting medicines.	Avoids noon dose, usually. Generic available.	Inappropriately, Dr. Leehey believes, all amphetamines are FDA approved down to age 3, while milder MPH is only approved down to age 6.
Adderall dextroamphetamine and amphetamine	tablet (scored) 5, 7.5, 10, 12.5, 15, 20, 30mg IR	1 or 2 times a day. XR may be once a day.	Child: 5-30 mg XR 10-20mg Adoles: 10-40 mg XR 10-30mg	IR onset: 30 min duration: 4-6 hrs	Similar to MPH-Pg. 1	IR Usually once or twice a day. Two doses usually cover a whole day. The XR form should cover the whole school day but may require an afterschool IR boost. The XR capsule can be opened and sprinkled on food. Generics are available. Adderall is the most abused stimulant.	Adderall is combination of two types of dextroamphetamine and two types of amphetamine. Adderall is the most abused. Adzenys and Evekeo have similar potential as they are also combinations of both amphetamine and dextroamphetamine.
AdderallL-XR	capsule: 5, 10, 15 20, 25, 30mg XR		Adults: 10-50 mg XR 10-30mg	XR onset: 30-60 min duration: 8-10 hrs		25% L and 75%D - amphetamine Stimulants, especially amphetamines, can help narcolepsy.	

continued

TABLE 2—Continued

Medication	Form	Dose/Schedule	Dose Range	Onset / duration	Most Common Side Effects	Pro	Precautions
Eveko D and L amphetamine sulfate	tablet (scored) 5, 10mg IR	once to twice or rarely 3 times a day	Child: 2.5–20mg Adoles: 5–30mg Adult: 5–40mg	onset: 30 min duration: 4-6 hrs	Similar to MPH–Pg. 1 Same as Adderall IR	Very similar to Adderall IR tablets. Is a 50/50 racemic mix of L and D amphetamine New 2016, Brand	Precautions same as Ritalin (MPH) but more so regarding growth, heart, blood pressure, tics, speedy, agitation, anger and abuse.
Adzenys XR ODT oral disintegrating tablet D and L amphetamine	tablet: 3.1, 6.3, 9.4, 12.5, 15.7, 18.8 mg XR	Once a day in AM Start 3.1 to 6.3 based on age and weight	Child: 3.1–9.4 Adoles: 3.1–18.8 Adult: 3.1–18.8	onset: 30-60 min duration: up to 12 hours	Similar to MPH–Pg. 1 Same as Adderall XR	This is equivalent to Adderall XR and is the only orally disintegrating ADHD med. New 2016. Brand	Inappropriately, Dr. Leehey believes, all amphetamines are FDA approved down to age 3, while milder MPH is only approved down to age 6.
Dyanavel XR oral suspension D and L amphetamine	liquid suspension 2.5mg/ml (1 ml = 1 cc)	Once a day in AM Start 2.5 mg Max 20 mg	Child: 2.5–10mg Adoles: up to 20mg Adult: up to 20mg	onset: 30-60 min duration: up to 12 hours	Similar to MPH–Pg. 1 Same as Adderall XR	This is simply an Adderall like mixed amphetamine XR option in a liquid form. Does not need refrigeration. Comes ready mixed, shake before using. New 2016. Brand.	Adderall is combination of two types of dextroamphetamine and two types of amphetamine. Adderall is the most abused. Adzenys and Eveko have similar potential as they are also combinations of both amphetamine and dextroamphetamine.

continued

TABLE 2—Continued

Medication	Form	Dose/Schedule	Dose Range	Onset / duration	Most Common Side Effects	Pro	Precautions
Vyvanse (lisdexamfetamine)	capsule: 10, 20, 30, 40, 50, 60, 70 mg XR	Once a day in AM	Child: 10-50 mg Adoles: 20-70 mg Adult: 20-70 mg	onset: 30-45 min duration: 8-12 hrs	Similar to MPH–Pg. 1	Longer duration. Capsule can be opened and sprinkled on food. Pro – drug avoids IV and snorting routes of abuse. Brand only. May be gentlest amphetamine.	Precautions same as Ritalin (MPH) but more so regarding growth, heart, blood pressure, tics, speedy, agitation, anger and abuse. Inappropriately, Dr. Leehey believes, all amphetamines are FDA approved down to age 3, while milder MPH is only approved down to age 6. Adderall is combination of two types of dextroamphetamine and two types of amphetamine. Adderall is the most abused. Adzenys and Evekeo have similar potential as they are also combinations of both amphetamine and dextroamphetamine.

Note: This table is intended to be a summary guide, not a full and complete list.
Source: Created by Kevin Leehey, M.D, August 2016 • www.leeheymd.com. Retrieved from www.leeheymd.com/charts/adhd_1.html

TABLE 3: NON-STIMULANT MEDICATIONS FOR ADHD

Medication	Form	Dose/Schedule	Dose Range	Onset / duration	Most Common Side Effects	Pro	Precautions
Strattera (atomoxetine)	capsules 10, 18, 25, 40, 60, 80, 100mg	Once or twice daily. Start in AM. Give evening if sedation.	Based on weight, 0.5 to 1.5mg/kg, target 1-1.4 mg/kg	onset 30-60 min duration: 5-8 hrs, steady state	Stimulant side effects but milder (see Ritalin); plus sedation, nausea possible.	Increases norepinephrine (NRI) stimulant-like action but lasts all day. Not a controlled substance. No direct dopamine effect so may be better tolerated.	Takes 2 to 4 weeks for maximum effects. Must be taken 7 days a week. Only available as brand.
Tenex (guanfacine)	tablets 1.0 mg 2.0 mg	Begin in evening. May need 3 times/day. No patch form. Must take 7 d/wk.	child: 1.0-5.0mg Adoles: 1.0-4mg Adult: 2.0-6mg		Less sedating than Clonidine, but can cause sedation, sometimes (25%) nightmares. May lower blood pressure.	Less sedating than Clonidine. Same other benefits. Can be given 2 or 3 times/day. May need 1-2 weeks to build up. Helps tics, hyperactivity. Does not cut appetite. Invented to treat high blood pressure. Generic available.	Will not help attention as much as stimulants. Do not stop suddenly, same as Clonidine. May rarely have unexpected heart effects.
Intuniv (guanfacine ER)	tablets 1, 2, 3, 4 mg	Intuniv usually AM, once a day		onset 30-45 min duration: 4-8 hrs	Intuniv is once a day in AM, longest duration, least sedating, often smoother and is a new brand.		

continued

TABLE 3—Continued

Medication	Form	Dose/Schedule	Dose Range	Onset/duration	Most Common Side Effects	Pro	Precautions
Catapres (clonidine)	0.1 mg 0.2 mg Patch (TTS-1/2/3)	Begin in evening due to sedation. May need to build up to 4 times/day. Patch on skin lasts 5-7 days. Must take 7 d/wk.	Adoles: 0.1-0.6mg Patch up to TTS-3	duration: 3-5 hrs patch 4-7 days duration	Very sedating. May lower blood pressure, dizziness. Skin irritation common with patch.	Helps tics. Helps severe hyperactivity and impulsivity. May need 1-2 weeks to build up. Does not cut appetite. Invented to treat hypertension. Has been used to treat opiate and/or nicotine withdrawal. Older, generic available.	Avoid if serious depression. Partial effect on attention. Taper off slowly to avoid rebound hypertension or agitation. May rarely have unexpected heart effects.
Kapvay (clonidine ER)	tablets 0.1, 0.2mg	Kapvay usually AM May be given BID			Kapvay is similar to Intuniv.		

Note: This table is intended to be a summary guide, not a full and complete list.
Source: Created by Kevin Leehey, M.D, August 2016 • www.leeheymd.com. Retrieved from www.leeheymd.com/charts/adhd_1.html

REFERENCES

APA Practice Central. (2016, May 26). *Young children with ADHD can benefit from behavior therapy, center for disease control and prevention announces.* Retrieved from http://apapracticecentral.org/update/2016/05-26/adhd-behavior-therapy.aspx

American Academy of Pediatrics. (2011, November). Clinical practice guideline–ADHD: clinical practice guideline for the diagnosis, evaluation, and treatment of attention-deficit/hyperactivity disorder in children and adolescents. *Pediatrics, 128*(5). doi:10.1542/peds.2011-2654

Center for Disease Control and Prevention. (2018, March 20). *Data & statistics (for ADHD).* Retrieved from www.cdc.gov/ncbddd/adhd/data.html

Harstad, E. B., Weaver, A. L., Katusic, S. D., Colligan, R. C., Kumar, S., Chan, E., Voigt, R. G., & Barbaresi, W. J. (2014, October). ADHD, stimulant treatment, and growth: A longitudinal study. *Pediatrics, 134*(4), e935–e944. doi: 10.1542/peds.2014-0428

Herbert, A., & Esparham, A. (2017, April 25). Mind-body therapy for children with attention-deficit/hyperactivity disorder. *Children, 4*(5), 31. Retrieved from https://www.ncbi.nlm.nih.gov/pubmed/28441363

Hvolby, A. (2015). Associations of sleep disturbance with ADD: Implications for treatment. *Attention Deficit and Hyperactivity Disorders, 7*(1), 1–18. Retrieved from https://www.ncbi.nlm.nih.gov/pmc/articles/PMC4340974/

Kasparek, T., Theiner, P., & Filova, A. (2015). Neurobiology of ADD from childhood to adulthood: Findings of imaging methods. *Journal of Attention Disorders, 19*(11), 931–943.

Khoury, J., & Doghramji, K. (2015, December). Primary sleep disorders. *The Psychiatric Clinics of North America, 38*(4), 683–704.

Konofal, E., Lecendreux, M., & Cortese, S. (2010). Sleep and ADHD. *Sleep Medicine, 11,* 652–658.

Lougy, R. A., DeRuvo, S. L., & Rosenthal, D. (2007). *Teaching young children with ADHD.* Thousand Oak, CA: Corwin Press.

Novotney, A. (2015, July/August). Are preschoolers being overmedicated? *Monitor on Psychology, 46*(7), 66–67.

Smith, B.L. (2011, July-August). ADHD among preschoolers. *Monitor on Psychology, 42*(7), 50–52.

Spruyt, K., & Gozal, D. (2011, April) Sleep disturbances in children with attention-deficit/hyperactivity disorder. *Expert Review of Neurotherapeutics, 11*(4), 565–577.

Chapter 13

ADHD APPROACHES THAT REQUIRE MINIMAL ASSISTANCE FROM PROVIDERS

Perhaps a "total" approach of incorporating a variety of traditional and alternative methods could be the most comprehensive and effective way of treating and managing ADHD. The intention of this and the following chapter is to present some, but not all, of the more promising alternative and less conventional approaches and treatments for ADHD. Some families may choose to use these approaches to avoid using medications. Others may use these approaches along with parent behavior management training and medication to maximize their efforts. This chapter will discuss the less conventional approaches that can be implemented at home with minimal or no assistance from providers. The next chapter will present alternative treatments from specialized providers. Before utilizing nutritional, dietary, or supplement approaches, parents should discuss these first with the child's or adolescent's psychiatrist or primary care physician.

While there are many different types of alternative treatments and supplements that claim to improve ADHD, many lack adequate or substantial research to support their effectiveness. As with other medical and psychological disorders, there can be anecdotal reports that claim to treat these conditions. The alternative supplements market is a massive business, and most websites sell these products without regulation. Some of these products may even help certain individuals due to biochemical individuality. However, too often, alternative treatments do not work, and families can become disheartened, waste money, and delay or avoid more proven and effective treatments. Additionally, despite the fact that some alternative approaches for physical and mental health conditions are popular, their use may not always be shared with health care providers. Research has found that many physicians tend to underestimate the widespread use of alternative treatments to address psychological and behavioral difficulties because they tend to overestimate parents' willingness to disclose their use (Schab & Trinh, 2004).

DIETARY APPROACHES FOR ADHD

While there is no official healthy "ADHD Diet," there are four specific dietary approaches that can maximize brain functioning and reduce ADHD symptoms. Dietary changes for healthier eating is a long-run process that requires commitment and a family lifestyle change in food shopping and eating patterns. Healthy or unhealthy dietary choices are habits, and it will take time to implement healthier choices. This can be particularly challenging with children with ADHD who are easily frustrated when they don't get their way. Families should make small diet changes slowly if they are unable to make big ones right away. Parents can reward their children and teen's cooperation in this dietary shift with special privileges and positive consequences that are not food related. A diet focused on reducing ADHD symptoms can consist of the four following approaches.

1. Eating healthier and better-quality foods
2. Eating a higher protein, lower simple carbohydrates and low sugar diet
3. Eliminating foods and drinks with artificial colors, additives, sweeteners and preservatives
4. Eliminating foods to which children and teens may be sensitive or allergic

Toxic Foods

Unfortunately, we live in a world that exposes us to an increasing number of toxins every day in our food, water, air, and home products. There are foods in the United States that have been found to be routinely toxic with unsafe residues from pesticides and various food preparation processes. The research on the following foods is from extensive independent tests run by the FDA and the USDA. The chemical contaminants commonly used in some food preparation have been found to be carcinogenic and neurotoxins for children. Beef, pork, and poultry were found to have the highest levels of pesticides of all foods, and more than any plant foods. Many chemical pesticides are fat-soluble and accumulate in the fatty tissue of animals. Antibiotics, drugs and hormones are often used in animal husbandry, all of which humans consume when they eat non-organic meats. Similarly, milk, cheese, and butter also pose a high risk for pesticide contamination ("The Dirty Dozen–Contaminated Foods," 2013).

The following fruits and vegetables were found to have between 25 and 45 commonly utilized pesticides and chemicals in FDA testing, and 68 to 94 percent of these foods were found to have contaminations that were considered dangerous and above safe levels. These include strawberries, raspberries, cherries, apples, pears, tomatoes, potatoes, spinach, coffee, peaches, nectarines, grapes, celery, and red and green bell peppers ("The Dirty Dozen–Contaminated Foods," 2013).

Additionally, other toxic chemicals called endocrine disruptors (such as Bisphenol A or BPA and Polybrominated diphenyl ethers or PBOE) negatively impact various healthy human hormones by accumulating in hormone producing organs. These may cause ADHD-like symptoms for some. Endocrine disruptors are almost inescapable because they are everywhere in modern life and are found in a range of everyday foods and common household chemicals and products. They seem to be harmful even in low quantities, affecting the way thyroid, estrogen, and androgen hormones are created, transmitted, and metabolized. They can impact developing brains and reproductive systems. These can be transmitted to fetuses prenatally and are frequently present in higher concentrations in infants and young children. Hundreds of studies have explored how the mechanisms of these endocrine disruptor chemicals impact animals' hormones. More recent studies with humans support the negative impact on children's learning and behavior. Also, some researchers suspect the cumulative effect of endocrine disrupting chemicals has been contributing over the past two decades to the rise of neurodevelopmental disorders in children (Lu, 2015).

Unfortunately, because there are so many exposures to endocrine disruptors from the vast number of products, detection of these toxic effects will be extremely difficult. These endocrine disruptors have been found in a number of animals that are commonly consumed, particularly meat and chicken that are fed antibiotics, hormones, and other chemicals. They are also in canned foods, and fruits and vegetables exposed to routinely used herbicides and pesticides. Additionally, these toxicants are found in household cleaning products, personal care products (soap, shampoo, toothpaste, moisturizer), drinking water, vinyl products, house dust, plastics that leech into food and water, and office products. Lastly, despite their omnipresence, eating organic foods and using non-toxic and natural products can reduce exposure to endocrine disruptors.

Unhealthy Diets and ADHD

Research has found that diets high in refined sugars and saturated fats, and low in fruits and vegetables are consistently associated with greater risks of ADHD. One study from Spain found that children and adolescents who had unhealthy diets and did not eat a Mediterranean diet had higher rates of ADHD. They reported that children and teens with ADHD ate less vegetables, fruit, rice, and pasta. Also, those with ADHD skipped breakfast and ate fast food more frequently. Further, low consumption of fatty fish and high consumption of candy, sugar, and soft drinks were associated with higher rates of ADHD. Similar findings exist around the world. A cross sectional study of children in Iran found a higher prevalence of ADHD was associated with greater sweets and fast-food consumption. A study of Australian teens determined an unhealthy western style diet was significantly associated with ADHD. Other studies have confirmed that skipping or replacing breakfast with sugary drinks impairs episodic memory and attention in children (Rios-Hernandez, et al., 2017).

Unhealthy diets can contribute to ADHD in a number of ways. Low-nutrient foods and beverages can cause deficiencies from lower intake of needed vitamins and minerals (such as iron, zinc, and omega-3 fatty acids), as well as deplete them. These diets can also cause higher consumption of toxic food additives. ADHD itself can contribute to poor diets from impulsive eating of high sugar and fatty foods. These choices can also contribute to obesity, and research has supported the significant association between obese children and ADHD (Rios-Hernandez et al., 2017).

Healthy Diets and Quality Foods

To improve the quality of diets, parents should commit to minimizing or eliminating the purchases of junk foods, fast foods, processed foods, and drinks with excessive levels of sugars and any artificial sweeteners. These include desserts, fruit juices, sodas, soft drinks, foods or drinks with high-fructose corn syrup, and foods and beverages with artificial food additives, colorings, and preservatives. Looking at food and beverage labels while shopping is a habit, and any ingredient that is long and difficult to pronounce means the item probably should not be purchased.

Parents can model healthier eating habits and not purchase or bring home these foods. While this can be difficult, if they are not in the house, they will not be consumed. Most people develop routines of consuming certain foods and beverages, and many develop emotional attachments to the items they like. These factors can create barriers to change and creating new healthy habits. If parents have difficulties reducing or eliminating junk foods, they may want to soul search, talk out, or journal upon deeper possible reasons for this. Finally, parents may need to slowly reduce unhealthy food purchases, and gradually replace them with healthier items.

In addition to reducing the purchase and consumption of poor-quality foods and beverages, families can also eat healthier to potentially decrease ADHD and enhance overall health. This would include consuming more organic, natural, and locally grown foods, as well as increasing protein and reducing fat intake. Eating high quality organic, fresh, pesticide-free and chemical-free foods will reduce exposure to toxic endocrine disruptors as well. While there is little research on how healthy eating alone can impact ADHD, good nutrition should create a more positive foundation for the brain and body ("ADHD Diets," 2015). Research of healthy diets in Korean children found traditional diets of high intakes of grains, bonefish, and kimchi (seasoned vegetables) and low consumption of fast foods and soft drinks were associated with lower probabilities of ADHD (Rios-Hernandez et al., 2017). Indeed, whatever is good for the brain will also probably be helpful in addressing ADHD. Good nutrition helps maximize digestion, optimize metabolism, stabilize blood sugar levels, and provides the body with essential building blocks. These are all critical for developing sustainable energy and optimal brain functioning ("ADHD Diets," 2015). While eating organically grown food is the healthiest option, locating and purchasing costlier organic foods can be challenging. If families cannot afford or commit to eating organic foods, they can start avoiding the previously mentioned toxic foods.

Lastly, families can consider taking multivitamins to enhance their nutritional intake. Unfortunately, however, the topic of taking multivitamins has been controversial. Only a few studies have investigated the use of multivitamins and minerals to treat ADHD, and results have varied. Essentially there are two perspectives on this approach. Some providers have suggested that children and adolescents take a high-quality multivitamin to improve health, particularly those with ADHD. The American Medical Association has recommended that everyone should take a vitamin supplement. Micronutrients play an important part in the creation and effectiveness of neurotransmitters, and multivitamins may enhance these processes and potentially improve brain-functioning (Stevens, 2016).

Other providers and research, however, state that multivitamins and other supplements are not necessary, particularly if children and teens are eating healthy and balanced diets. Further, if children and teens are eating nutrient-rich diets, they can exceed recommended daily limits if they take a multivitamin. William Walsh, Ph.D. of the Walsh Research Institute does not recommend the use of multivitamins or supplements without specific testing first. He believes this approach is like trying to create a one-size shoe for everyone. Due to biochemical individuality, each person's nutritional needs are different and these supplements can be harmful (Walsh Research Institute, 2005–2016b).

Ultimately, it will be up to each family if they wish to try multivitamins. Supplements can be useful if specific micronutrient deficiencies exist. After taking the multivitamins, parents can monitor for positive effects and negative reactions. While this would not prevent potential unwanted effects, this "try and see" approach would focus on ending their use if indicated or no positive results occur. Proper supervision by a provider would be the safest approach and could increase effectiveness with this process. The supplementation approach will be addressed further in the next chapter.

High Protein, Low Simple Carbohydrates and Low Sugar Diet

A high protein diet may be helpful in decreasing ADHD, and possibly assisting medications for ADHD to work longer ("ADHD Diets," 2015). Amino acids are the building blocks of protein that promote the production of neurotransmitters and enzymes which are essential for healthy brain functioning. By adding quality protein to one's diet, ADHD may be improved. Good sources of proteins are meat, poultry, fish, eggs, and dairy products. The organic versions of these foods can be the heathiest.

Sugar and simple carbohydrate foods can cause sluggishness and inattention (Amen, 2013), and diets high in these foods can worsen ADHD for most. Thus, reducing sugar and simple carbohydrates, such as refined or white flour foods, pasta, white bread, potatoes, rice, and cereals, while increasing complex carbohydrates, such as vegetables, whole grain foods, peas, and beans may improve ADHD (Amen, 2013; "ADHD Diets," 2015). Breakfasts with higher protein, lower simple carbohydrates, higher healthy fat, and low sugar can improve school functioning by enhancing concentration and decreasing hyperactivity and restlessness. This type of diet can also minimize blood sugar swings which cause irritability and inattentiveness, and may help ADHD medications work longer. High sugar breakfasts, including certain cereals, muffins, and pancakes with syrup should be avoided. Instead, brain-functioning can be enhanced during mornings with eggs, toast with peanut butter, smoothies or yogurt with flax oil, protein shakes, nitrate-free bacon or sausage, and egg and sausage on English muffin (Amen, 2001).

It is important to note that due to biochemical individuality, not everyone with ADHD will improve with a higher protein, lower simple carbohydrates and low sugar diets. Improvement may range from minimal to substantial. Finally, Amen (2001) reported that individuals with his Type 3 Overfocused ADD (a combination of ADHD and obsessive-compulsive symptoms), can worsen from higher-protein, lower-carbohydrate diets. Instead, these individuals require a more balanced diet of carbohydrates and protein to enhance dopamine and serotonin neurotransmitter levels.

Artificial Colors and Additives

Claims that artificial food colors and additives can have negative effects on the behavior of children first became popular in the 1970s. Ben Feingold was an early pioneer in these perspectives. Artificial food coloring has no nutritional value, is made from petroleum or crude oil, and is only used to make food more desirable to children. Feingold and others stated that certain children demonstrate ADHD-like difficulties, learning problems, and behavioral symptoms due to their greater sensitivities to food coloring and additives as compared to the general population (McCann et al., 2007). The Fiengold Diet approach advocates a diet that eliminates artificial food colors, naturally occurring salicylates in fruits and vegetables, specific food preservatives, and artificial flavors. Foods with red, blue, and yellow artificial coloring dyes are especially believed to be toxic. Natural and synthetic salicylates are chemicals found in beauty and health products, many medications, perfumes, and preservatives. People with salicylate intolerance can experience stomach upset, rashes or itchy skin, headaches, breathing difficulties or asthma, swelling of various body parts, and bedwetting. While the effectiveness of the Feingold and similar diets to reduce ADHD has been debated, they have been popular and widely used (Schab & Trinh, 2004).

While subsequent studies in the 1970s failed to confirm the effectiveness of the Feingold diet with ADHD, studies have indicated that a small subgroup of preschool children experienced adverse responses to additives and preservatives and may benefit from their elimination (Millichap & Yee, 2012). Others have stated research supports that most ADHD is not caused by food sensitivities or allergies. Barkley reported food additives and preservatives can cause a slight increase in inattentiveness and activity in only 5 percent or fewer children, and most are preschool age (Barkley, 2013). However, there seems to be increasing interest in food additives' effects on ADHD (Millichap & Yee, 2012).

Bateman et al. (2004) conducted an important population-based study in the United Kingdom that found artificial food coloring and sodium benzoate, a common food preservative, significantly caused hyperactivity in three-year-old children. This was one of the largest controlled trials that explored the impact of artificial food additives on hyperactivity in children. Prior to the study, the children were determined to have ADHD, no ADHD, hyperallergic sensitivities, or no sensitivities. The children were initially given a diet that eliminated artificial colorings and the food preservative sodium benzoate for one week. Then they were given a daily drink that contained artificial food colorings and the preservative or a placebo mixture, in addition to the special diet. Results indicated there were significant decreases in hyperactive behaviors during the initial phase of the diet without artificial additives. Also, there were significantly greater increases in hyperactivity when subjects drank the additives beverage versus the placebo. The study reported substantially increased hyperactivity for the children taking the artificial food colorings and sodium benzoate, regardless if they had prior hyperactivity or hyperallergic problems or not. Finally, the authors concluded that all children would benefit from the removal of artificial food colors and sodium benzoate from their diets (Bateman et al., 2004).

There are other findings that indicate food colorings and allergies can impact attention and behavior. Schab and Trinh (2004) conducted a meta-analysis of a number of studies and their findings strongly suggested that artificial food colors do promote increased hyperactivity in children diagnosed with ADHD (Schab & Trinh, 2004). Jean-Jacques Dugoua, N.D., member of the Nutritional Magnesium Association and chief medical officer at the Liberty Clinic in Toronto, Canada stated that the yellow dye tartrazine has been found to worsen ADHD symptoms. The dyes Red 3 and Red 40, Blue 1 and Blue 2, Green 3 and Orange B are also believed to cause learning problems and ADHD-like symptoms (Chiarello-Ebner, 2009). A literature review that examined 35 years of research on dietary sensitivities and ADHD symptoms indicated that 65 to 89 percent of children with suspected food additive sensitivities negatively reacted to artificial food colors. Additionally, some children are more allergic than others to common non-salicylic foods and artificial food additives, and this can make their sensitivities more complicated (Millichap & Yee, 2012).

A group of researchers conducted an important community-based study to explore if artificial food coloring and the common food preservative sodium benzoate would affect behavior on groups of three- year-old and eight or nine-year-old children. The findings were significant and found that this mix of additives did increase the hyperactivity levels of both groups of children. This study replicated findings of the earlier Bateman et al. (2004) study. The research concluded that the findings of these two studies provide strong support that food additives exacerbate ADHD symptoms. The findings also indicated that the increased ADHD effects are evident in children with ADHD as well as in the general population (McCann et al., 2007).

These enlightening studies seemed to influence the United Kingdom in 2009 and the European Union in 2010 to change their food regulations and the restriction of artificial food colorings (Kleinman et al., 2011). The British government required that the food and restaurant industries eliminate the use of specific food dyes by the end of 2009. The European Parliament of the European Union passed legislation in July, 2010 that requires a warning notice on all foods that contain certain food dyes which states these "may have an adverse effect on activity and attention in children." Curiously, certain products made by major United States multinational corporations still contain these food dyes in the United States, while natural or no colorings are used for these same products in the United Kingdom (Kobylewski & Jacobson, 2010).

The safety of artificial food colorings, additives and preservatives is related to concerns and debates regarding how human health is impacted by the ingredients and technologies used by the food industry. These controversies also include the role of irradiation in food-processing, health risks connected to plastics in food and beverage containers, the meat industry's use of hormones and antibiotics, and the use of genetically modified foods (Kleinman et al., 2011).

While much research has indicated that genetics are a large cause of ADHD, these studies also suggest the possibility that artificial food coloring and additives may interact with certain underlying genetic factors to activate ADHD in some individuals. While this possibility needs further research, if these colorings and additives increase the risk of ADHD development in even a subgroup of children, then it seems critical to identify this risk group to alter their diet. This approach is used with other children's conditions, such as phenylketonuria. More research will need to be conducted to address the larger and governmentally-impacted food policy decisions that affect children across the world regarding potentially unsafe food practices (Kleinman et al., 2011).

Kobylewski and Jacobson (2010) shared health risk concerns about the use of artificial food dyes and the problems with the United States' Food and Drug Administration's (FDA) approval process for their use. The FDA regulates the safety of additives and their impact on public health. It has created legal limits for food dyes containing carcinogenic agents. However, their process seems to have a number of flaws. Studies of nine dyes approved by the FDA suggest these dyes can cause significant health problems, including hyperactivity. First, tolerances were based on dye usage from 1990, while per capita usage has approximately doubled since then. Second, they did not seem to consider that food dyes pose increased risks to children because they are more sensitive to carcinogens and consume more dyes per unit of body weight than adults. Finally, the FDA has not considered the potentially substantial cumulative risk of food dyes consumed together and over time (Kobylewski & Jacobson, 2010).

Unfortunately, skin tests for allergies and intolerances to food additives, dyes, and coloring have been unreliable. Elimination diets are necessary to identify the specific intolerances to these additives (Millichap & Yee, 2012). Further, the removal of foods and beverages with the offending additives and colorings will be the only way to prevent negative reactions.

The American Academy of Pediatrics has now agreed that eliminating food colorings and preservatives from the diets of children with ADHD is a reasonable objective. Families should avoid artificial coloring in foods and drinks, particularly red and yellow dyes (which are the majority of dyes), and food additives, such as aspartame, MSG (monosodium glutamate), sodium benzoate, and nitrates ("ADHD Diets," 2015).

Food Sensitivities and Allergies

In addition to sensitivities to chemical additives, people can also have specific sensitivities and allergies to natural foods. One study reported that a restricted diet produced significant improvements in ADHD symptoms. In this study, researchers restricted the diets of children with ADHD to rice, white meat, water, certain fruits and vegetables. The diet excluded tomatoes, dairy, wheat, oranges and eggs. The study found that 64 percent of the children showed significant improvements in their ADHD and ODD symptoms. The researchers concluded that children with ADHD should be given the special diet to help their parents determine which foods may worsen their conditions ("Study supports restricted diet for kids with ADHD," 2011). Based on these and other findings, some families may wish to explore addressing food intolerance and allergies as an approach to improve ADHD and ADHD-like difficulties. While not accepted as a standard ADHD treatment approach, this may reduce symptoms for some and may be particularly helpful for children who do not respond to ADHD medications.

Food intolerance and food allergies have similarities but are different. Food allergies can be more serious, and often emerge suddenly. Small amounts of food can ignite the allergy; the reaction occurs each time the food is eaten or exposure happens, and for some these can be life-threatening. Food allergies occur when the immune system falsely believes the food is harmful and attacks it. Symptoms can include chest pain, itchy skin, hives, rash, difficulty breathing or swallowing, sudden blood pressure drop ("Food Allergy, or Something Else?," 2015), coughing, swollen eyelids or lips, diarrhea, and vomiting. The most common children's food allergies are cow's milk, eggs, peanuts, tree nuts, soybeans, and wheat ("Food Allergies: Suspect, Test, Avoid," 2015).

In contrast, food intolerance often occurs gradually, may only happen if the food is eaten often or in larger amounts, and is not life-threatening. Food intolerance typically occurs when food irritates the stomach and the body cannot digest it properly. Symptoms include heartburn, headaches, gas, bloating, cramps, nervousness, or irritability. The most common is lactose intolerance, which is a sugar in milk and dairy products. Others include sulfites and various food additives ("Food Allergy, or Something Else?," 2015). Finally, an interesting aspect of food allergies and sensitivities is that some people will crave the offending foods.

Unfortunately, food allergy testing can be controversial and diagnosing it can be difficult. Allergy testing with skin-testing, IgG, and blood tests may be unreliable and produce many false positives. Patients can test positive with skin-tests for different foods and may be advised to avoid these, but they may not be truly allergic to them. Experts stress the importance of confirming specific suspected food allergies with detective work regarding what was eaten, and working with physicians to avoid blind testing. Once a food allergy is determined, the only treatment is avoidance, and newer guidelines emphasize repeated testing to see if the food allergy remits with time. Many children with food allergies can eventually become tolerant. Most commonly, tolerance occurs with cow's milk, wheat, eggs, and soybeans, while it is least likely to occur with peanuts, seafood, and tree-nut allergies ("Food Allergies: Suspect, Test, Avoid," 2015).

Diagnosing food sensitivities can be complex, time-consuming, and sometimes too demanding for families and pediatricians. Elimination diets are often the best way to explore food sensitivities and allergies, but adherence can be difficult. An elimination diet removes the most common allergy foods or other suspected foods for two weeks, and then slowly adds each item back every three days, with the child being encouraged to eat higher amounts of the food for four days. If there is a sensitivity, negative reactions or behavioral problems should be observed within four days. After removal, it may take 10 to 14 days for behavioral improvements to result (Millichap & Yee, 2012). It is important to know that there are no cures for food allergies and sensitivities, just avoidance of the offending foods.

For families who wish to try elimination or oligoantigenic diets and modifications, it will be important to closely examine all labels for the food items or additives that should be eliminated. Another way is to gradually remove food items one at a time and notice if the ADHD symptoms reduce or cease. Careful food journaling and observations are important in this process. It is unclear how many children with ADHD-like symptoms would benefit from restrictive and additive/preservative-free diets. Perhaps these approaches are better for medication-resistant children and highly motivated parents. Despite being healthy, adherence to these restrictive diets can be difficult. They require a large commitment and food lifestyle changes. For most, focusing on removing only the identified offending foods will be easier than maintaining a more restrictive diet.

Another controversial food topic associated with ADHD is gluten, casein, and whey allergies and sensitivities. Gluten is a protein found in wheat, barley, and rye, and casein is a protein found in milk. While much of the evidence is anecdotal, some parents have reported that their children's behavior, learning and language have improved on gluten-free/casein-free (GFCF) diets (Chiarello-Ebner, 2009). These diets are gaining in popularity, and these options are increasing in stores and restaurants. More research is needed on these diets and their impact upon ADHD. However, determined families can start with an elimination of wheat, dairy, barley and rye from child and teen diets (one food group at time) and track if the ADHD-like symptoms improve or not.

OMEGA-3 FATTY ACIDS

There are two types of essential fatty acids, omega-3s and omega-6s. Most individuals in the United States receive more than adequate omega-6s but inadequate levels of omega-3s (National Resource Center on ADHD, 2013). Fatty acids are involved in a number of significant neurological functions, including helping brain cells communicate and interact with neurotransmitters, such as dopamine and serotonin (American Pharmacists Association, 2012). Omega-3 fatty acids have anti-inflammatory properties and can affect central nervous system cell membrane fluidity which can change dopamine and serotonin neurotransmission (Bloch & Qawasmi, 2011). Because humans cannot make omega-3 fatty acids by themselves and most do not consume enough fish in their diets, fish oil supplements that contain the omega-3 fatty acids can be an important supplement. Omega-3 fatty acids in fish oil can improve mental focus, but do not seem to reduce hyperactivity or impulsivity (Barrow, 2008). In addition, these supplements have been found to improve a number of other conditions, including cardiovascular health, vision, memory, joints, immune functioning, skin, and mood.

There is evidence suggesting that some children with ADHD have low levels of essential fatty acids (American Pharmacists Association, 2012). Previous research has shown that there are differences in omega-3 fatty acid composition in individuals with and without ADHD (Bloch & Qawasmi, 2011). Some with ADHD seem to have greater omega-3 deficits, and may benefit more than others from supplementation (Millichap & Yee, 2012). Signs of fatty acids deficiency include dry skin, dry hair, broken nails, frequent urination, excessive thirst, and follicular keratoses or small hard bumps on the backs of arms or front of thighs (Stevens, 2016). However, they are not critical to determine who will benefit from supplementation, and many can benefit even if they lack these signs.

In spite of the promising results of some studies, other research has shown no positive results from treating children with ADHD with omega-3 fatty acids. Some have indicated that benefits from omega-3 supplements were relatively modest compared to FDA-approved medication for ADHD. Research showed that at least three months of omega-3 supplementations are needed to demonstrate results (National Resource Center on ADHD, 2013). A review study reported that there is reasonable evidence for a modest benefit of taking omega-3 fatty acids to improve symptoms of inattention when compared to placebo (American Pharmacists Association, 2012). Other studies indicated that omega-3 fatty acids can be used along with ADHD medications. However, without specific blood testing for omega-3 deficiencies, the effects of supplementation on ADHD symptoms will be unknown until attempted (Millichap & Yee, 2012).

While more conventional psychiatric and psychological treatment providers may be skeptical or unenthusiastic about using omega-3 fatty acids to treat ADHD, there are a number of national and international studies that support its effectiveness for some children and adolescents. One study found that while a majority of children ages 8 to 18 did not seem to respond to taking omega-3 fatty acids, a subgroup of 26 percent of the study showed a more than 25 percent reduction of ADHD symptoms. This subgroup tended to have Inattentive ADHD and co-existing neurodevelopmental disorders (Johnson et al., 2009).

An important meta-analysis study of ten randomized trials of 699 children examined the effectiveness of taking omega-3 fatty acids supplements for children with ADHD. The researchers examined studies that lasted between seven weeks and four months. Their findings demonstrated that omega-3 fatty acids supplements (especially with higher doses of EPA, which is one of the basic forms of omega-3 fatty acids), were modestly effective in treating ADHD in children. However, compared to ADHD medications, such as stimulants or atomoxetine, the efficacy of the omega-3 supplements were only moderate. The study suggested that due to the benign side-effects and modest efficacy, omega-3 supplements may be reasonable to decrease ADHD for families who do not wish to use medication (Bloch & Qawasmi, 2011). Finally, perhaps the results of reduced ADHD symptoms from the meta-analysis findings would have been greater if all the studies used supplements for six months or longer.

Eating Fish to Increase Omega-3 Intake

To increase omega-3s, children and adults with ADHD should consider taking omega-3 fatty acid fish oil supplements and/or eating foods high in omega-3 fatty acids. Eating non-toxic fish three times or more a week can be an excellent way of increasing omega-3 fatty acids. When eating fish, it is recommended that fish are cooked in healthy ways. Families should not eat deep fried fish, such as in fried fish or frozen fish sticks, because it may be cooked in oils high in very unhealthy trans fats (National Resource Center on ADHD, 2013). Foods rich in omega-3 fatty acids are salmon, shrimp, flax seed oil, whole grains, very dark leafy green vegetables like spinach, walnuts, and pumpkin, flax and chia seeds. While flax seed and flax oil are the richest plant source of omega-3 fatty acids, these are less potent and effective sources of omega-3 fatty acids.

While eating more fish can be a good way to increase omega-3 fatty acids intake, some fish can be toxic and should be avoided. Certain fish do not live in healthy environments and can be infected with high levels of pollutants and mercury. Fish are increasingly exposed to manufacturing toxins and mercury from industrial factories that pollute oceans and rivers. These toxins are absorbed by aquatic plant life and small water organisms, which are eaten by larger fish. Mercury biologically accumulates as it moves up the food chain, and this makes the larger fish more contaminated and dangerous to eat. Some of the larger species fish that have higher risks of mercury are tuna, orange roughy, shark, swordfish, cod, and halibut. Smaller fish lower in the food chain are healthier to eat (Ryan, 2016).

People assume that farmed fish are safe, but many fish farms can be harmful. Industrially farmed fish are crammed into tanks which can cause health issues. They are often fed unnatural diets of antibiotics, hormones, and foods not native to them which can cause them to be sick. However, there are safer fish options. For wild-caught fish, select smaller species of fish, and buy fish certified by the Marine Stewardship Council to ensure that the fish were caught in responsible ways. For farmed fish, the label should state that the fish were free of hormones and antibiotics, farmed in low-density herbicide-free tanks or pens, and were fed a natural diet. Smaller fish with lower mercury risks include shrimp, tilapia, crab, catfish, oysters, and anchovies (Ryan, 2016).

Taking Quality Omega-3 Fish Oil Supplements

Despite the benefits of eating healthy fish three or more times per week, this may be difficult for some families. Therefore, taking purified omega-3 fish oils supplements may be a good alternative. Omega-3s can improve ADHD symptoms but may not completely eliminate them, and can be taken with stimulant medication.

Eicosapentaenoic acid (EPA) and docosahexaenoic acid (DHA) are the two basic forms of omega-3 fatty acids found in fish oils. The amounts of EPA and DHA can vary in these supplements. As a general rule, supplements should have at least three times the amount of EPA to DHA. The higher rate of EPA seems to generate better improvements in ADHD symptoms, aggression, and mood swings. Fish oil supplements typically come from fish that live mostly in cold-water and are fatty fishes, such as salmon, tuna, and sardines (Barrow, 2008). However, there are other sources of omega-3 fatty acids from oceans, such as small crustaceans called krill.

Some studies have shown that at least three months of daily consumption of omega-3 fatty acid supplements are needed to increase fatty acids levels in brain cells and produce positive results, although some benefits may be seen earlier. Unfortunately, there are no universal guidelines at this time for the proper dosage and length of time for using omega-3s for ADHD. Research has varied in the daily dosages provided for children with ADHD, ranging from low doses of 300 to 450 mg to very high doses. Barrow reported that children can take up to 2.5 grams and adults can take up to 5 grams of fish oil daily. High doses of omega-3 fish oils can cause diarrhea, nausea, and gastrointestinal discomfort (Barrow, 2008). Amen (2013) shared that children can take between 1000 mg to 2000 mg per day, and at six months omega-3 supplements tend to be effective, but typically not earlier. Others found that fish oils with both EPA and DHA were more effective than single agents, and effective doses were about 1000 mg with more EPA than DHA, and that at least three months were required for positive results (American Pharmacists Association, 2012). Additionally, because it takes time for the fish oil to build up in a person's system, it should be taken daily to be effective. Finally, omega-3 supplements should be taken with food.

There are several points to know when buying omega-3 fatty acid supplements. Liquid forms of omega-3s tend to be more effective than capsules or pills because they are absorbed better. However, liquid fish oils will cost more, require refrigeration, are typically sold only in health food stores, and are messier than pill forms. They may have an unpleasant taste as well. Also, some fish oils can be from questionable sources and may have high levels of heavy metals, like mercury, and other toxins. Families should only purchase higher quality purified fish oils that are pharmaceutical grade or have molecular distillation. Look on the label for these phrases. The molecular distillation process removes pesticides, polychlorinated biphenyls (PCBs), mercury, and other heavy metals. Families should not purchase lower quality and inexpensive omega-3 fatty acids supplements that do not state they are specially purified or molecularly distilled. However, despite these statements, it may be unclear if lower quality supplements are actually as purified as they claim. Any fish oils supplements that smell funny or rancid should be thrown out or returned to the store.

Liver oil and cod liver oil should be avoided for fish oil supplements. Also, while flax seed oil can have good levels of omega-3 fatty acids, this is not the recommended form to take for children with ADHD (National Resource Center on ADHD, 2013).

Parents should know that "no burps" or "odorless" types of fish oil supplements may be better tolerated by children and teens, and should reduce the fishy taste or aftertastes of some fish oils. Younger children may cooperate more with swallowing the liquid forms of flavored fish oils than taking large fish oil capsules. These capsules can be big and hard to swallow, and may even be a safety factor as a swallowing risk for younger children. There are some fish oil capsules that come in smaller sizes that make them easier to swallow. Be aware that liquid fish oil may be higher quality, more expensive, and harder to find than the fish oil capsules. Parents should visit health food or nutritional stores for these liquid versions.

If a child or teen consistently takes an adequate dose of quality fish oil for at least 6 months, but does not show ADHD improvement, then this would probably indicate that the fish oil is not helpful. Conversely, if a family is doing a number of things to manage a child's ADHD and there has been improvement, it may be unclear what is exactly helping, including any one specific supplement, such as omega-3 fish oils. Millichap & Yee (2012) stated that while many parents are initially enthusiastic about supplements, in almost all cases, medication is required, particularly for more moderate to severe cases of ADHD.

Individuals with a condition called Pyrrole Disorder will not respond positively to fish oil supplements. Pyrrole disorder is a biochemical abnormality that causes the overproduction of pyrrole molecules and deficiencies in zinc and vitamin B-6. Individuals with pyrrole disorder will worsen from taking omega-3 fish oils, and this can occur within one month. Those with this condition require omega-6s and not omega-3s, and a special urine test can determine if a person has pyrrole disorder (A. Mensah, personal communication, 09/25/14). Please refer to the next chapter for more information on pyrrole disorder.

INCREASE SLEEP

Sleep difficulties have been discussed previously, including guidelines on the suggested number of hours for children and adolescents. This section will discuss how lesser sleep can increase ADHD and ADHD-like difficulties. Hopefully this will motivate families to increase sleep as a specific intervention to address ADHD and optimize brain-functioning.

Lack of adequate sleep is known to cause neurobehavioral, neurocognitive, and functional impairments that can resemble ADHD-like presentations. Observational studies in neurotypical children have demonstrated that shorter sleep duration can produce ADHD-like behaviors (Hvolby, 2015). Chronic partial sleep deprivation in children and adolescents has been called an unrecognized epidemic. Most people do not appreciate how critical quality sleep is for brain development, and how it impacts daytime functioning, mood, and behavior (Breus, 2005). If children or teens receive inadequate amounts of sleep or experience poor sleep quality, such as from enlarged tonsils or sleep-disordered breathing, then ADHD-like symptoms, inattention, and/or behavioral problems can occur. True ADHD can worsen as well (Greene, 2014). Inadequate sleep quantity and quality can limit the refreshing and deep delta wave sleep that children require.

Some may question how sleep deprivation can closely mimic ADHD. Adults who receive inadequate amounts of sleep may be lethargic and distracted, while children without adequate sleep can become the opposite and exhibit ADHD-like symptoms, moodiness, and other behavioral difficulties. Indeed, there are a number of studies that demonstrate the negative relationship of sleep difficulties upon ADHD-like presentations. Insufficient sleep has been found to cause decreased short-term memory and attentional abilities, inconsistent performance, delayed response time, and irritability (All About Sleep, 2011).

Additionally, child and adolescent sleep problems have been associated with higher levels of concentration problems, ADHD-like symptoms, difficulties modulating emotions and impulses, problematic behaviors and lesser frustration tolerance (Greene, 2014). Insufficient and persistent sleep problems have also been associated with difficulties involving alertness, energy, social skills, and school performance, as well as greater depression and learning challenges. Students with poor grades are more likely to sleep less, go to bed later, and have more irregular sleep/wake habits. One study showed that students with C to F grades obtained about 25 fewer minutes of sleep and went to bed about 40 minutes later than A and B students. For some, even 20 fewer minutes of sleep can significantly affect their behavior (Breus, 2005).

Several studies have reported that greater total sleep, earlier bedtimes, and later rising times during weekdays are associated with better grades. As adolescents age, they experience lesser parental control, increased social and academic demands, and sleep often becomes a lower priority. Most teens have insufficient sleep, with an average of 7.5 hours, with more than 25 percent typically sleeping 6.5 or less hours per night. Sleep-deprived teens have increased risks for impaired memory, negative moods, lowered motivation, drowsy driving and increased automobile accidents. Further, children and adolescents rarely complain about sleep problems. Adolescent sleepiness is so prevalent than it can appear normal. Parents may overestimate the amount of sleep children and adolescents obtain because they may be unaware when they actually fall asleep, night awakenings (Breus, 2005), or if other sleep conditions or problems exist.

Sadly, sleep duration for children and adults has decreased in many countries. In the United States, it is estimated that a third of children suffer from inadequate sleep. One study found that children who had fewer than 7.7 hours of sleep had higher hyperactivity and impulsivity scores and higher ADHD total scores when compared to children who slept more. In the study, short sleep duration was a statistically significant predictor of hyperactivity and impulsivity, and sleeping difficulties were associated with these problems and inattention ("Inadequate Sleep Leads to Behavioral Problems, Study Finds," 2009).

It seems clear that a proper amount of sleep each night is critical for optimal brain functioning for children and adolescents, and is particularly true for those with ADHD. Parents should spend time to explore if their children and teens are obtaining enough sleep. If they are not, they can make it a priority to maintain sleep schedules and healthy sleep hygiene to ensure that adequate sleep is achieved nightly. Indeed, many families that have invested in healthy sleep practices and raised their expectations for increased sleep have experienced improvements in the child's ADHD. Chapter eight provides ways to achieve these goals to increase the amount and quality of sleep.

CONSISTENT EXERCISE AND PHYSICAL ACTIVITY

A number of research studies have shown that exercise and physical activity can help children and teens who have ADHD. One study found that children who had daily aerobic exercise before school helped to reduce ADHD symptoms at school and home, as well as improvements in peer behavior and moodiness. The students from kindergarten to second grade engaged in moderate to vigorous physical activity for 31 minutes before each school day for 12 weeks. The physical activity involved continuous activity at a rate that caused the children to breathe heavily. While all children in the study showed improvements, those with ADHD symptoms seemed to benefit more. Other research demonstrated that physical activity can have positive effects on children with ADHD, including improved brain-functioning and reading and math skills (Hoza et al., 2015).

Another study found that daily physical exercise for 26 minutes for eight weeks significantly reduced symptoms of ADHD in grade-school children. One clinician even suggested exercise should be considered as medication for ADHD. Even very light physical activity can trigger the brain to release dopamine and serotonin. These brain chemicals prompted by activity can improve cognitive performances and mood (Hamblin, 2014). An interesting study reported that a single 20-minute bout of moderately intense aerobic exercise improved neurocognitive functioning, scholastic performance, and inhibitory control in children with ADHD (Pontifex et al., 2013).

Based on solid findings about exercise's positive impact on ADHD, the American Academy of Pediatrics has determined that physical exercise was a Level Two treatment option for ADHD. This means it has good support as an evidence-based child and adolescent intervention for ADHD (Practicewise, 2016).

Exercise and physical activity are critical for children's development, whether children have ADHD or not. Children who are physically active have lower rates of stress anxiety, obesity, and are less vulnerable to health problems later in life. So, while exercise is not a miracle cure for ADHD, it can help children improve their functioning and quality of life. Also, unless there is some medical reason for not exercising, consistent exercise and physical activity can be an addition to other ADHD treatments. A challenge of incorporating regular activity and exercise will be to make it appealing. Some children struggle with organized sports and fitting in with a team. Children with ADHD may struggle with coordination, staying interested, and following rules. Also, the social and competitive aspects of organized sports may not be compelling. If a child has these challenges, parents can explore other kinds of activities such as swimming, running, or martial arts. Parents should talk with their child about activities and sports they prefer. An ongoing reward program can help with compliance as well. Additionally, families can do more physical activities together, such as regular walking or bike rides (Jacobson, 2016).

The U.S. Department of Health and Human Services has recommended school-age children should engage in one or more hours of physical activity daily. Exercise seems to be especially important for the healthy development of the brain's executive functions (Holton & Nigg, 2016). Other health experts concur, and suggest the activity should be at moderate to intense levels. When people exercise, the mixture and amounts of neurotransmitters improve, including dopamine. Stimulant medications work by increasing the amount of dopamine available in the brain, and so it can be said that exercise works in some ways similar to ADHD medications. Also, exercise is believed to work on children's brains by enhancing blood flow to the brain, thereby increasing brain activity in parts related to attention and behavior. Exercise can boost the effectiveness of medications that treat ADHD as well ("Exercise for children with ADHD," 2016).

If families will use exercise and activity as an effective intervention to reduce ADHD symptoms, there are several factors to consider. The exercise should be a structured expectation that is consistent and daily, or five days a week at a minimum. It should also be at a moderately intense level, raise the heart rate, should be at least 30 minutes in length, and may have specific start or stop times. All activities and sports are not equal, and so they will need to be adequately intense and year-round, not just during certain parts of the year. Also, when the exercise or activity isn't done, then it may be assumed the child or teen will not receive as much of the benefits for that day. Additionally, the activity would be best done in the morning before school, but this may be impractical. Compliance may be an ongoing challenge, and it can be difficult to incorporate exercise and physical activities each day, particularly for busy families. Ongoing predetermined daily rewards can be used to improve compliance and motivation. Finally, it would seem logical that the greatest success for consistent physical activity would result from an activity the child enjoys and one that can be accessed each day (such as martial arts or swimming).

GREEN TIME

Similar to physical activity, parents can consider increasing green time for children and adolescents. Green time is regular walking, playing, or doing sports in outdoor green environments with grass or trees. One group of researchers found in several studies that children with ADHD showed symptom improvements when they had routine play in green environments, including milder symptoms immediately after their play and overall improved concentration and impulse control. The researchers also learned that children with high hyperactivity tended to have milder symptoms if they played regularly in an open green setting, such as an expansive lawn or soccer field, compared to children who played in constructed larger environments or indoors (University of Illinois at Urbana-Champaign, 2011).

Other research found that children with ADHD had improved concentration after a twenty-minute walk in a park but not after a walk in an urban non-green area (Taylor & Kuo, 2009). Collectively, the research suggests that common after-school and weekend activities done in relatively natural outdoor environments can be effective in reducing symptoms of ADHD. One study demonstrated that it was the green setting along with activities, and not the activities alone, that produced the positive results. Also, these green effects also occurred for children with Inattentive ADHD without hyperactivity, and the results did not occur just from discharging extra energy in children with hyperactivity. Finally, the green effects were noticed in children who lived in communities of various sizes, different regions of the United States, and at different income levels (Kuo & Taylor, 2004). Lastly, parents can maximize results by combining regular physical exercise and activity in green settings to reduce ADHD symptoms.

EXCESSIVE SCREEN TIME AND VIDEO GAME PLAYING

The topic of screen media use of computers, TVs, smart phones, tablets, and/or iPads, and ADHD has been concerning. There has been some research suggesting a connection. One study found that at ages one to three, the number of hours of television viewed each day was associated with attention problems by age 7. Another study reported that children who watched a fast-paced children's cartoon television show displayed immediate cognitive performance deficits on a wooden puzzle game right after watching the show, compared to other children who did not watch it (Mahone & Schneider, 2012). National data for children and teens with ADHD ages 5 to 17 indicated that 32 percent were more likely to watch TV in excess of one hour a day, and were 29 percent less likely to participate in sports.

Indeed, greater screen time use co-exists with lesser physical activity (Holton & Nigg, 2016).

Screen time that involves excessive video game use is also a growing concern, particularly for those with ADHD. Research has discovered that children and adolescents with attention or impulse problems spent more time playing video games, even when earlier attention problems, age, gender, socioeconomic status and race were statistically controlled. It suggested that video game playing and attention problems and impulsivity can mutually influence each other, with children who have greater attention difficulties and impulsivity spend more time playing, which then further increases their attention and impulsivity problems. The study also found that children and teens who had attention problems or impulsivity were attracted to and sought out video games more (Gentile et al., 2012). Additional research found that male children and teens with ADHD had greater video game access in their rooms and had greater problematic video game use when compared to neurotypical boys. The study also reported that inattention was strongly associated with pathological gaming (Mazurek & Engelhardt, 2013).

Unfortunately, children and teens with ADHD are at greater risk of developing pathological video game use and becoming addicted to video games. The American Medical Association has acknowledged that this is an area worthy of study, and The American Psychiatric Association has decided more research is needed. Gaming disorder is in the International Classification of Diseases (ICD-11) due to their findings that excessive video or digital gaming can cause impairments and pathological patterns of behaviors in some players. A national study found that 8.5 percent of game users have video game addiction or pathological video gaming, and these rates are similar for countries other than the United States. Another large study of children and adolescents found that 7.6 percent to 9.9 percent had pathological video gaming, and that 84 percent of this group had pathological gaming after two years, indicating it was not a temporary phase (Gentile et al., 2011).

What are the signs of pathological video game playing? These include playing video games 24 hours a week or more (which is over three hours each day), not being able to decrease the amount of game playing, not sleeping or decreased sleep due to game play, feeling compelled to play, feelings of agitation when not playing, arguments related to game playing, missing meals or lateness related to game play, gaming interfering with social relationships and/or homework or schoolwork, and spending excessive money on game play (Warner, 2007).

There are a number of factors that place children and adolescents at greater risk for video game addiction. These includes those who are more impulsive, have poor emotional regulation, and lower social competence and empathy. One study found that youths who played video games an average of 31 hours per week were at higher risk for addiction, compared to those who played 19 hours a week and never developed pathological gaming. The study found that once players had pathological gaming, they had increased levels of anxiety, depression, and social phobia. Also, they experienced poorer relationships with their parents, lower grades, and were exposed to more violent games. Finally, children who played more violent games also began to have more aggressive fantasies, more beliefs that aggression was normal, and engaged in more aggressive behaviors (Gentile et al., 2011).

Additional research on pathological video gaming has discovered those with video game addictions spent 24 hours a week playing games (which is about twice as much as other children), were more likely to have game systems in their bedrooms, had poorer grades, more attention problems in school, and more health problems. Some studies have suggested that the most addictive video games are fantasy role-playing games, particularly for children who are unpopular or shy. Pathological gaming seems to interfere with everyday life, impacting family and peer relationships, school functioning, and can produce withdrawal effects if they are denied games (Dewar, 2009-2013).

Many parents will acknowledge that children and teens can be exhausting in their begging and demands for screen time and video games. While screen time can provide welcome breaks for parents, lengthy screen time each day is unhealthy. The American Academy of Pediatrics has taken a cautious perspective on screen use and has recommended no screen time for children under two years. They have recommended no more than one to two hours per day of quality media and television for older children, and the removal of TVs and screen media from children's bedrooms (Mahone & Schneider, 2012).

Because children and teens with ADHD are at higher risks of developing video game addiction, parents should be diligent in protecting them by limiting and monitoring their video game use on computers, cell phones, tablets, iPads and laptops. Having rules and limits for screen time and video game use is one of the most important things parents can do to manage these problems. Children and teens can earn daily screen time and video game use after they perform their chores, homework, and other expected behaviors each day. To be safe, children and teens should spend no more than one hour of video game use per day. Also, increased screen time takes away from physical activity, reading, and socializing, and can contribute to children and teens becoming overweight. Screen use before bedtime and in bed can cause difficulties falling asleep and obtaining healthy amounts of sleep as well.

Warner (2007) presented additional approaches parents can take to reduce and manage the risk of pathological video gaming. Parents should not permit children and teens to have a computer, cell phone or gaming system in their bedroom. Rather, these items should be located and used in community areas of the home. Parents should check and follow age-based ratings and content descriptions of video games before children and teens acquire them. Parents can use clear expectations with negative consequences for not complying with parental approval of all new games purchased. Discussions should be regularly held with children and adolescents regarding internet safety, particularly if they play multiplayer online role-playing games. Caregivers should talk to the parents of the children's friends about the video games they play, and what their child is permitted to play. In addition, discussing their children's limits on content and time playing can be addressed. Caregivers should also play some video games with their children so they can learn more about their child's games. Parents can have frequent causal conversations about the games they play and their experiences.

Families are encouraged to develop the routine of using a kitchen timer or inexpensive egg timer each time a child or teen has video game time, and particularly if excessive use is a problem. This may be difficult to practice at first, but will help limit and manage excessive use. Finally, parents can consult with an experienced psychotherapist if they are concerned about video game use.

MIND-BODY PRACTICES

Mind-body practices of mindfulness meditation, yoga, and tai chi can be utilized to decrease ADHD and have the advantages of low cost, can be done in many settings, and have little to no side effects (Herbert & E-sparham, 2017). While there is growing research on their effectiveness and their costs are low, these approaches are probably best perceived as adjunct interventions for ADHD. More research is needed to demonstrate their effectiveness and ways they can be better integrated into ADHD treatment.

One of the largest challenges with the mind-body approaches will be making a long-term commitment to these practices. While studies have shown that there were short-term benefits after several weeks or a few months, the prolonged reduction of symptoms will probably require consistent dedication. Understandably, this can be difficult for most children and teens with ADHD. The topic of persistence has been critical to the other practices discussed in this chapter, such as diet, supplement use, exercise, limiting screen time, and maintaining healthy sleep practices. Because those with ADHD struggle with boredom, motivation, and consistency, they will be at great risk for not maintaining healthy practices. Parents will have to structure these activities regularly, may need to do the activities along with the child or teen, and may need to reward heavily for daily compliance.

Also, if children or teens are truly interested in these practices, they will probably be more motivated to maintain these.

Additionally, these practices may be initially difficult, particularly for children or teens with moderate to severe ADHD. They can improve their skills over time, but the initial learning period may be frustrating or boring. Perhaps using these approaches for shorter periods over an extended time may be helpful, along with rewards. Finally, families can examine these approaches on YouTube for more information and to watch how they are performed. The following summarizes interesting research reported by Hebert and Esparham (2017) on the effects of mind-body practices upon ADHD.

Mindfulness Meditation

Mindfulness meditation has been described as a process of focusing one's attention on the present experience, moment by moment. With practice, sustained awareness to the present moment can bring many positive results. Numerous studies have shown its benefits, including brain activation changes, enhanced mood, lower stress and anxiety, and increased connectivity among executive functioning brain regions. Research of teens and adults with ADHD found significant improvements after taking an 8-week mindfulness training. Another study of teens, parents, and their tutors who used mindfulness training for 8 weeks reported improved attention and executive functioning (Herbert & Esparham, 2017).

While it may seem like children or teens with ADHD cannot maintain their focus long enough to use mindfulness, this is not necessarily true. Even toddlers can learn to use mindfulness and attend to their breath, but it will be for shorter periods. Parents can use mindfulness apps and practice with their children at night before bed, which may be calming and help sleep onset. Over time this may become more desirable and useful to children and teens, and this can be used as coping with emotional management skills. Although mindfulness will not cure ADHD, with practice it may improve some symptoms, as well as possibly enhance patience and frustration tolerance.

Yoga

Yoga is an ancient Indian practice that teaches the use of certain breathing techniques and poses. It has been studied as an intervention for a number of conditions. One study found children with ADHD who completed three weeks of two 30-minute yoga sessions at school experienced shorter and longer-term improvements in their focusing abilities. Another study of boys with ADHD on medication showed that after 20 yoga sessions, improvements resulted and the breathing and relaxation techniques were helpful for restlessness and sleep. Another researcher found that an 8-week yoga program significantly improved sustained attention in children with ADHD (Herbert & Esparham, 2017).

Tai Chi

Tai chi is an ancient Chinese martial art that uses slow movements, deep breathing and balanced body weight. Research of teens with ADHD found that after five-weeks of tai chi, they experienced significantly decreased anxiety, hyperactivity and daydreaming, and improved conduct (Herbert & Esparham, 2017).

MOVING TOWARD A HEALTHIER LIFESTYLE

An interesting study found that a combination of unhealthy lifestyle behaviors existed in children with ADHD when compared to neurotypical children. The researchers examined children ages 7 to 11, and controlled for IQ, ADHD medication use, household income, and other psychological conditions. They found that children with ADHD were almost twice as likely to have more unhealthy behavioral routines. These findings suggest guidelines for increasing healthy behaviors, including drinking more than three cups of water a day, reducing or eliminating artificially sweetened and caffeinated drinks, reading more than one hour a day, limiting screen time to one hour per day, increasing physical activity to one hour or more per day, and improving the quality and amount of sleep. Finally, healthy behaviors seem to influence each other and are more powerful as a cumulative process. For example, physical activity can reduce screen time, increase water consumption, and enhance sleep (Holton & Nigg, 2016).

While previously mentioned, it is important to reiterate that it can be challenging to begin the process of implementing the healthier practices discussed in this chapter, as well as reducing exposure to the toxins in daily life. There are stages of change, and some families will not be initially ready to make these lifestyle adjustments. Of course, these decisions are commitments that begin with the parents, and some may need to reflect or read more on these topics. Family changes involving buying and eating healthier foods, using supplements, improving sleep, increasing physical activity and reducing screen and video time should be considered a process. These will take time and patience. Some may wish to work on altering one practice at a time. Change is difficult for most people, and it is easy to default to old familiar habits. However, if parents can explain to all family members the reasons for these lifestyle changes, and increase their use of rewards for compliance, they may increase the families' cooperation and "buy in" for these modifications.

While not addressed in this book, there are other ways to increase a healthier home environment and decrease toxin exposures, in addition to altering shopping choices and switching to more natural and organic foods and beverages. While these are costlier and more time consuming at first, they can change people's lives for the better and should be considered investments in wellness. Some of these healthy choices include using whole house or reverse osmosis kitchen water purifiers, whole house air purifiers (newer versions can be attached to furnace systems), using glass food storage containers instead of plastic ones, not microwaving food in plastic containers, removing lead exposure from homes (including addressing old lead-based paint and lead plumbing, and eliminating certain candles), reducing exposure to vinyl products (such as shower curtains, mini-blinds and sofas), using the more "natural" and less toxic versions of home care and cleaning products, wearing clothes with natural fibers and reducing the use of polyester and other unnatural clothing fibers, and reducing or eliminating the use of toxic chemicals at home (such as outdoor pesticides and lawn chemicals). This topic is vast, and those interested can research this more. However, making even some of these changes can produce a healthier home environment and promote improved well-being for the entire family. Of course, positive communication and parenting practices, respectful relationships, and having laughs and fun together all contribute to a healthy family as well.

SUMMARY POINTS

- Dietary approaches for decreasing ADHD include eating healthier and better-quality foods; eating a higher protein, lower simple carbohydrates and low sugar diet; eliminating foods and drinks with artificial colors, additives, sweeteners and preservatives; and identifying and eliminating foods that cause food sensitivities or allergies.
- Quality omega-3 fish oil supplements may decrease symptoms.
- Increase sleep duration to optimize brain functioning.
- Utilize consistent exercise and physical activity for improvements, and incorporate "green time," or regular playing and activities in outdoor green environments.
- Children and teens with ADHD are at increased risk for excessive screen use and pathological video game playing. Limit screen time to one hour per day.

- Mindfulness meditation, yoga, and tai chi may help.
- Families can strive for a healthier lifestyle by creating new routines over time.

REFERENCES

ADHD Diets. (2015). Retrieved from http://www.webmd.com/add-adhd/guide/adhd-diets

All About Sleep. (reviewed 2011, January). Retrieved from http://kidshealth.org=KisHealth&lic=1&ps=107&cat_id=190&article...

Amen, D. (2001). *Healing ADD.* New York, NY: Berkley Books.

Amen, D. (2013). *Healing ADD* (revised edition). New York, NY: Berkley Books.

American Pharmacists Association. (2012, February). Omega-3 fatty acids for pediatric ADHD. *Pharmacy Today, 18*(2), 6. Retrieved from http://pharmacytoday.org/article/S1042-0991(15)31983-6/fulltext

Barkley, R. (2013). *Taking charge of ADHD* (3rd ed.). New York, NY: The Guilford Press.

Barrow, K. (2008). ADHD supplements: Facts about fish oil. *The ADDitude guide to alternative ADHD treatment.* New Hope Media, New York, NY. Retrieved from www.additudemag.com

Bateman, B., Warner, J. O., Hutchinson, E., Dean, T., Rowlandson, P., Gant, C., Grundy, J., Fitzgerald, C., & Stevenson, J. (2004). The effect of a double blind, placebo controlled, artificial food colourings and benzoate preservative challenge on hyperactivity in a general population sample of preschool children. *Archives of Disease in Childhood 89,* 506–511.

Bloch, M. H., & Qawasmi, A. (2011, October). Omega-3 fatty acid supplementation for the treatment of children with attention-deficit/hyperactivity disorder symptomatology: Systematic review and meta-analysis. *Journal of the American Academy of Child & Adolescent Psychiatry, 50*(10), 991–1000.

Breus, M. J. (2005). *Back to school, back to sleep.* Retrieved from www.webmd.com/sleep-disorders/features/fixing-sleep-problems-may-improve-child-grades-and-behavior?print=true

Chiarello-Ebner, K. (2009, October 9). Autism and ADD: The nutrition-behavior link. *WholeFoods Magazine.* Retrieved from http://reviewitproducts.blogspot.com/2009/09/whole-foods-magazine-october-issue.html

Dewar, G. (2009-2013). *Video game addiction: An evidence-based guide.* Retrieved from http://www.parentingsscience.com/video-game-addiction.html

The Dirty Dozen—Contaminated Foods. (2013, July). Retrieved from www.prevention.com/print/25479

Exercise for Children with ADHD. (2016). Retrieved from http://www.webmd.com/add-adhd/childhood-adhd/exercise-for-children-with-adhd?print=true

Food Allergies: Suspect, Test, Avoid. (2015). Retrieved from www.webmd.com/allergies/guide/food-allergy-testing

Food Allergies, or Something Else? (2015). Retrieved from www.webmd.com/allergies/guide/foods-allergy-intolerance.

Gentile, D. A., Choo, H., Liau, A., Sim, T., Li, D., Fung, D., & Khoo, A. (2011, February). Pathological video game use among youths: A two-year longitudinal study. *Pediatrics, 127*(2), e319–3329. doi:10.1542/peds.2010-1353

Gentile, D. A., Swing, E. L., Lim, C. G., & Khoo, A. (2012). Video game playing, attention problems, and impulsiveness: evidence of bidirectional causality. *Psychology of Popular Media Culture, 1*(1), 62–70.

Greene, A. (2014). *Dr. Alan Greene on sleep deprivation and ADD/ADHD.* Retrieved from www.parents.com/parents/templates/story/printable... storyid=/templatedata/hk/story/data/1524.xml&catref=...

Hamblin, J. (2014, September). *Exercise is ADHD medication.* Retrieved from http://...antic.com/health/archive/2014/09/exercise-seems-to-be-beneficial-to-children/380844/

Herbert, A., & Esparham, A. (2017, April 25). Mind-body therapy for children with attention-deficit/hyperactivity disorder. *Children, 4*(5), 31. doi: 10.3390/children4050031

Holton, K. F., & Nigg, J. T. (2016, April 28). The Association of lifestyle factors and ADHD in children. *Journal of Attention Disorders.* doi: 10.1177/1087054716646452

Hvolby, A. (2015). Associations of sleep disturbance with ADD: Implications for treatment. *Attention Deficit and Hyperactivity Disorders, 7*(1), 1-18. Retrieved from https://www.ncbi.nlm.nih.gov/pmc/articles/PMC4340974/

Hoza, B., Smith, A. L., Shouldberg, E. K., Linnea, K. S., Dorsch, T. E., Blazo, J. A., Alerding, C. M., & McCabe, G. P. (2015, May). A randomized trial examining the effects of aerobic physical activity on attention-deficit/hyperactivity disorder symptoms in young children. *Journal of Abnormal Child Psychology, 43*(4), 655–667.

Inadequate Sleep Leads to Behavioral Problems, Study Finds. (2009, April 28). Retrieved from www.sciencedaily.com/releases/2009/04/090427131313.htm

Jacobson, R. (2016). *ADHD and exercise.* Retrieved from http://childmind.org/article/exercise-and-adhd/

Johnson, M., Ostlund, S., Fransson, G., Kadesjo, B., & Gilbert, C. (2009, March). Omega-3/omega-6 fatty acids for attention deficit hyperactivity disorder—A randomized placebo-controlled trial in children and adolescents. *Journal of Attention Disorders, 12*(5), 394–401.

Kleinman, R. E., Brown, R.T., Cutter, G. R., DuPaul, G. J., & Clydesdale, F. M. (2011, June). A research model for investigating the effects of artificial food colorings on children with ADHD. *Pediatrics, 127*(6). doi: 10.1542/peds.2009-2206

Kobylewski, S., & Jacobson, M.F. (2010, June). Center for Science in the Public Interest. *Food dyes—A rainbow of risks.* Retrieved from https://cspinet.org/new/pdf/food-dyes-rainbow-of-risks.pdf

Kuo, F. A., & Taylor, A. F. (2004, September). A potential natural treatment for attention-deficit/hyperactivity disorder: Evidence from a natural study. *American Journal of Public Health, 94*(9), 1580–1586.

Lu, S. (2015, October). Chemical threats. *Monitor on Psychology, 46*(9), 63–68.

Mahone, E. M., & Schneider, H. E. (2012, December). Assessment of attention in preschoolers. *Neuropsychology Review. 22*(4), 361–383.

Mazurek, M. O., & Engelhardt, C. R. (2013, August). Video game use in boys with autism spectrum disorder, ADHD, or typical development. *Pediatrics, 132*(2), 260–266.

McCann, D., Barrett, A., Cooper, A., Crumpler, D., Dalen, L., Grimshaw, K., Kitchin, E., Lok, K., Porteous, L., Prince, E., Sonuga-Barke, E., Warner, J., & Stevenson, J. (2007). Food additives and hyperactive behaviour in 3-year old and 8/9-year old children in the community: A randomized, double-blinded, placebo-controlled trial. *Lancet, 370*(9598), 1560–1567. doi: 10.1016/S0140-6736(07)61306-3

Millichap, J., & Yee, M. (2012, February). The diet factor in attention-deficit/hyperactivity disorder. *Pediatrics, 129*(2), 330–337. Retrieved from http://pediatrics.aappublications.org/content/early/2012/01/04/peds.2011-2199

National Resource Center on ADHD. (2013, May). *Fish oil supplements and ADHD*. Retrieved from http://www.chadd.org/Understanding-ADHD/About-ADHD/Treatment-of-ADHD/Complementary-and-Other-Interventions/Fish-Oil-Supplements-and-ADHD.aspx

Pontifex, M. B., Saliba, B. J., Raine, L. B., Picchietti, D. L., & Hillman, C. H. (2013, March). Exercise improves behavioral, neurocognitive, and scholastic performance in children with attention-deficit/hyperactivity disorder. *The Journal of Pediatrics, 162*(3), 543–551.

Practicewise. (2016). *Blue menu of evidence-based psychosocial interventions for youth*. Retrieved from https://www.practicewise.com/Community/BlueMenu. Also listed on the American Academy of Pediatrics mental health website (www.aap.org/mentalhealth)

Rios-Hernandez, A., Alda, J. A., Ferran-Codina, A., Ferreira-Garcia, E., & Izquierdo-Pulido, M. (2017, February). The Mediterranean diet and ADHD in children and adolescents. *Pediatrics, 139*(2), e2016–e2027. doi: 10.1542/peds.2016-2027

Ryan, S. (2016). *Which fish are the safest & healthiest to eat?* Retrieved from http://greenopedia.com/healthy-sustainable-fish/

Schab, D., & N. Trinh (2004, December). Do artificial food colors promote hyperactivity in children with hyperactive syndromes? A meta-analysis of double-blind placebo-controlled trials. *Journal of Developmental and Behavioral Pediatrics 25*(6), 423–34. Retrieved from https://www.ncbi.nlm.nih.gov/pubmed/15613992

Stevens, L. J. (2016). *Solving the puzzle of your ADD/ADHD child*. Springfield, IL: Charles C Thomas Publisher, Ltd.

Study supports restricted diet for kids with ADHD. (2011, February 3). Retrieved from http://www.reuters.com/article/us-adhd-diet-idUSTRE7130AI20110204

Taylor, A. F., & Kuo, F. E. (2009, March). Children with attention deficits concentrate better after walk in the park. *Journal of Attention Disorders, 12*(5), 402–409.

University of Illinois at Urbana-Champaign. (2011, September, 11). *For kids with ADHD, regular 'green time' is linked to milder symptoms*. Retrieved from http://www.sciencedaily.com/releases/2011/09/110915113749.htm

Walsh Research Institute. (2005–2016b). *Biochemical individuality and nutrition.* Retrieved from www.walshinstitute.org/biochemical-individuality-nutrition.html

Warner, D.E. (2007, December). Video games: When does play become pathology? *Current Psychiatry, 6*(12), 27–38.

Chapter 14

ALTERNATIVE ADHD TREATMENTS FROM PROVIDERS

NEUROFEEDBACK

Biofeedback is a process of electronically monitoring and learning to change involuntary bodily activities. Neurofeedback is a type of biofeedback that helps children and adults modify their brain wave activity during sessions over time. It is not electroconvulsive or electroshock therapy, it is not a talk therapy, and is not painful in any way. In neurofeedback, a person plays a special video game, watches a movie, or just views a monitor while wires and sensors connected to the head share information with a computer program. The computer then provides feedback to the person indicating poor performance in the screen activity if certain unwanted brain waves occur. Abnormal waves may vary in speed, or may not be within a desired zone. More traditional neurofeedback training is a classical conditioning process of associating healthier brain states with a mildly rewarding activity, such as success in a video game.

Our emotions, thinking and behaviors result from communicating neurons in the brain. Brain waves result from the electrical pulses and activity from the incredible amount of communications among millions of neurons. Neurofeedback detects and alters these electrical patterns. Different brain wave frequencies result from the various activities that occur during the day and night. Beta waves are the alert and normal awake state, alpha waves are the state of calm and relaxation where there is no thinking, theta waves occur during meditation and deep relaxation, and delta waves are the state of deep and dreamless sleep. Children and adults with ADHD or other conditions have specific brain wave imbalances that create symptoms and difficulties.

Neurofeedback works by teaching the person to have more normal wave activity by retraining the brain's neural connections. This learning process occurs automatically during sessions, and participants do not have to "work at" improving their brain waves. However, the length of sessions and results can vary based on the individual, their conditions, the provider, and type of neurofeedback utilized. Results can range from minimal to highly successful outcomes. Researchers do not know exactly how neurofeedback works, but over time it can produce a variety of often permanent brain improvements.

Neurofeedback stimulates the brain by creating and strengthening new neural pathways which can actually change the brain. One study found that neurofeedback produced structural changes of the white and grey matter of the brain. Research has also found that electroencephalography or EEG neurofeedback can help improve a variety of conditions including anxiety, mood disorders, and sleep. However, most of the clinical evidence for neurofeedback involves ADHD (Weir, 2016). While everyone differs in their responses, neurofeedback can also treat learning disorders, sensory processing difficulties, migraines, tic conditions and Tourette's Syndrome.

Neurofeedback is perhaps the only ADHD treatment that, when effective, can reduce some or even all ADHD symptoms, and the results can be permanent. Neurofeedback can also help to reduce or eliminate ADHD medication use. Additionally, it can be combined with other treatments to help maximize results, including psychiatric medications, occupational therapy, psychotherapy, tutoring or educational therapy. Neurofeedback sessions can be administered to children starting at about age 5, but they need to remain still and cooperative.

In a neurofeedback study of randomly controlled trials, researchers found that EEG neurofeedback improved inattention symptoms in children. Another study reported that EEG neurofeedback was more effective in reducing ADHD symptoms than cognitive behavioral therapy (Weir, 2016). So, while these and other studies have shown that it is an effective ADHD treatment, more research seems needed until it is accepted as a standard treatment. Until this occurs, most health insurance companies are reluctant to approve coverage.

While still somewhat controversial despite the growing research, neurofeedback seems to be increasingly more accepted for treating ADHD. The American Academy of Pediatrics has determined that neurofeedback is a Level One treatment option for ADHD, which means it has the best support as an evidence-based child and adolescent intervention for ADHD (Practicewise, 2016). Additionally, even if true ADHD does not exist, it can treat a number of ADHD-like presentations. For example, high beta waves can cause nervousness, anxiety, and racing thoughts which may mimic ADHD-like difficulties.

Often neurofeedback practitioners will start with a Quantitative EEG (QEEG) evaluation to identify the imbalanced brain areas and to help guide treatment sessions. These QEEG tests are essentially brain maps that explore brain wave frequencies and other aspects of brain functioning. QEEGs are typically conducted at the beginning of neurofeedback treatments to create baselines for ongoing sessions. These tests can help to confirm if a child or adult has true ADHD and/or other conditions. This diagnostic approach can cost about $500, or more, but unfortunately, most insurance plans do not cover QEEG testing.

While not definitive by itself, QEEG tests can be up to 90 percent accurate (Hallowell & Ratey, 2005), but other clinicians doubt their accuracy for determining ADHD. QEEGs can detect or suggest the possible presence of other conditions, including sensory processing deficits, sensory motor problems, visual and auditory processing problems, traumatic brain injuries, learning conditions, attentional shifting difficulties, OCD, anxiety, and hyperactivity. QEEGs may also possibly detect inadequate sleep or open mouth breathing problems as well. Additionally, QEEGs can suggest seizure disorders or show seizure activity, and in some cases, parents may not be aware that these have occurred. Referenced EEG (REEG), or medication sensitivity testing, can be performed during a QEEG brain map that can provide prescribers information regarding the effectiveness of ADHD medications. This can help physicians focus on which medications will be more effective for patients, with less trial and error.

There are various types of neurofeedback treatment systems. EEG treatments address brain waves, while HEG (hemoencaphalography) treatments address blood flow in the brain. Amplitude training is the oldest form of neurofeedback, typically lasts 40 to 80 weeks, and usually is twice a week. With amplitude training, individuals may begin to see initial improvements by 15 to 20 weeks. QEEGs may then be performed after 20 or 40 sessions to track progress. However, some providers may have increased effectiveness treating ADHD with newer neurofeedback technology and fewer sessions as well. This includes coherence training, Z-score training, connectivity guided, and LENS (Low Energy Neurofeedback System). These and other powerful neurofeedback systems can require as little as 12 to 15 sessions for treatment of ADHD. LENS does not even use a screen, only sensors, and sessions can last several to 15 minutes. Sometimes different neurofeedback systems can be combined for even greater impact, such as using LENS with coherence or Z-score training, with the combined sessions lasting about 35 minutes total. New technology is constantly emerging for neurofeedback systems, and new treatments offer exciting possibilities for the present and future.

The biggest drawbacks to neurofeedback are its expense (and this will depend on how many sessions are required), poor or no coverage by most health insurance plans (with PPOs plans being the most likely to cover this), and it can be time consuming (typically requiring two or three office sessions per week, with sessions lasting from 30–60 minutes). Costs can vary depending on the provider, length of sessions, the types of initial diagnostic procedures, and neurofeedback systems used. Each session cost can range from $60 to $150, and the entire treatment may cost between $2000 to $4500, or more. However, payment for these treatments is often session by session, so families do not need to pay this entire amount at once. While these costs are high, improving someone's brain functioning for life may be worth the financial and time commitments. Also, the costs of ongoing ADHD medication and other related services should be compared to the price of neurofeedback services, especially if the neurofeedback is effective and can reduce or eliminate other treatments.

Finally, there are a variety of professionals who provide this treatment, including clinical psychologists, master's level mental health practitioners, nurses, and even chiropractors. Neurofeedback is less regulated than other clinical services, and as with any provider, some will be more effective or better trained than others. Families should seek out neurofeedback professionals who are properly trained and board certified in neurofeedback. It is preferable that they have mental health licenses as well. Neurofeedback treatment may be more difficult to find outside of metropolitan areas. For more information, parents can visit YouTube or other websites to learn more about the various neurofeedback treatments.

TREATING CERTAIN MINERAL AND VITAMIN DEFICIENCIES

The approach of treating ADHD with micronutrients is alternative to traditional treatment standards, and is generally less understood and respected by a number of pediatricians and primary care physicians. However, it may be more common than once believed. One large study reported that 20 percent of children and teens with ADHD used dietary supplements (Center for Disease Control and Prevention, 2018). There are a number of vitamins, minerals, micronutrients, herbs and supplements that have received research and anecdotal evidence regarding their effectiveness of improving various conditions, including ADHD. Only some of the most researched and effective for decreasing ADHD will be presented here. This section is a basic approach, and focuses on zinc, magnesium, iron, B and D vitamin deficiencies. Digestion problems and conditions are another topic related to nutrition that can potentially impact ADHD and other conditions, but this will not be addressed in this book. As with any new dietary or supplemental approach, any of these micronutrient testing and supplement approaches should first be discussed with the child's physician or other knowledgeable health care providers.

When taking supplements and multivitamins, it is important to know that every child and adult is biochemically unique and different. As a result, some people may benefit from taking specific vitamins, minerals, or supplements, while others may not benefit or can become worse after taking these same products. This is why some providers stress the importance of testing before use. In addition to biochemical individuality, the impact of supplements and multivitamins will also vary due to a number of other factors, including the dosage and quality of the products, overall diet, and the actual nutrient deficiency levels. As a result, it could take weeks to months before results are evident. Also, supplements may not be accurate in the amounts of nutrients listed. Product quality can differ as well, and the more inexpensive ones may be lower quality. Some supplements may even have unhealthy unlisted ingredients.

Deficiencies of specific minerals and vitamins have been documented in children with ADHD, including magnesium, iron, zinc, and B vitamins, and particularly B6. However, the results of prior studies that explored taking minerals or vitamins to reduce ADHD symptoms have been inconsistent (Harvard Medical School, 2009). Despite these, some newer research has shown impressive findings regarding their use.

To utilize this approach, families can first evaluate possible specific imbalances by asking pediatricians or primary care physicians for special blood and/or urine testing to determine if the child or teen has these deficiencies or imbalances. In theory, if deficiencies are detected, then supplementation could improve ADHD symptoms. Families can also ask for more comprehensive micronutrient testing to explore a wider range of vitamin, mineral, and nutrient imbalances. However, some pediatricians and physicians may be reluctant to do this or not believe in this approach. Clinicians should also know that they may not be popular with some pediatricians or family practice physicians if they encourage families to use this approach.

While this specialized testing will take time and money, it can be the most accurate and safest approach before supplementation is begun. Some clinicians and researchers have reported concerns that individuals can actually have excessive levels of micronutrients, and taking supplements may increase their symptoms and/or worsen their functioning.

To obtain testing and treatment with micronutrient and supplements, families may need to visit other providers if their physicians cannot or will not provide nutrient testing and supplementation guidance. Dietitians and naturopathic physicians may be knowledgeable or helpful with these approaches. Naturopathic doctors are alternative providers who use natural healing and holistic health care approaches, and do not provide prescription medications or surgeries. As with many alternative approaches, naturopathic providers are controversial. Some do not believe that naturopaths are science-based or helpful, while others have reported great benefits from their services. Only some states in the United States have licensed naturopath providers, and some naturopaths would say that licensure in their field is not necessary. Finally, there are many micronutrient testing companies and services on the internet that claim they can provide accurate testing. As with many things on the web, it is uncertain which testers are legitimate or helpful. Working with knowledgeable and respected providers can be the safest and most effective ways to receive micronutrient testing and treatment.

If referrals cannot be obtained, or if parents do not wish to obtain this nutrient testing initially, families can try more conventional ADHD treatments first. If there are no significant or only partial improvements, then the family could attempt this nutrient and micronutrient testing process. It should be noted that if iron, zinc, magnesium, B and D vitamins, or other micronutrient deficiencies exist but are not tested, then these will probably not be detected. If the micronutrient deficiencies and/or related medical conditions truly exist, they may ultimately be easier to correct than using more traditional treatments to treat the ADHD-like problems. Finally, although not recommended by some, another approach would be to start certain supplements without initial deficiency testing and monitor results. Laake & Compart (2013) suggested initially taking magnesium, vitamin D, zinc, essential omega-3 fatty acids, probiotics, and multivitamins, and discontinue these if negative effects occur.

Zinc

Zinc is an essential trace mineral and nutrient that is important for a number of bodily functions. Zinc's role in brain functioning is just starting to be appreciated. Scientists believe that low zinc levels can impact ADHD through its influence on dopamine-related brain signaling. Low zinc levels have also been associated with a range of brain disorders, including ADHD, depression, Alzheimer's and Parkinson's diseases. Some research has suggested that adding 30 mg of zinc each day can help reduce the need for ADHD medications (Healthline Editorial Team, 2005–2016). A high percentage of children and adolescents with ADHD have been found to have zinc deficiencies (Walsh, 2014; Healthline Editorial Team, 2005–2016). In one study, zinc supplements were found to enhance the benefit of ADHD stimulant medication (d-amphetamine), with the dose being 37 percent lower when zinc was taken (Millichap & Yee, 2012).

Zinc deficiency can cause children to become picky-eaters. As it progresses, taste aversion increases and taste perception decreases. It can limit foods children eat, and cause family conflicts (Laake & Compart, 2013). Zinc deficiency is also linked to slow growth, poor appetite, frequent sicknesses, and white spots on fingernails (Stevens, 2016).

Zinc testing is generally less common (Laake & Compart, 2013). This testing can measure zinc levels in serum, red blood cells, and through hair analysis. High serum copper levels are often present with zinc deficiencies, so serum copper testing may also be helpful. The recommended daily allowances (RDA) for zinc are 5 mg for ages 4 to 8, 8 mg for ages 9 to 13, 11 mg for boys ages 14 to 18, and 9 mg for girls ages 14 to 18. More than 10 mg of zinc daily should not be taken without physician direction (Stevens, 2016).

Magnesium

Magnesium is a common deficiency in children with ADHD. It is necessary for more than 350 biomedical bodily reactions, including neurotransmitter functioning. It has a calming effect on the nervous system and can improve attention and sleep while decreasing hyperactivity (Laake & Compart, 2013). Magnesium deficiency can result from diets higher in processed foods, soda and salt. Deficiency signs include a lack of desire for a range of foods, irritability, trouble falling and staying asleep, restless legs syndrome, muscle spasms, pins and needles skin sensations, nighttime teeth grinding, and bed wetting (Stevens, 2016).

One study found that 95 percent of children with ADHD had a magnesium deficiency. Another study reported that giving magnesium-deficient children 200 mg of magnesium daily decreased their hyperactivity (Chiarello-Ebner, 2009). Research reported that taking a combination of vitamin B-6 and magnesium for two months significantly improved inattention, hyperactivity, and aggression. After the study concluded, participants reported that their symptoms returned when they stopped taking these supplements (Healthline Editorial Team, 2005–2016).

While this testing is less common (Laake & Compart, 2013), many experts do not believe magnesium tests are accurate or helpful, so determining deficiency can be challenging. For supplementation, children require 6 milligrams of magnesium per body pound (for example, a 40-pound child may try 240 mg). Magnesium supplements can cause gas or diarrhea, and children with kidney disease will require physician approval (Stevens, 2016).

Iron

Iron deficiency has been believed to be a potential contributing cause of ADHD in some children. Iron deficiency during infancy can cause slower brain development and decreased school performance later in childhood. Researchers found in one study that 84 percent of children with ADHD had low iron levels, compared with 18 percent of children who did not have ADHD. Curiously, the children in the study that were the most inattentive, impulsive, and hyperactive also had the most severe iron deficiencies. The researchers did not know exactly why the children with ADHD had lower iron levels, and they did not have malnutrition. Low levels of iron in the brain have been known to affect the activity of the neurotransmitter dopamine, and this may be an explanation of the link between ADHD and iron levels (Buchan, 2004). Additionally, iron is needed by tyrosine hydroxylace to function effectively (Amen, 2013), and tyrosine hydroxylace is involved with the production of dopamine. Deficiencies in iron are also common in people who have restless legs syndrome and anemia, and each of these conditions can cause ADHD-like symptoms.

In another study involving iron deficiencies and ADHD, 23 children ages 5 to 8 with low iron levels received 80 mg per day for 12 weeks. Their ADHD symptoms appeared to improve, as compared to controls. The iron supplementation was well tolerated and the effects were similar to use of stimulants (Konofal et al., 2008). Indeed, there seems to be a subgroup of children with ADHD and low iron that benefit from iron supplementation. To test for iron levels or when anemia is suspected, physicians can order serum ferritin tests. If low iron exists, physicians may recommend eating more iron-rich foods and/or taking iron supplements. Iron supplementation should not occur without medical supervision because it can cause severe side effects or death (Stevens, 2016).

B Vitamins

Vitamins B6, B12, and folinic acid play important roles in ADHD, and are essential nutrients needed for brain and nerve development, functioning, and methylation. Methylation is a process critical for regulating gene expression, building neurotransmitters, creating enzymes, synthesizing DNA, and creating cellular energy. B6 may be one of the most useful supplements in treating ADHD (Laake & Compart, 2013). Also, it seems a subgroup of children with ADHD can benefit from taking individual B-vitamins. However, taking B vitamins when deficits do not exist may increase hyperactivity (Stevens, 2016). The neurotransmitter dopamine has been found to have increased production with B6. This is important because dopamine deficiencies are involved with ADHD.

While testing for B12 is common, testing for all B vitamin and methylation deficits is uncommon and probably will not be performed by physicians. For deficits, B vitamin complexes or multivitamin supplements can be taken (Laake & Compart, 2013). Stevens (2016) recommended starting with 10mg of vitamin B6 per day for two weeks, continuing this if improvement occurs and ending if they worsen. Next, they can try 20 mg of vitamin B1 per day for two weeks, continuing with improvement and ceasing if they worsen. Lastly, parents can give 400 micrograms of folic acid daily. If a negative reaction occurs to any, then multivitamins with minerals will not work most likely.

Vitamin D

Vitamin D is vital to our health. It promotes the absorption of calcium and healthy bone growth, modulates cell growth and neuromuscular functioning, and reduces inflammation. Very few natural foods contain vitamin D, and fatty fish can be one of the best sources. In the United States, fortified foods provide the majority of vitamin D intake for Americans, such as milk. Sunlight can be an important source of vitamin D as well (National Institutes of Health, 2018). Sun exposure to arms and legs without sunscreen in later spring through summer for at least 15 minutes should provide adequate vitamin D levels for the general population (Rusinska et al., 2018).

Vitamin D impacts ADHD in various ways. Stimulant ADHD medications slow the body's recycling of dopamine between neurons to make more dopamine available. One step that limits dopamine is controlled by the protein enzyme tyrosine hydroxylase. Vitamin D encourages DNA to make tyrosine hydroxylace, and zinc is required to assist vitamin D bind to DNA for the production of tyrosine hydroxylace. Additionally, vitamin D deficiency can cause a lack of absorption of iron, zinc, and calcium (Amen, 2013), which can also affect ADHD symptoms.

A 25(OH)D test is the most accurate for checking vitamin D levels and to detect deficiencies. It is also called the 25-hydroxy vitamin D test, and can be ordered by physicians. The recommended daily allowance for vitamin D for children and adolescents ages one to 18 is 600 IU per day, and is determined for those with a minimum of sun exposure (National Institutes of Health, 2018). Other experts have recommended somewhat higher dosage levels. Children and adolescents who are obese or larger may require higher doses, and those with vitamin D deficiencies should utilize greater dosages as indicated from the 25(OH)D test results (Rusinska et al., 2018).

THE WALSH BIOCHEMICAL IMBALANCES APPROACH AND ADVANCED NUTRIENT THERAPY

The Walsh Biochemical Approach and Advanced Nutrient Therapy provide a similar but more comprehensive and effective diagnostic and treatment method than treating the mineral and vitamin deficiencies approach discussed in the prior section. These are revolutionary because these methods can significantly improve a number of psychological and neurodeveloptal disorders in children and adults, including ADHD. This approach can improve brain imbalances and functioning with greater effectiveness and fewer side effects than many current psychiatric medications. Unfortunately, it is not yet well known within the behavioral health treatment community.

Overview of the Walsh Approach and Advanced Nutrient Therapy

Psychiatric medication has been the standard and most popular treatment for ADHD and other psychological conditions. However, some alternative approaches can be effective and may even become future standards. The Integrative Medicine for Mental Health organization (www.immh.org) advocates a more alternative, whole body, and orthomolecular approach to treat mental health conditions by using multiple fields of medicine and nutritional sciences. These approaches can be used along with traditional medical approaches and psychotherapy. They support the use of laboratory analysis for the evaluation and treatment of underlying biomedical issues that can include food allergies, nutritional deficiencies, toxicities, infections, and genetic disorders. They believe that by focusing on a person's unique biochemical, genetic, and nutritional status, customized treatment approaches can be used to create better wellness outcomes (Integrative Medicine for Mental Health, 2016).

For the past several decades, mental health treatment has focused on the imbalances of brain chemistry and the use of drugs to alter the activity of neurotransmitters. In the early 1970s, prescription drugs were the only method known to have a substantial impact on the brain's molecular processes. This medication approach has been highly successful and has helped millions of people in the treatment of ADHD, depression, schizophrenia, and other conditions (Walsh Research Institute, 2005–2016a).

Biochemical factors influence us in profound ways, and massively impact our physical and psychological health. Humans bodies have about 60 chemical elements that play an important role in our gene expression. More than 95 percent percent of our bodies are composed of four elements: oxygen, carbon, nitrogen, and hydrogen. The remaining five percent are micronutrients and macronutrients that are essential for proper production of neurotransmitters, hormones, and immune functioning. The micronutrients of minerals and vitamins are necessary in small amounts, while macronutrients such as magnesium, potassium, and calcium are required in larger amounts. These nutrients perform a variety of vital functions, including driving chemical reactions, building cell structures and bones, and regulating the body's pH (Mensah Medical, 2016).

Biochemical imbalances can be impacted by diet and stressful life events, and often are affected by genetics and epigenetics (Mensah Medical, 2016, February 27). Most people with serious psychological conditions are born with predispositions due to genetically-aberrant levels of certain neurotransmitters (Walsh Research Institute, 2005–2016a). Our inherited genes are not only from our parents, but from ancestors on both sides of our family trees. Epigenetics is the influence of environmental factors in an individual's life that turns genes on and off without altering the DNA sequence. Without a healthy balance of micro and macronutrients, epigenetics will activate inherited genes to cause a diseased state. Specific lab testing to determine nutrient compounds can help balance these deficiencies (Mensah Medical, 2016, February 27).

Early pioneers in the nutritional treatment of mental illness were Abram Hoffer, M.D., Ph.D. and Carl Pfeiffer, M.D., Ph.D. They experienced success in treating mental illness by using high doses of certain nutritional supplements. William J. Walsh, Ph.D. and these earlier pioneers have created a revolutionary approach to the understanding and treatment of complex brain and mental health conditions that is separate from psychiatric medications (Walsh Research Institute, 2005–2016a). Walsh worked with Pfeiffer, and he later advanced Pfeiffer's work to determine the specific biochemical imbalances that cause a number of behavioral health conditions, including ADHD (Mensah Medical, 2016).

The Walsh approach recognizes that behavioral health and psychological difficulties can result from nutrient imbalances that alter brain levels of essential neurotransmitters, disrupt gene expression of enzymes and proteins, and cripple the body's protection against environmental toxins. Walsh's database of millions of chemical factors found in thousands of patients' blood, urine, and tissue samples has identified significant and specific biochemical imbalances in those with ADHD, ODD, conduct disorder, learning disorders, autism, bipolar disorder, depression, anxiety, obsessive-compulsive disorder, schizophrenia, violent and aggressive behaviors, and Alzheimer's disease. Their clinical protocol consists of a medical history, specialized comprehensive lab testing, identification of the specific types of chemical imbalances, and individualized treatment designed to normalize brain chemistry (Walsh Research Institute, 2014–2016).

His Advanced Nutrient Therapy is a natural method of correcting the neurotransmitter activity. Based on a person's testing results, Advanced Nutrient Therapy utilizes individualized blends of vitamins, minerals, amino acids and essential oils. Walsh is the president of the non-for-profit Walsh Research Institute that has advanced these perspectives (Walsh Research Institute, 2005–2016a). In addition to research and promotion, Walsh has trained physicians and medical practitioners in this method since 2000. This approach has produced thousands of reports of recovery from serious behavioral health conditions (Walsh Research Institute, 2014–2016).

Advanced Nutrient Therapy is different from vitamins and minerals purchased at health food stores. Diet changes, over-the-counter multivitamins, and trial-and-error use of various supplements can be inadequate to address each person's individual nutritional deficits and related genetic conditions. Without testing, people will not know what diets and supplements they require. Advanced Nutrient Therapy uses a custom blend created by nutrient pharmacies based on specific lab testing results that have determined each person's unique biochemical imbalances, nutritional overloads and deficiencies (Mensah Medical, 2016).

Some may not believe in a nutrient approach because it seems weak and lacks real clinical potency. Psychiatric medications that affect neurotransmitters are believed to be the most powerful and effective ways of treating psychological conditions (Walsh Research Institute, 2005–2016b). However, an important fact that is not appreciated by most people is that the primary raw materials necessary for the creation and synthesis of many neurotransmitters are nutrients, including vitamins, minerals, amino acids, and other natural biochemicals obtained from foods (Walsh Research Institute, 2005–2016a). Our brain is a chemical factory that produces neurotransmitters and other vital brain chemicals 24 hours a day. If the brain lacks the needed amounts of these nutrient building blocks, then serious difficulties with neurotransmitters should be expected (Walsh Research Institute, 2005–2016b).

For example, some individuals with depression have pyrrole disorder, which is genetically caused and grossly depletes vitamin B-6. Those with pyrrole disorder cannot create sufficient serotonin because B-6 is a critical co-factor needed in the final steps of its synthesis. Many of these individuals benefit from the psychiatric medications Paxil, Prozac, Zoloft and other selective serotonin reuptake inhibitors (SSRIs). However, similar benefits can be achieved by giving these individuals sufficient amounts of B-6 along with additional augmenting nutrients, but without the medication side effects (Walsh Research Institute, 2005–2016b).

A large and important advantage of this nutrient approach is the absence of side effects that psychiatric medications can cause. Advanced Nutrient Therapy and similar orthomolecular approaches utilize natural chemicals. The foreign molecules and synthetic compounds in psychiatric prescription medications can cause the unpleasant side effects. Indeed, some psychiatric medications can cause serious and challenging side effects which may reduce or even prevent long-term compliance. The Advanced Nutrient Therapy approach has no side effects and can be used along with psychiatric medications to maximize results (Walsh, 2015).

Walsh presents an essential concept in his approach called biochemical individuality. We all possess biochemical factors that influence many aspects of our lives, including our behavior, personality, mental health, allergic tendencies, and immune functioning. Besides identical twins, each person has unique biochemical individuality that results in diverse nutritional needs. Some people are genetically suited for a vegetable-based diet, while others are not. Some individuals can satisfy their nutritional needs from their diet alone, while others require nutritional supplements or medications to overcome their genetic flaws. Because of genetic differences in the way our bodies process foods, most people are quite deficient in specific nutrients and overloaded in others. Even with an ideal diet, most have specific nutrients at very low levels, and they may require many times the recommended daily allowance to achieve healthy levels (Walsh Research Institute, 2005–2016b).

Walsh cautions against the use of vitamin supplements without specific testing because this practice may cause overload and serious health problems. Walsh and his team have learned after studying the biochemistry of 10,000 individuals that the greatest biochemical imbalances and difficulties are usually caused from nutrients that are stored in the body in excessive amounts, and not in depleted levels. The most common overloads of nutrients are iron, copper, folic acid, calcium, manganese, methionine, choline, and omega-6 fatty acids. Curiously, these same nutrients can be lacking in some people (Walsh Research Institute, 2005–2016b).

Biochemical individuality explains why some psychiatric medications work well for some people, but not for others. Because we all have unique genetic predispositions that affect how our bodies process food and what we require for healthy levels of functioning, only individualized testing can determine what imbalances exist and what specific treatments are necessary for proper brain balancing. The predominant approach in using psychiatric medications is "try and see." However, in the future, testing will probably be routine to determine which psychiatric medications and supplements should be used for each person. While some drug-gene testing (also called pharmacogenetics tests) from saliva or blood samples is utilized now to determine the best psychiatric mediations for certain psychological conditions, it is not universally used yet. The Walsh approach is science-based and is not against psychiatric medication use (he has presented at an annual American Psychiatric Association meeting!). The testing that the Walsh protocol and similar practitioners use can actually determine which psychiatric medications will work and which will not.

The Most Common Walsh Biochemical Imbalance Conditions

As stated previously, Walsh has created decades of research that indicates there are specific biochemical imbalances that can cause psychological conditions. He has a massive database of 1.5 million chemical data from 10,000 patients with behavioral disorders and 5,600 patients with ADHD (Walsh, 2014). Based on this large database, Walsh found patterns of specific biochemical imbalances that can be determined by testing, including significant abnormalities in certain nutrients needed for neurotransmitter production. The most common biochemical imbalance conditions are overmethylation, undermethylation, copper overload, zinc deficiency, folate deficiency, folate overload, pyrrole disorder, glucose dyscontrol, toxic heavy-metals (such as lead, mercury, cadmium), toxic substances (such as pesticides and organic chemicals), malabsorption (problems with stomach, digestion, and intestine), and essential fatty acids imbalances (insufficient omega-3 and excessive omega-6 levels, but sometimes the converse). Individuals can have one or more of these conditions (Walsh, 2015; Walsh Research Institute, 2005–2016b). As stated previously, methylation is a process critical for regulating gene expression, building neurotransmitters, creating enzymes, synthesizing DNA, and creating cellular energy (Laake & Compart, 2013).

The Walsh Approach for Treating ADHD and ODD

Since 1976, Walsh has conducted more than 12 outcome studies to explore the effectiveness of Nutrient Therapy on patients with ADHD and behavioral disorders. He believes that with his testing and treatment approaches, children and adolescents with ADHD, ODD, conduct disorder, learning disorders, violent behaviors and other conditions can dramatically improve. For Inattentive ADHD, he has found that many children have deficiencies in folic acid, vitamin B-12, zinc, and choline, and believes they can improve after taking supplements for these nutrients. For those with predominantly hyperactive and impulsive difficulties, they often have a metal metabolism disorder with excessive copper levels and zinc deficiency. This imbalance in metals is associated with low dopamine and elevated norepinephrine and adrenalin activity. While stimulant medications for ADHD can elevate dopamine activity, Walsh has stated that his nutrient therapy can balance copper and zinc levels with similar results. Combined ADHD conditions often have more than one chemical imbalance. Many have a seriously elevated copper/zinc ratio, but may also have a methylation disorder, toxic overload, pyrrole disorder, or other imbalances. Children and teens with ODD often have undermethylation problems, and those with conduct disorder often have the chemical signature of severe pyrrole disorder and undermethylation (Walsh, 2014).

Unfortunately, this specialized orthomolecular and biomedical approach is provided by a small number of licensed clinical practitioners and labs. The Walsh Research Institute website (www.walshinstitute.org) offers a directory of these providers. Fortunately, however, some providers offer these testing and treatment services from a distance, with lab work and telemedicine consultation services provided remotely by phone or Skype. These testing and treatment services are typically not covered by health insurance.

After the initial diagnostic lab services and clinician evaluations and consultations, the cost of the specialized nutrient compounds from specific pharmacies can be approximately $100 per month. This will vary based on the conditions being treated. These treatments for ADHD will take longer than stimulant medications to be effective. Treatment compliance with taking the nutrient compounds long term and lack of immediate results are two of the largest challenges with this approach. Children with ADHD require about three months for full results, and adults with ADHD can take more than six months before progress is observed (W. J. Walsh, personal communication, October 19, 2014). Lastly, those who wish to learn more about the Walsh approach can visit YouTube to view videos of William J. Walsh, Ph.D. discussing his perspectives.

There are other orthomolecular and alternative providers that may use similar approaches to the Walsh approach. The Integrative Medicine for Mental Health website has a clinician registry directory of providers who utilize various approaches to treat ADHD and other behavioral health conditions (www.immh.org/find-a-practioner). While it is unclear how effective they may be, some seem to use testing to detect and treat biochemical imbalances.

BRAIN GYM®

While there is little research on the effectiveness of Brain Gym® exercises, some people believe it has been helpful in addressing ADHD, learning disorders, and other neurodevelopmental conditions. Brain Gym® is part of Edu-K or Educational Kinesiology, which uses methods to assist students in schools to improve learning and educational deficits. Edu-K was developed by Paul Dennison in 1980, and it involves a number of techniques to enhance hemispheric functioning and communication. Brain Gym® uses a series of easily performed activities to help children, teens, and adults to enhance learning and coordination. One example is an exercise called Lateral Repatterning, which involves enhancing homolateral and cross-crawl movements. The cross-crawl movement consists of alternatingly using one's hands to touch the opposite side's leg, with right hand to left leg, and then left hand to right leg. The Lateral Repatterning exercise uses the cross crawl with counting, humming, and certain eye movement patterns to produce a temporary state of increased learning and attention (Gallo, 1999). Brain

Gym® may be taught or utilized by some occupational therapists as well as other providers.

Dennison and Dennison (1987) stated that Brain Gym teaches individuals to become better hemispherically integrated. They have reported that some individuals do not achieve brain integration in childhood, and this can cause chronic hemispheric imbalances. This can occur when children do not crawl before walking. These special brain-balancing exercises cross the midline of the body to correct imbalanced brain states that reportedly promote brain integration and improve learning and attention.

These Brain Gym® exercises can be done before school or multiple times a day for increased effectiveness. The www.braingym.org website states that there are 26 special Brain Gym® exercises, movements, and activities that are similar to the movements done by children during the first years of life and involve coordinating the eyes, ears, hands, and whole body. Despite not being able to exactly explain why they work, they may bring improvements in attention and concentration, academic performance in reading and math, memory, physical coordination, and organizational skills (Brain Gym International, 2015). One website provides ten Brain Gym® exercises (www.myexerciseworld.com/brain-gym-exercises.html) that may help promote right and left-brain coordination, attention, learning, and memory abilities. This adjunct approach may be more effective when combined with other ADHD treatments and may not be as effective by itself. Parents can visit YouTube for more information about this approach.

BAL-A-VIS-X

While there is little research on the effectiveness of Bal-A-Vis-X exercises, some believe it has been helpful in addressing ADHD and other conditions. Bal-A-Vis-X is a series of 300 Balance/Auditory/Vision exercises that vary in complexity and are deeply rooted in rhythm. The exercises are done with sand-filled bags and racquetballs, and sometimes while standing on a balance board. This series of exercises promotes the mind and body to experience the natural symmetrical flow of a pendulum. It requires focused attention and cooperation, promotes self-challenge, and is fun for many children. It is typically offered by occupational therapists and can be done individually or in groups at schools as well. These exercises promote crossing the midline, as described above. Anecdotally, some children and parents have reported improvements in ADHD, coordination difficulties, behavioral problems, and learning disorder symptoms after utilizing this method over time. The founder stated that bouncing, catching, and tossing balls and bags in rhythmic sequences promotes various types of sensory integration (Hubert,

2001–2017). Additionally, this adjunct approach may be more effective when combined with other ADHD treatments, and may not be as effective in addressing ADHD by itself. Lastly, parents can visit YouTube for more information on Bal-A-Vis-X.

SUMMARY POINTS

- Neurofeedback treatment can provide permanent brain enhancements, reduce symptoms, and improve learning disorders, anxiety, and other conditions.
- Zinc, magnesium, iron, B and D vitamin deficiencies can cause ADHD symptoms. By evaluating these, identified deficiencies can be treated with supplements.
- The Walsh Biochemical Approach and Advanced Nutrient Therapy provide an innovative method to treat ADHD and other psychological conditions. Biochemical imbalances can be identified with blood and urine tests from special labs, and then pharmacy compounds can treat these with individualized blends of vitamins, minerals, amino acids and essential oils.
- Brain Gym® and Bal-A-Vis-X exercises may help reduce some ADHD difficulties.

REFERENCES

Amen, D. (2013). *Healing ADD* (revised edition). New York, NY: Berkley Books.

Boyles, S. (2004, December 17). *Study links low iron to ADD*. Retrieved from http://www.webmd.com/add-adhd/childhood-adhd/news/20041217/study-links-low-iron-to-adhd?print=true

Brain Gym International. (2015, October 27). Retrieved from www.braingym.org/about.

Centers for Disease Control and Prevention. (2018, March 20). *Data & statistics (for ADHD)*. Retrieved from www.cdc.gov/ncbddd/adhd/data.html

Chiarello-Ebner, K. (2009, October 9). Autism and ADD: The nutrition-behavior link. *WholeFoods Magazine*. Retrieved from http://reviewitproducts.blogspot.com/2009/09/whole-foods-magazine-october-issue.html

Dennison, P. E., & Dennison, G. E. (1987). *Edu-K for Kids*. Ventura, CA: Edu-Kinesthetics.

Gallo, F. (1999). *Energy psychology*. Boca Raton, FL: CRC Press.

Hallowell, E. D., & Ratey, J. J. (2005). *Delivered from distraction*. New York: Ballantine Books.

Harvard Medical School. (2009, June). *Diet and attention deficit hyperactivity disorder.* Harvard Mental Health Letter, Harvard Health Publications. Retrieved from https://www.health.harvard.edu/newsletter_article/Diet-and-attention-deficit-hyperactivity-disorder

Healthline Editorial Team. (2005–2016). Medically reviewed by Legg, Tim on 03/17/16. *Supplements to treat ADD.* Retrieved from http://www.healthline.com/health/adhd/treatments-supplements?print=true

Hubert, B. (2001–2017). *About Bal-A-Vis-X.* Retrieved on 09/07/17 from http://www.bal-a-vis-x.com/about.htm

Integrative Medicine for Mental Health. (2016). *About integrative medicine for mental health.* Retrieved from http://www.immh.org

Konofal, E., Lecendreux, M., Deron, J., Marchand, M., Cortese, S., Zaim, M., Mouren, MC., & Arnulf, I. (2008, January). Effects of iron supplementation on attention deficit hyperactivity disorder in children. *Pediatric Neurology, 38*(1), 20–6.

Laake, D. G., & Compart, P. J. (2013). *The ADHD and autism nutritional supplement handbook.* Beverly, MA: Fair Winds Press.

Mensah Medical. (2016). *Mensah Medical's CustomCoRx and Advanced Nutrient Therapy.* Retrieved from https://www.mensahmedical.com/becoming-a-patient/what-is-advanced-nutrient-therapy/

Mensah Medical. (2016, February 27). *Biochemical imbalances: What are they?* Retrieved from https://www.mensahmedical.com/what-are-biochemical-imbalances/

Millichap, J., & Yee, M. (2012, February). The diet factor in attention-deficit/hyperactivity disorder. *Pediatrics, 129*(2), 330–337. Retrieved from http://pediatrics.aappublications.org/content/early/2012/01/04/peds.2011-2199

National Institutes of Health. (2018, March 2). Office of Dietary Supplements. *Vitamin D, fact sheet for health professionals.* Retrieved from https://ods.od.nih.gov/factsheets/VitaminD-HealthProfessional/

Practicewise. (2016). *Blue menu of evidence-based psychosocial interventions for Youth.* Retrieved from https://www.practicewise.com/Community/BlueMenu. Also listed on the American Academy of Pediatrics mental health website (www.aap.org/mentalhealth)

Rusinska, A., Pludowski, P., Walczak, M., Borszewska-Kornacka, M., Bossowski, A., Chlebna-Soko, D., . . . & Zygmunt, A. (2018, May 31). Vitamin d supplementation guidelines for general population and groups at risk of vitamin d deficiency in Poland—Recommendations of the Polish society of pediatric endocrinology and diabetes and the expert panel with participation of national specialist consultants and representatives of scientific societies—2018 update. *Frontiers in Endocrinology, 9.* doi: 10.3389/fendo.2018.00246

Stevens, L. J. (2016). *Solving the puzzle of your ADD/ADHD child.* Springfield, IL: Charles C Thomas Publisher, Ltd.

Walsh, W. (2014). *Nutrient power.* New York, NY: Skyhorse Publishing.

Walsh, W. (2015, November 15). *Advanced nutrient therapies for mental disorders.* Retrieved from www.walshinstitute.org/uploads/1/7/9/9/17997321/cam_london_keynote_dr_walsh_11_07_15_final.pdf

Walsh Research Institute. (2005-2016a). *Advanced nutrient therapy.* Retrieved on 12/12/16 from www.walshinstitute.org/advanced-nutrient-therapy.html

Walsh Research Institute. (2005-2016b). *Biochemical individuality and nutrition.* Retrieved on 12/12/16 from www.walshinstitute.org/biochemical-individuality-nutrition.html

Walsh Research Institute. (2014-2016). *The Walsh approach.* Retrieved from www.walshinstitute.org/the-walsh-approach1.html

Weir, K. (2016, March). Positive feedback. *Monitor on Psychology, 47*(3), 51–55.

INDEX

A

Academic problem interventions, 156–167
  ADHD classroom approaches, 162–165
  collaboration with others, 165–166
  educational therapists, 161–162
  encourage reading at home, 159–160
  increase sleep, 208
  investigate decreasing grades, 157–158
  parent and school staff collaborations, 156–157
  summary points, 166
  teach study skills, 158
  tutoring services, 160–161
  weekly organizational reviews, 162
Acceptance, 44–45
ADHD, 3–21. *See also* Combined ADHD; Inattentive ADHD
  academic problems and, 10–11, 22–25, 38. *See also* Homework and school behavioral notebook systems
  adolescents with, 15–16, 97–104
  adults with, 16–17
  brain-functioning details about, 17–19
  causes of, 5–6
  co-existing disorders and, 4, 6, 13–14, 30–33, 100–101
  as a complex brain-functioning condition, 3–4, 17–19
  diet causing ADHD like symptoms, 194
  disclosure of diagnosis, 166
  genetic transmission of, xiv, 5, 200
  ODD and, 12
  parents with, 17, 43–44, 78, 83, 90–91
  positive aspects of, 47
  prevalence of, 3–5, 16
  problems associated with, 4, 7–10
  progression of, 14–15, 105
  sleep deficiency causing ADHD like symptoms, 207–208
  social problems and, 11–12
  summary points, 20
  types of, xvi, 6
  Walsh approach for treating, 235–236
ADHD alternative treatments from providers, 222–240
  BAL-A-VIS-X, 237–238
  Brain gym®, 236–237
  common Walsh biochemical imbalance conditions, 234–235
  neurofeedback, 222–225
  overview of Walsh Biochemical Approach and Advanced Nutrient Therapy, 231–234
  treating mineral and vitamin deficiencies, 225–230
  Walsh approach for treating ADHD and ODD, 235–236
  Walsh Biochemical Approach and Advanced Nutrient Therapy, 230–231
ADHD approaches requiring minimal assistance from providers, 192–221. *See also* Dietary approaches for ADHD
  cautions regarding, 192–221
  controlling screen time and video game playing, 211–214
  exercise and physical activity, 209–210
  green time, 25, 211
  increase sleep, 207–209
  mind-body practices, 214–216
  moving toward a healthier lifestyle, 216–217
  summary points, 217–218

ADHDology treatment model overview, 22–26
ADHD-Predominantly Hyperactive/Impulsive, 6
Adrenaline, 8
Advanced Nutrient Therapy, 26, 232–233
Advocates and consultants for assistance with official school plans, 152
Age, 3
  ADHD progression and, 14–15
  adolescents with ADHD, 15–16
  appropriateness for time-outs, 61, 63, 64
  at diagnosis, 4
  to discuss risky behaviors at, 102
  grief in adolescents, 44
  hyperactivity in young children, 34
  impact of TV watching on young children, 211
  to initiate neurofeedback treatment, 223
  management approaches for adolescents with ADHD, 97–104
  management approaches for young children with ADHD, 95–97
  medicating young children for ADHD, 179–181
  of medication initiation and side effects, 176
  occurrence of ADHD-Predominantly Hyperactive/Impulsive and, 6
  at onset of Inattentive ADHD, 6
  school performance changing with, 122
  screen time recommendations by, 213
  sleep habits and, 208
  sleep requirements and, 36
Aggressive behaviors, 72–73, 83, 112–113, 213
Allergies, 201–202
Allowance systems, 61, 67–71
Alternative and Additional ADHD Approaches and Treatment, 22–26
American Academy of Pediatrics
  on ADHD evaluation guidelines, 30
  on ADHD treatment, 93, 179–180, 209
  on diet, 200
  on neurofeedback, 223
  on screen use, 213
American Medical Association, 196, 212
American Psychiatric Association, 212
Amphetamine-based medications for ADHD, 186t–188t

Anger, 9, 12, 44, 84, 100, 105
Anxiety
  co-occurring with ADHD, 13, 16, 90
  co-occurring with inattentive ADHD, 6, 34
  in siblings of children with ADHD, 109
  treatment of, 25, 94, 223
  video game addiction as cause of, 213
Apps, software, and websites
  for access to school assignments, 130
  on ADHD, 43
  for data on school behaviors, 134
  for educational advocate referrals, 152
  for mindfulness activities, 215
  for monitoring teen electronic use, 99
  for parent/teacher communication, 157
The Association of Educational Therapists, 161
Atomoxetine (Strattera), 35, 174–175, 177
Attitudes of parents, 57
Auditory processing disorder (APD), 31, 33, 224
Autism, 25

B

Bal-A-Vis-X, 26, 237–238
Basal ganglia, 19
Behavior management essentials for ADHD, 49–75. *See also* Homework and school behavioral notebook systems
  address aggressive and suicidal behaviors, 72–73
  allowance systems for chore compliance, 67–71
  behavioral problems at school, 124
  behavior modification, 52
  be prepared out in public, 71
  consistency and timeliness with consequences, 53–54
  creating behavioral expectations, 60–61
  ignoring undesired behavior, 64–65
  intensive treatment needs, 73–74
  maintaining consequences, 72–75
  overview, 49–51
  respond to property destruction, 72
  rewards and praise for positive behaviors, 54–55
  summary points, 74–75

time-outs, 61–64, 96
token reinforcement and point systems, 65–67
use of behavioral expectations with consequences, 56–59
ways to improve compliance, 53–56
Behavior rating measures, 29
Behavior therapy, 179–180
Bibliotherapy, 107
Biochemical imbalance conditions, 235
Biochemical individuality, 234
Boredom, 103
Boredom Disorder aspect of ADHD, 8
Brain development, 103, 194, 207, 210, 228
Brain-functioning details about ADHD, 17–19
Brain Gym®, 26, 236–237. *See also* Neural pathways
Brain imaging methods, 17
Brain waves, 222, 224
Breathing exercises, 111–112
Bullying, 12, 124
Bupropion (Wellbutrin), 174
B vitamins, 229–230

C

Caffeine, 176
Casein, 202
Causes of and factors suggestive of ADHD, 31–32
Causes of problem behaviors, 82
Cell phone monitoring apps, 99
Centers for Disease Control and Prevention (CDC), 4, 179
Cerebral cortex, 18
Classroom approaches for ADHD, 162–165
Clonidine, 120, 174–175, 178
Coaching, 44, 60, 94–95
Co-existing disorders, 4, 6, 13–14, 30–33, 100–101
Combined ADHD. *See also* ADHD; Inattentive ADHD
 in adolescents, 15–16, 100
 age at onset of, 14
 behavioral manifestation of, 11–12
 dysgraphia in, 14
 frustration tolerance in, 9, 12
 medication response, 175

ODD in, 12
overview of, 6–7
progression over time, 15
school difficulties related to, 124, 131
self-control challenges in, 9
Concentration Deficit Disorder (CDD), 6, 34–35
Conduct disorder, 73, 76, 105. *See also* Oppositional defiant disorder (ODD)
Conflict resolution skills, 88, 107–109
Consistency, 24, 53, 64–65, 96, 136
Control
 in authoritarian parenting, 84
 of consequences, 52
 frontal lobe role in, 77
 healthy detachment aiding, 80–81
 parents regaining through time outs, 62
 planning as a tool for, 81
 siblings need for, 109–110
 teens escalating as a means of, 72–73
Coping activities, 111–112
Coping skills, 103. *See also* Emotional management skills
Corporeal punishment, 52, 84
Cost of neurofeedback treatment, 224–225
Cost of psychological testing, 29
Cost of special education services, 140
Curfews, 99

D

Danger to self or others, 97, 180
Depression
 co-occurring ADHD, 13, 16, 90
 co-occurring with Inattentive ADHD, 6, 13, 34
 in siblings of children with ADHD, 109
 treatment of, 25, 94
 video game addiction as cause of, 213
Detachment, 80–81
Developmental challenges, 105
Developmental stages, 87, 88, 97, 100
Dietary approaches for ADHD, 193–207. *See also* Nutrient Therapy approach; Supplements
 artificial colors, food additives and preservatives, 5, 195, 197–201
 deficiencies, 26, 32, 39–40, 195, 203, 225–230

eating fish to increase omega-3 intake, 204–205
Fiengold Diet approach, 198
food journaling, 202
food sensitivities and allergies, 201–202
healthy diets and quality foods, 195–197
high protein, low simple carbohydrates and low sugar diets, 197
medication interactions with, 176
monitoring for effects of, 196
omega-3 fatty acids, 203–204
omega-6 fatty acids, 207
overview of, xv–xvi
recommendations, 25, 197, 216
sleep enhancing foods, 119
toxic foods, 193–194, 204–205
unhealthy diets and ADHD, 194–195
Disability perspective, 23, 44–45, 82, 105, 109
Disclosure of ADHD diagnosis, 166
Divorce, 12, 17
Docosahexaenoic acid (DHA), 205–206
Dopamine, 18–19, 197, 203, 209–210, 229–230
Driving, 104
Dysgraphia, 14, 32, 130

E

Education about ADHD, xiv, 22–23, 43–47
Educational Kinesiology, 236–237
Educational therapists, 161–162
Eicosapentaenoic acid (EPA), 205–206
Electroencephalography, 223
Electronic screen devices, 36, 118–119, 211–214
Emotional management skills, 82, 110–113, 120. *See also* Coping skills
Employment difficulties, 16–17
Endocrine disruptors, 194, 196
Environmental factors in ADHD, 5
Environmental interventions, 217
Epigenetics, 232
European Union, 199
Evaluating ADHD and other co-existing conditions, 27–42. *See also* Sleep
  independent testing and assessments, 138
  medical problems to screen for, 35–40
  occupational therapy, 34, 138
  overview of in ADHDology treatment model, 22–23
  professional providers for, 27–29, 34–35, 38, 168–170, 172
  Quantitative EEG (QEEG) evaluation, 223–224
  school evaluations, 139–140
  screening for conditions with ADHD-like symptoms and/or coexisting disorders, 30–33
  Sluggish Cognitive Tempo (SCT), 34–35
  summary points, 40
  Unger family case example, xi–xiv
Exercise, 25, 209–210
The Explosive Child (Green), 109

F

Family dynamics, 49–50, 73
Family Medical Leave Act (FMLA), 91
Family structures, 51
Family therapy, 88–89, 93–94
Fiengold Diet approach, 198
Financial costs of ADHD, 4
504 Plans, 23, 125, 127, 130
Food and Drug Administration (FDA), 97, 200
Frustration Disorder aspect of ADHD, 9, 12

G

Gaming disorder, 212
Gender
  ADHD prevalence and, 4, 90
  co-existing disorders in females, 13
  Inattentive ADHD in females, 6
  marriage to partners with ADHD, 17
  menstrual period and ADHD symptoms, 15–16
  mothers of children with ADHD, 89
Genetic transmission of ADHD, xiv, 5, 200
Gluten, 202
Gratitude, 119
Green time, 25, 211
Grey matter, 18, 223
Grieving process after diagnosis, 23, 44–46, 82, 97–98, 109
Guanfacine, 174–175, 178

H

Health insurance plan limitations, 28-30, 161, 223-224, 236
Hearing tests, 33
HEG (hemoencaphalography) treatments, 224
Home. *See* Parental effectiveness at home
Homework and school behavioral notebook systems, 122-137. *See also* Academic problems and ADHD; Behavior management essentials for ADHD
   academic problems at school, 122-123
   behavioral problems at school, 124
   combining the homework and school behavioral notebook systems, 135-136
   homework notebook system, 125-128
   homework suggestions, 128-130
   sample combined plan, 136-137
   school behavioral notebook system, 130-135
   summary points, 137
   ways to manage school difficulties, 124-125, 134, 136
Hormones, 15-16
Hyperactivity in young children, 34

I

Imbalances of power, 73
Inattentive ADHD. *See also* ADHD; Combined ADHD
   behavioral manifestation of, 11
   behavioral manifestations of, 9
   bullying of children with, 12
   differentiating from SCT, 34
   green time aiding, 211
   medication responsiveness, 175
   omega-3 supplementation aiding, 204
   overview of, 6-7
   peer relationships of children with, 106
   Walsh approach for treating, 235
Inconsistency, 8, 9, 17
Individual Education Plans (IEPs), xv, 23, 125, 127, 130
Individual psychotherapy, 74, 89, 91, 93-94, 107, 169. *See also* Psychotherapy

Individuals with Disabilities education Act (IDEA), 141-142, 144-146
Inmates, 16
Input from children, 57, 108
Insight improvement, 53-54, 86
The Integrative Medicine for Mental Health organization, 231, 236
Intermittent reinforcement, 55-56
International Classification of Diseases (ICD-11), 212
Interventions for ADHD, 93-114
   ADHD coaching, 94-95
   conflict resolution skills, 107-109
   discussion topics for teens, 101-102
   emotional management skills, 110-113, 120
   enhancing social skills, 106-107
   expect changes over time, 104-105
   family and individual therapy, 93-94, 101, 102, 107, 110, 113
   management approaches for adolescents, 97-104
   management approaches for young children, 95-97
   sibling issues, 109-110
   summary points, 114
   treating ODD, 105-106
Iron, 228-229

J

Journaling, 37, 119-120, 173, 177, 195, 202

L

Lateral Repatterning exercise, 236
Learning disorders, 25, 32, 122, 151, 160
Listening, 88

M

Magnesium, 228
Managing ADHD at home, xiv, 22, 24. *See also* Parental effectiveness at home
Marine Stewardship Council, 205
Mecury in fish, 205-206
Medical conditions to screen for, 30-31, 35-40
Medication treatment for ADHD, 168-191
   in ADHDology treatment model, 23, 25

amphetamine-based medications for ADHD, 186t–188t
benefits of, 86, 94, 106–107, 159, 168, 170–171
dietary considerations with, 176, 197
differences between psychiatrists and psychologists, 168–170
drug-gene testing, 234
interfering with sleep, 36, 120, 175–176
journaling for tracking, 173, 177
mechanism of, 18, 210, 230
"medication holidays," 177
medication sensitivity testing, 224
methylphenidate-based medications, 97, 182t–185t
monitoring effectiveness of, 82, 105, 134
necessity of, 170–171
non-stimulant medications, 189t–190t
pediatricians vs psychiatrists for, 172
pharmacogenetics tests, 234
pros and cons of using and not using, 171
rebound effect of stimulants, 175–176
to reduce dangerous behaviors, 97
right medication at the right dose, 175
routines for and monitoring administration of, 178–179
side effects of, 175–176, 179–180, 182t–190t, 233
sleep problem treatment, 118, 120, 178
summary points, 181
teen compliance with, 98
that stops working, 178
timing of, 177
to treat ODD, 105–106
types of ADHD medications, 173–174, 182t–190t
under-medicating in, 172
understanding the prescribing process, 172–173
Unger family case example, xv
wearing off, 61, 100–101, 127, 129, 158, 177
for young children, 179–181
zinc enhancing effects of, 227
Melatonin, 118, 120, 178
Menstrual period and ADHD symptoms, 15–16
Mental health, 73–74, 83, 89–91. *See also specific conditions*

Methamphetamine-based stimulant medications, 173–174
Methylation, 229, 235
Mind-body practices, 214–215
Mindfulness, 111–112
Mindfulness meditation, 215
Misconceptions about ADHD, 7
Modeling behavior, 78, 81
Molecular distillation process, 206
Money management problems, 16
Motivation, 64, 67–68, 70, 131
Motivation Disorder aspect of ADHD, 7
Motor disorders to screen for, 31
Mouth breathing, 37–38
Myelination, 103

N

Naturopathic doctors, 226–227
Neural pathways, 19, 25. *See also* Brain Gym®
Neurodevelopmental conditions to screen for, 31
Neurofeedback, xv, 25, 74, 160, 222–225
Neuroplasticity, 171
Neurotoxins, 4
Neurotransmitters
    dopamine, 18–19, 197, 203, 209–210, 229–230
    effect of diet on, 196–197, 203, 228, 231, 233, 235
    exercise impacting, 210
    imbalances and deficiencies in, 4, 18, 232
    serotonin, 197, 203, 209, 233
Norepinephrine, 18
Notice, Accept, and Cope (NAC) method, 110–113
Nutrient Therapy approach, 74. *See also* Diet

O

Obesity, 195, 230
Obsessive-compulsive symptoms, 197
Obstructive sleep apnea, 31, 36–37
Occupational therapy, 34, 96, 138, 146, 151–152, 237–238
Official school plans: 504s and IEPs, 138–155

accommodations and recommendations for, 150–152, 160–161
after implementation of, 153
alternative or therapeutic schools, 153–154
educational advocates and consultants, 152–153
504 Plans, 143–144
IEPs under IDEA, 144–146
importance of providers outside of the school, 138–143
overview of, 141–143
in private schools, 146–147
process of requesting, 147–149
sample documents, 149–150
summary points, 154
Omega-3 fatty acids, 203–204
Omega-6 fatty acids, 234–235
1-2-3 Magic (Phelan), 43, 62
1-2-3 Magic Teen (Phelan), 62
Oppositional defiant disorder (ODD). *See also* Conduct disorder
aggressive and suicidal behaviors in, 72–73
antagonizing behavior in, 78
arguing with children with, 76, 81
interfering with sleep, 36
overview of, xiii–xiv, 12–13
parental reactions to, 84
treatment for, 94–95, 105–106
Walsh approach for treating, 235–236
Organization Disorder of ADHD, 8–9
Other Health Impairment (OHI), 142, 145
Otolaryngologists, 38

P

Parental effectiveness at home, 76–92. *See also* Managing ADHD at home
abusive parenting, 83–84
address parental ADHD, 90
address parental stresses and increase self-care, 89–90
avoid power struggles, 80, 108
calmly give consequences, 77–78
changing unproductive thinking, 79
child's perspective of adult life, 82
Family Medical Leave Act (FMLA), 91
ineffective parenting styles, 83–86

learn to expect certain behaviors, 81–82
parent-child/teen relationship improvement, 86–89
prioritizing problems, 125
stop excessively talking, 76–77
summary points, 92
work on healthy detachment, 80–81
Parent management training, 93–94
Parents
attitudes of, 57
family structures, 51
improving individually, 93–94
using parental power, 76–78
positive focus for, 54–55
roles of, 24–25
single parent families, 49
Parents with ADHD, 17, 43–44, 78, 83, 90–91
Performance Disorder of ADHD, 7–8
Pesticides, 193
Phelan on parental approaches, 88
Poor Self-Awareness Disorder aspect of ADHD, 10
Positive aspects of ADHD, 47
Power phrases, 112
Power struggles, 80, 108
Premack reinforcement principle, 61
Prenatal substance exposure to screen for, 31
Primary care physicians, 27–28
Problems associated with ADHD, 4, 7
Procrastination, 9
Progression of ADHD, 14–15
Property destruction, 72
Proprioceptive sensory processing disorder, 34
Psychological conditions to screen for, 31
Psychological testing, 27–29, 138–139, 169
Psychotherapy, 44–45. *See also* Individual psychotherapy
Putting on the Brakes: Young People's Guide to Understanding ADHD (Quinn & Stern), 43
Pyrrole Disorder, 207, 233, 235

Q

Quantitative EEG (QEEG) evaluation, 223–224

R

Rebound effect of stimulants, 175–176
Rehabilitation Act of 1973 (Section 504), 141–142
Risky behaviors, 15–16, 100–102, 105
Routines, 50, 60–61, 128. *See also* Structure

S

Salicylates, 198
Salience network, 19
Self-awareness, 10
Self-care practices, 78, 90
Self-Control Disorder aspect of ADHD, 9
Sensory processing disorders to screen for, 31, 96
Serotonin, 197, 203, 209, 233
Serum copper, 228
Sexuality, 100
Shaming, 133
Sibling issues, 109–110
Side effects of medication treatment for ADHD, 175–176, 179–180, 182t–190t
Single parent families, 49
Sleep
   bedtime and sleep time, 117–118
   bedtime routine, 61
   consistent sleep schedules, 116–117
   creating positive associations, 57, 62–63, 118–119
   difficulties falling asleep, 119–120
   disorders to screen for, 31, 35–38
   EEG neurofeedback aiding, 223
   increasing, 207–209
   medication side effects impacting on, 175–176
   medication treatment for, 118, 120, 178
   obstructive sleep apnea, 31, 36–37
   overview of, 24, 115
   prevalence of problems with, 14
   problems and disorders, 35–38
   professional interventions to assist with, 120
   screen time and sleep, 118–119, 213
   sleep hygiene, 116–120
   sleep journals, 37
   sleep requirements, 36, 115–116
   sleep studies, 120
   summary points on, 120

Sluggish Cognitive Tempo (SCT), 6, 34–35
Social phobia, 213
Social problems and ADHD, 11–12
Social skills, 106–107
Social workers in schools, 146
Sodium benzoate, 198–199
Software. *See* Apps, software, and websites
Spirituality, 45–46, 112
Stages of grief, 44
Stimulants. *See* Medication Treatment for ADHD
Stress-reducing plan, 89–90
Structure, 8, 52, 82, 96–97, 102, 163. *See also* Routines
Study skills, 158
Substance abuse, 15–16, 100–104
Suicidal behaviors, 72–73
Supplements. *See also* Dietary approaches for ADHD
   B vitamins, 229–230, 233
   iron, 228–229
   magnesium, 228
   multivitamins, 196
   nutrient overload, 234
   omega-3 fatty acids, 203, 205–207
   omega-6 fatty acids, 234–235
   testing before use of, 226
   treating mineral and vitamin deficiencies, 225–227
   vitamin D, 230
   Walsh Biochemical Approach, 26, 230–236
   zinc, 227–228, 230
Support groups, 43

T

Tai Chi, 216
Taking Charge of ADHD (Barkley), 43
Teenagers with ADD and ADHD (Dendy), 43
Time, concept of, 59
Time-Disorder aspect of ADHD, 10
Time-outs, 61–64, 96
Together time, 86–87, 106, 110
Trauma, 77
Triggers of problem behaviors, 82
Tutoring services, 160–161
Type 3 over-focused ADD, 197
Tyrosine hydroxylace, 229–230

U

United Kingdom, 199
U.S. Department of Health and Human Services, 210

V

Vestibular sensory processing disorder, 34
Visual problems, 32
Visual processing disorders (VPDs), 32–33

W

Walsh Biochemical Approach, 26, 74, 196, 230–236

Websites. *See* Apps, software, and websites
Whey allergies, 202
White matter, 18, 223

Y

Yoga, 215–216
YouTube resources, 107, 215, 237–238

Z

Zinc, 227–228, 230

CHARLES C THOMAS · PUBLISHER, LTD.

THE HANDBOOK OF CHILD LIFE
(2nd Edition)
by Richard H. Thompson
642 pp. (7 x 10) • 7 illustrations • 14 tables
$59.95 (paper) • $59.95 (ebook)

ART THERAPY WITH STUDENTS AT RISK
(3rd Edition)
by Stella A. Stepney
344 pp. (7 x 10) • 39 illustrations (12 in color) • 27 tables
$44.95 (paper) • $44.95 (ebook)

RESEARCH IN REHABILITATION COUNSELING
(3rd Edition)
by Phillip D. Rumrill and James L. Bellini
358 pp. (7 x 10) • 3 illustrations • 10 tables
$49.95 (paper) • $49.95 (ebook)

POSITIVE BEHAVIOR SUPPORTS IN CLASSROOMS AND SCHOOLS
(2nd Edition)
by Keith Storey and Michal Post
318 pp. (7 x 10) • 15 illustrations • 52 tables
$42.95 (paper) • $42.95 (ebook)

TREATING SEXUAL ABUSE AND TRAUMA WITH CHILDREN, ADOLESCENTS AND YOUNG ADULTS WITH DEVELOPMENTAL DISABILITIES
by Vanessa Houdek and Jennifer Gibson
186 pp. (8.5 x 11)
$28.95 (paper) • $28.95 (ebook)

AUDITORY-VERBAL PRACTICE
(2nd Edition)
by Ellen A. Rhoades and Jill Duncan
322 pp. (7 x 10) • 4 illustrations • 14 tables
$55.95 (paper) • $55.95 (ebook)

TECHNOLOGY IN MENTAL HEALTH
(2nd Edition)
by Stephen Goss, Kate Anthony, LoriAnn Sykes Stretch, and DeeAnna Merz Nagel
456 pp. (7 x 10) • 12 illustrations • 6 tables
$81.95 (paper) • $81.95 (ebook)

BEHAVIORAL GUIDE TO PERSONALITY DISORDERS (DSM-5)
by Douglas H. Ruben
272 pp. (7 x 10) • 31 illustrations • 1 table
$42.95 (paper) • $42.95 (ebook)

SOCIAL AND CULTURAL PERSPECTIVES ON BLINDNESS
(2nd Edition)
by C. Edwin Vaughan and Fredric K. Schroeder
274 pp. (7 x 10) • 6 tables
$39.95 (paper) • $39.95 (ebook)

CASE STUDIES IN SPECIAL EDUCATION
by Tera Torres and Catherine R. Barber
198 pp. (7 x 10) • 1 illustration • 3 tables
$31.95 (paper) • $31.95 (ebook)

SYSTEMATIC INSTRUCTION OF FUNCTIONAL SKILLS FOR STUDENTS AND ADULTS WITH DISABILITIES
(2nd Edition)
by Keith Storey and Craig Miner
272 pp. (7 x 10) • 14 illustrations • 32 tables
$36.95 (paper) • $36.95 (ebook)

RENTZ'S STUDENT AFFAIRS PRACTICE IN HIGHER EDUCATION
(5th Edition)
by Naijian Zhang
640 pp. (7 x 10) • 6 illustrations • 5 tables
$69.95 (hard) • $69.95 (ebook)

CASE STUDIES IN APPLIED BEHAVIOR ANALYSIS FOR STUDENTS AND ADULTS WITH DISABILITIES
by Keith Storey and Linda Haymes
344 pp. (8.5 x 11) • 29 illustrations • 4 tables
$53.95 (paper) • $53.95 (ebook)

RESEARCH IN SPECIAL EDUCATION
(2nd Edition)
by Phillip D. Rumrill, Jr., Bryan G. Cook, and Andrew L. Wiley
278 pp. (7 x 10) • 2 illustrations • 9 tables
$42.95 (paper) • $42.95 (ebook)

INTRODUCTION TO HUMAN RELATIONS STUDIES
by George Henderson and Wesley C. Long
364 pp. (7 x 10)
$62.95 (paper) • $62.95 (ebook)

HELPING STUDENTS WITH DISABILITIES DEVELOP SOCIAL SKILLS, ACADEMIC LANGUAGE AND LITERACY THROUGH LITERATURE STORIES, VIGNETTES, AND OTHER ACTIVITIES
by Elva Duran, Rachael Gonzales, and Hyun-Sook Park
608 pp. (8.5 x 11) • 26 illustrations • 4 tables
$49.95 (comb-paper) • $49.95 (ebook)

FACEBOOK.COM/CCTPUBLISHER

FREE SHIPPING ON WEBSITE ORDERS
On retail purchases through our website only to domestic shipping addresses in the United States

TO ORDER: 1-800-258-8980 • books@ccthomas.com • www.ccthomas.com

SIGN UP TODAY FOR OUR e-NEWSLETTER AND RECEIVE e-ONLY SPECIALS AT WWW.CCTHOMAS.COM